Organizational Change as a Development Strategy

Studies in
Development Management

Series Editor: *Louis A. Picard*
National Association of Schools of
Public Affairs and Administration and
the University of Nebraska at Lincoln

A series of books prepared by
The National Association of Schools
of Public Affairs and Administration
and
The Development Program Management Center of
The United States Department of Agriculture,
sponsored by
The Bureau for Science and Technology of
The United States Agency for International Development

• **Books in the Series** •

- Management Training Strategies for Developing Countries
  John E. Kerrigan and Jeff S. Luke

- Development Administration and U.S. Foreign Aid Policy
  Dennis A. Rondinelli

- Creating Opportunities for Change: Approaches to Managing
  Development Programs   *Louise G. White*

- Organizational Change as a Development Strategy: Models and
  Tactics for Improving Third World Organizations   *Jerald Hage
  and Kurt Finsterbusch*

Organizational Change as a Development Strategy

Models & Tactics for Improving Third World Organizations

Jerald Hage and
Kurt Finsterbusch

Lynne Rienner Publishers • Boulder & London

Published in the United States of America in 1987 by
Lynne Rienner Publishers, Inc.
948 North Street, Boulder, Colorado 80302

Library of Congress Cataloging-in-Publication Data
Hage, Jerald, 1932–
  Organizational change as a development strategy.

(Studies in development management)
  Bibliography: p.
  Includes index.
  1. Economic development projects—Developing
countries—Management.   2. Organizational change—
Developing countries.   I. In Finsterbusch, Kurt, 1935–
II. Title.   III. Series.
HC59.72.E44H34   1987   338.9′0068   87-12730
ISBN 1-55587-012-0 (lib. bdg.)

Printed and bound in the United States of America

The paper used in this publication meets
the requirements of the American National Standard
for Permanence of Paper for Printed Library
Materials Z39.48-1984   ⊗

To Madeleine and Meredith

For their inspiration and support
in our efforts to develop knowledge
that improves the human condition

Contents

Figures

Series Foreword

Webster defines management as "the judicious use of means to accomplish an end." Applying management concepts to economic and social development programs in the Third World is a complex and multifaceted task because the manager must deal with elusive goals, changing environments, and uncertain means, and because optimal directions for organizing donor programs to assist the management of Third World programs have been ambiguous. The comparatively new field of economic and social development management is challenged to create more useful intellectual resources for both developing country management and donor cooperators.

Specialists in the field—managers, analysts, consultants, educators, and trainers—have found that to trace the academic base of development management is to draw a broad and interdisciplinary framework. Members of the development fraternity continually call attention to the diversity of the subject areas that are critical to the judicious management of social and economic change.

The need to develop a better understanding of development program management both in theory and practice has prompted the preparation of the current NASPAA/DPMC series. The Rondinelli book, analyzing the development management work that has been funded over the past fifteen years by the Agency for International Development (AID), examines some of the major research contributions to the development management field. The White, Hage-Finsterbusch, and Kerrigan-Luke volumes synthesize, probe, and order the academic bases for practice aimed at strengthening development management. Their subjects—development program management, organizational change strategies for more effective program management, and management training strategies for promoting improved program management—are purposely interrelated. The focus is on development programs in the Third World.

These books order and organize complex subjects. They thereby invite collateral analytic work by specialists in related concentrations and with related perspectives. In particular, we seek stronger links with work by Third World specialists, for although the authors have sought a Third World perspective, they have relied heavily on literature available in the United States.

The fifth book in the series presents the development management writing of one person. The Performance Management Project has valued the work of David Korten, chiefly in Asia, throughout his close to five years of work under the Project. His writings growing out of this work have found a wide and appreciative audience among those concerned with management for greater development strength at the grass roots. The Performance Management Project and NASPAA are pleased to include a compendium of his writings in this series and to have the opportunity to emphasize this aspect of development management.

The impetus and subsequent funding for the research discussed in this series came from the Performance Management Project in the Office of Rural and Institutional Development of AID's Bureau for Science and Technology. The research should be useful to both practitioners and educators interested in international development and related fields. A major purpose of the books, from the funder's point of view, is to make more explicit the links between the assimilated knowledge and skills of the development management practitioner and the literature base that supports development practice. This required creative, developmental work. We are grateful to the authors for their considerable investment in time and thought that have brought these results.

The organizations that have implemented the Performance Management Project—the National Association of Schools of Public Affairs and Administration, the Development Program Management Center and its cooperator, the International Development Management Center of the University of Maryland—have for a number of years undertaken a variety of practical and analytical work with developing country organizations for improved management. The NASPAA/DPMC Studies in Development Management series reflects an interaction between the individual authors and the experienced practitioners associated with the two implementing organizations.

I would like to express my appreciation to an extraordinary group of people connected with the Performance Management Project who have contributed to this series. These books build on the work of many practitioners and academics who have been associated with the Performance Management Project over the past seven years. Particular thanks go to Wendell Schaeffer, Louise White, and Merlyn Kettering, Project coordinators for the management training, organizational change, and program management books respectively; to the series editor, Louis Picard; and to the editorial committee who, from its inception, provided this venture with important direction and analytic support strengthened by practical experience. They and I, in turn, are grateful to the specialists outside the Project who have contributed substantially through their critiques of the manuscripts. We want to make appreciative note of the understanding, leadership, and support that the books in this series have received from Kenneth L. Kornher, chief of the USAID division which is responsible for institutional development and management research. Christopher Russell, Jerry French, Eric Chetwynd, John O'Donnell, and Robert McClusky also have provided valuable agency support to this project's research activities.

> *Jeanne Foot North*
> Project Officer
> The Performance Management Project
> Office of Rural and Institutional Development
> Bureau for Science and Technology
> Agency for International Development

Preface

The administration of development activities in Third World countries is a difficult but rewarding task. As a result, development administrators express a peculiar blend of pessimism and optimism. They talk constantly about failures in donor-funded projects and the nearly insurmountable political, economic, attitudinal, organizational, social, and cultural factors that mitigate against effective projects—it is amazing that anyone stays in this apparently hopeless field. On the other hand, we have noticed the enthusiasm and dedication of many development administrators and their confidence that they know how to improve projects and programs. Seldom are they able to carry out projects the way they wish they could; nevertheless, they stick to their guns and fight for their dreams against awesome odds. The professional development administration literature mirrors in academic garb the pessimism/optimism tension of the administrators.

This book is optimistic. We take into account the difficulties of projects in less developed countries but focus on the organizational forms and managerial technologies that are the most effective in various situations. We utilize a contingency theory of organizations that identifies the most effective organizational forms for markets of various levels of technological complexity. We examine twelve case studies of organizational change in Third World countries in terms of an analytical framework that is based on the organizational change literature of the Western developed countries. From the synthesis of all these sources we derive lessons for change agents.

We have have coauthored this book. Our different expertise and perspectives have enriched our joint effort. Hage views development from the perspective of organizational change; Finsterbusch views it from the perspective of community change and social impacts. Our work has been partially funded by a grant from the National Association for Schools of Public Affairs and Administration; Hage was the principal investigator and Finsterbusch the research associate on the project (which explains the ordering of authors for this book). Nevertheless, the entire volume is jointly coauthored and the work, pain, errors, insights, credit, glory, blame, responsibility, and royalties are shared equally.

Our effort has benefited from the encouragement, assistance, support, and comments of many people. At various times Rudi Klauss, Louis Picard, Wendell Schaeffer, Beth Shields, and Louise White have served as project monitors providing us with leeway or guidance as required and support, which was essential. We benefited tremendously from the review of our manuscript in various stages by Derick Brinkerhoff, Edward Connerley, Larry Cooley, Marcus Ingle, Merlyn Kettering, Moses Kiggundu, Kenneth Kornher, David Korten, Jeanne North, Samuel Paul, Charles Perrow, William Siffin, Morris Solomon, Russell Stout, and Dwight Waldo. They have not always agreed with what we have written, nor have we always agreed with their criticisms, but we have always found the dialogue helpful for improving our manuscript. We were fortunate to engage the able assistance of Farid Alatas and Warren Van Wicklin III in collecting the literature data base and critiquing our ideas. Finally, we thank Renate Edmundson most gratefully for endless typing and retyping.

Prologue:
Organizational Change as a
New Development Strategy

Since the end of the World War II, there has been a concerted effort
to solve the problem of underdevelopment in Third World countries.
A variety of approaches has been used, from extreme central planning to a heavy reliance on market mechanisms. National donor
agencies, such as the U.S. Agency for International Development
(USAID) and La Cooperation, and international donor agencies,
such as the World Health Organization (WHO), the Food and Agriculture Organization (FAO), and the World Bank, are trying to
help countries achieve their development goals. In the course of
four decades a variety of strategies has been tried including capital
investments in economic infrastructure, education and the development of human capital, technology transfer, integrated rural
development, population control, and the like.

Most of these approaches to development emphasized one or
more of the factors of production, i.e., capital, labor, technology,
human capital, or resources. The commonly accepted theory was
that increasing the factors of production would increase economic
production and raise standards of living if population growth were
kept within reasonable limits. But things did not work out as
planned; the factors were increased but economic growth was less
than expected. Eventually it became widely recognized that the
factors of production require conducive institutional arrangements
to have their full effects. Now USAID and other donor agencies
have institution building as one of their major objectives. An important part of institution building is the improvement of productive
and administrative organizations, the subject of this monograph.

1

Although organizations are only one type of institution (families and markets are other examples), they are critical to economic development. Most goods and services are produced by organizations and most development projects are implemented by them. In fact, the production function actually takes place in organizations, because capital, labor, technology, human capital, and materials are utilized by organizations and transformed into goods and services. Therefore, if organizations can be made more productive, the economy will grow and people will be better off generally. The strategy of improving organizations, however, does not substitute for the strategy of increasing the factors of production; rather, it complements it. Organizational improvement multiplies the benefits of increasing the factors of production.

The objective of this monograph is to show how to improve organizations in less developed countries (LDCs). It analyzes how organizations should be structured and how they can be changed to the appropriate structure. We begin with the Western literature on organizational change which prescribes how to improve organizations in the West. We then look at Third World case materials to discover which of these prescriptions work in LDCs and which do not, and to identify non-Western patterns of success.

Both the theory and the case materials agree on two important points. First, the structure of the organization has a profound effect on its degree of productivity. Second, the type of structure which is effective depends upon environmental conditions. At least six different models of organizations can be effective in Third World countries depending on their settings. Four of these models have been developed in Western organizational theory and observed in Third World countries. The other two are not found in organizational theory but were found in the Third World case materials. Thus, a major focus of this book is to set forth various conditions in Third World countries and to describe those structures which are most appropriate for, and thus more effective in dealing with, the differing circumstances.

In the past, too many development change agents, whether nationals or foreigners, have had a single-image formula for the structure of organizations. Some advocated decentralization; others bureaucracy; still others structured flexibility. Each of these approaches has advantages but none is adequate or even desirable in all situations. The central thesis of this monograph is that development change agents need to construct a variety of organizational structures within the same country. There is no single panacea.

Another complicating factor is the great variability of institutions in the Third World and between the Third and First Worlds. Each developing society has created its own institutional arrangements through centuries of social evolution. Many have had a colonial veneer laid on top of the local institutions, and usually it remained only a veneer. In the societies where colonial control has existed for a century or more, institutional hybrids have resulted. This is as true of organizations as it is of other kinds of institutions. Given this variability, are the organizational models of the West applicable to the Third World? We try to answer this question using Third World case materials and the answer we find is a qualified yes—the main qualification being the necessity to employ the correct strategies of organizational change.

The change agent needs to know not only which structures are appropriate for which conditions, but also how to change organizations in the appropriate direction. This is a complex problem which requires answers with many components, including motivation for change, levels at which intervention should occur, combination of tactics which works best, level of resources needed, and methods of data collection. Seldom do change agents work with a strategy as extensive and complex as the one which we propose. However, changing organizations in developing countries is a complex task and requires a multifaceted and carefully articulated approach.

Any strategy of organizational change in developing countries must confront the political realities and cultural values which influence the organization. These factors cause many efforts to improve organizations to fail. We have chosen successful projects precisely because we believe that they will provide insights into how to cope with these twin issues of political power and cultural preferences. We also describe the case studies thoroughly to show how organizations can be changed.

The first two chapters in this book review theories and strategies of organizational change. Chapter 1 reviews briefly the three major literatures on organizations—organizational development, organizational theory, and organizational design—from the perspective of how organizations should be structured and designed, and how they might be changed. It uses a framework which encompasses all three strategies and includes fundamental assumptions, major concepts, intervener targets, change points, intervention levels, and change tactics. Organizational development emphasizes changing employee attitudes, group processes, and job designs by means of training, group discussion, sensitivity training groups (T-groups), and problem-solving groups. Organizational theory emphasizes restructuring the organization in the direction prescribed by contingency theory (a dominant perspective in both this and organizational design), as best suited to achieving either efficiency or innovativeness in its market situation. It usually utilizes the change tactics of decree, data collection, group discussion, and restructuring. Organizational design emphasizes improving strategic planning, changing structures for greater efficiency, and improving managerial technologies. It favors the change tactics of decree, group problem solving, and restructuring.

All three schools of organizational change build motivation for change by identifying performance or output gaps. The most influential individuals or groups within an organization, or the most powerful people outside of it, must perceive the organization as failing on a valued performance or output dimension before it can be changed. Each school tends to focus on different performance or output gaps, but they all identify and use gaps to build support for change. The demonstration of performance and output gaps was also found in all of the case studies of organizational change in less developed countries presented in this monograph. Thus, this practice transfers readily to a Third World context.

Since contingency theory is the strategy used in the analysis of Third World cases, Chapter 2 is devoted to explicating it. The premise of contingency theory is that different environmental situations (contingencies) call for different organizational forms. Two contingencies are emphasized: market demand and technological sophistication. Market demand varies from large demand and mass markets to local demand and individual or batch markets. Technologies range from simple to complex. When these two dimensions are crisscrossed, they produce a fourfold table containing the four major organizational forms in contingency theory: simple technology/small market equals craft organization; simple technology/large demand equals mechanical organization; complex technology/small demand equals organic organization; and complex technology/large demand equals mechanical-organic organization.

Contingency theory began by developing and contrasting the two organizational forms of mechanical and organic. The mechanical organization fits Weber's model of bureaucracy and is centralized, hierarchical, specialized in tasks, formalized, and large scale. It is efficient, produces in quantity, provides a standardized service or product, and capitalizes on economies of scale. The organic organization has mainly the opposite traits and is decentralized, relatively nonhierarchical, based on teamwork and networks, specialized around professional expertise, nonformalized and small scale. It is innovative or adaptive, produces quality and nonstandardized goods and services in small numbers, and does not benefit from economies of scale. A major thesis of contingency theory is that organizations can not be both efficient (low cost per unit of output) and innovative (number of new outputs or procedures) at the same time—they must emphasize one or the other performance in their principles of organization. Often, however, organizations overemphasize one and encounter problems from the lack of the other; then they must be changed in the other direction. Even innovative organizations must try to keep their costs down and efficient organizations must occasionally innovate to stay, or become more efficient. The two performances must be traded off and the appropriate combination created for the circumstances.

The mechanical-organic and craft organizations lie between the mechanical and organic forms on the above dimensions, but the mechanical-organic lies closer to the mechanical and the craft lies closer to the organic. The mechanical-organic combines the two forms by having a mechanical production and control system but having an organic department for research and development or for other highly technical tasks. The craft organization was the traditional and dominant organinization form until the industrial revolution. Most are family businesses or partnerships and they function effectively in local markets with low capital and skill requirements. These four models of organizations can be used by development change agents to determine the direction in which specific organizations should be changed.

The literature on development administration is generally pessimistic. Many books focus on the difficulties of implementing projects or effectively administrating programs. We are more interested in what works than in what does not work, so we focus on a variety of success stories. Our cases vary from moderately to highly successful and our task is one of testing whether organizational change strategies explain these positive results.

Our methodology has been to select critical cases of organizational change. We have been seriously hampered in this effort by a lack of cases at the organizational level of analysis. There are many prescriptions in the literature but few concrete descriptions of successful organizational change. This is an intellectual tragedy. Many natural experiments have been tried but the efforts are not reported thoroughly in the literature.

Chapters 3 and 4 examine case studies and draw lessons for change agents. In Chapter 3, six cases are examined in which the purpose of the project was to change the organization(s). In Chapter 4, six cases are examined in which the purpose of the project was to improve services to communities, with organizational change or creation taking place to achieve this purpose. These two sets of cases represent two different institution-building strategies —the first is to improve organizations and the second is to develop local urban and rural communities. As we review these cases, our major concern is how relevant organizational development, organizational theory, and organizational design strategies are for these two types of institutional development in developing countries.

Our major conclusion is that the three literatures on organizations are relevant to Third World contexts. Many of the successful interventions demonstrate the utility of contingency theory, for example. Many organizations were moved in the direction of being made effective bureaucracies by the addition of managerial technologies. Other organizations were moved in the direction of being made more organic and thus responsive to the needs of the clients.

In Chapter 5 we analyze the change efforts made in the Third World countries from the perspective of organizational theory. Our analysis suggests many lessons for development change agents. Some of these lessons reflect findings and theorems based on organizations in the developed world while some are relatively unique to Third World countries. In fact, we find a disjuncture between the literatures on organizations and development activities in the West and those in Third World countries. We hope that this monograph will help to close this gap and facilitate mutual learning. The developed countries can learn from the developing countries as well as vice-versa. There are many interesting experiments going on in less developed countries; we report several of these and the lessons that they provide.

Finally, in the Epilogue we articulate our work on organizational change with the problem of institutional development. We propose a strategy of organizational change which suggests what changes should be made and how to make them. We use six models of organizations to indicate the appropriate direction of change for different sets of contingencies. Our recommendation on how to change organizations is to use many tactics, although we point out that some tactics are more important than others. Finally, we discuss the two problems of power and scarce resources and indicate how to deal with them.

1

Organizational Change as a Strategy for Development

For more than three decades donor agencies such as the U.S. Agency for International Development (USAID), the World Bank, and La Cooperation, as well as government agencies in less developed countries (LDCs) in Asia, Africa, and Latin America, have intervened in organizations.[1] The interventions usually have been for short-term projects and any organizational changes were typically unplanned. With time, however, organizational interventions have become more intentional. Recently, donors and LDC governments have funded projects to add new outputs,[2] increase participation by beneficiaries,[3] create new organizations, decentralize decision making, or devolve administration.[4] At the same time, LDCs want to make their organizations more effective relative to long-term development goals. Given the current interest in improving organizations, now is a propitious time to review what has been learned about organizational change in LDCs and to begin constructing a program of research and training to make organizational change more effective.

Organizational change, whether in the developed or underdeveloped world, is extremely complex. There are dozens of variables that significantly affect organizational effectiveness, and perhaps hundreds which may be important in specific cases.[5] We handle this complexity by using a systems framework that relates strategies of organizational change to the desired ends, available means, and salient features of the context. By classifying variables as components of an organizational system and by analyzing how

9

they contribute to the achievement of goals, we use a logical framework to analyze organizational change.

Change agents must know which performance or output of an organization they want to affect and what structural arrangements can improve that performance. *The basic assumption of this monograph is that high attainment on different performances requires different structures.*[6] No single organizational model, whether bureaucracy or "ad hocracy," centralized or participatory, can claim always to be the best. In organizational theory this view is called the contingency approach to the study of organizations and is the major perspective used throughout this monograph.

This first chapter describes what is known about the practice of organizational change in the developed world and provides a foundation for the analysis of cases in the following chapters. It has four sections. The first gives a definition of organizations which designates those social collectives to which organizational theory applies. The definition of organizations is followed by a discussion of the performance-and-output gap approach to producing change in an organization. All change is at least implicitly designed to affect some output or performance; change agents need to make this objective explicit. Two performances—efficiency and innovation—are especially important since they require organizations to be structured very differently.

The third section reviews three basic literatures of organizational change: (1) industrial psychology or human relations, (2) the sociology of organizations, and (3) management research. Each of these literatures has an explicit or implicit change strategy. In human relations the strategy is explicit and is called organizational development. In the sociology of organizations it is implicit and we call it organizational theory, the term most often used in business schools. In management science the change strategy is called organizational design and is explicit. All three begin by identifying performance and output gaps in order to build pressure for change, but each focuses on different factors to improve performance and increase outputs. They also frequently differ in the kinds of outputs or performances that they try to impact. We compare these three literatures using our system's framework which focuses on culture-strategy, internal processes-functions, structures, resources-inputs, performance-output gaps, and environmental context.

The final section relates the above material to the rest of the study. We employ a special methodology, which is reflected in the monograph's arrangement and is described in this concluding section.

Definition of Organizations

All theories must define the unit(s) to which they apply. This monograph is based on a contingency theory of organizational change, so then we need to define an organization and compare it to other kinds of social collectives. Our definition must be precise in order to prevent inappropriate applications of organizational theory and organizational design. Although some principles of organizational theory can be applied to other social collectives, such as voluntary associations, groups, families, or nations, these collectives are guided by other principles and much of organizational theory does not apply.

To designate properly the social units which are appropriate for organizational theory we use a strict definition of an organization which includes seven elements:

1. At least five years in existence
2. Minimum size of ten members
3. Members are paid employees
4. Full-time annual workers
5. A division of labor with occupational skills
6. A single core technology or product/client group
7. Specific goals[7]

These seven elements define an organization as follows:

> a social collective which has existed for at least five years, including at least ten paid employees who work largely full time throughout the year, use essentially the same core technology, and are arranged in a variety of prescribed positions designed to achieve some specific collective output(s).

The first five characteristics can be made into continuums such as duration, size, extent of reliance on salary, and so forth. In most cases, however, we emphasize a specific turning point such as is found in a temperature scale when ice turns into water at zero degrees. In this sense the definition stresses the turning point rather than the continuum underlying it. This emphasis is useful because it tells us at what point along the continuum an organization materializes and organizational theory becomes applicable. It is apparent, however, that our turning points are not as precise as the temperature at which water freezes. A collective does not become magically an organization when the tenth member is added.

We recognize that organizations are commonly defined in sociology as social systems that are explicitly designed to achieve specific goals.[8] This definition, however, encompasses many social collectives that do not conform to a common set of organizational principles. For example, it includes instrumental voluntary associations and task groups, which are very different from organizations as we have defined them.

Some of the specific details of our narrow definition of organizations may seem to be quite arbitrary and yet they are essential. Research has shown that once the number of employees is less than ten, small-group dynamics take over and it is best to apply the principles of social psychology rather than organizational theory.[9] Concretely, what this means is that the mix or "chemistry" of personalities becomes very important for the success of the small group and small-group processes dominate. For this reason we will call social collectives with less than ten paid members, but with all the other characteristics, task or working groups. As the number of paid workers increases beyond ten, the organizational or formal characteristics tend to dominate.

The number of ten employees has many practical implications for development administration. Most of the businesses in Burkina Faso (Upper Volta), for example, have less than ten employees. Organizational theory change strategies, therefore, do not apply to most of these businesses nor to many other social institutions in Third World countries because they are based on small collectives and operate according to kinship or group principles. One would want to use other strategies to improve their performance; this problem is addressed in Chapter 5 and also in the Epilogue.

Size, of course, can be treated as a continuum. As organizations grow beyond ten, other changes occur which can be relevant for a change agent. One branch of organizational design has focused on the different kinds of crises or performance gaps which occur at different stages of growth in size. As size increases, the organization subdivides into departments and eventually into divisions, with new problems of coordination arising.

Duration, like size, is a continuum but differences in age are relatively unimportant past the formative period. The first few years of an organization are unique and often benefit from high motivation. As a result, pilot projects often succeed while the organization which follows their pattern fails. Organizational theory applies to relatively fixed organizational structures and routines and these require time to build. Permanence changes the nature of social collectives and produces certain kinds of problems in the process. As organizations become older, traditions or bureaucratic procedures become more and more institutionalized. The converse is that the organization becomes more and more difficult to change. Since organizational theory presumes a fair amount of stability, we will call any organization which has been in existence for less than five years an embryonic organization. Some theorems of organizational theory may apply to embryonic organizations, but they should be retested.

Not only do many social collectives in Third World countries have few paid employees, but often their workers are not full time or permanent, working intermittently instead. When this is a problem, their performance may be improved by transforming these task groups into organizations. For example, when a volunteer fire department provides inadequate service, a regular fire department could be formed.

Local social collectives that have been in existence for more than five years and are designed to achieve specific objectives, but have nonpaid members, are usually called instrumental voluntary associations. Because they do not have paid members they have a whole series of special problems which are uncommon in organizations. Participation and compliance of community members is problematic, leadership (and especially charismatic leadership) becomes more critical, and early success is practically required for their survival. In Chapters 2, 4, 5, and the Epilogue special attention is given to instrumental voluntary associations because they provide a number of opportunities for institution building in LDCs. Although they are not organizations in the technical sense of that term, some organizational principles do apply to them.

A division of labor with occupational skills is one of the most distinctive characteristics of organizations. While it is true that families have the positions or roles of husband and wife, father and mother, and peer groups have leaders, lieutenants, and followers, most organizations have a variety of positions or roles that usually have specific occupational skills. Family roles and roles in groups are not occupations, but roles in organizations are. Even relatively small organizations have a variety of occupations. A small print shop may have three or four printers, a manager-owner, several salespersons, a number of assemblers of print orders, and so forth. The number of job titles in a large organization may number in the hundreds. Admittedly, not all titles are occupations but the variety of titles does represent a division of labor. *It is this division of labor that gives organizations their productive advantage over work groups, primary groups, and even associations, especially when it comes to achieving complex goals.*

The next component of our definition is a single core technology or product/client group. These are complicated concepts and we discuss them at some length. These criteria are necessary to distinguish multiple organizations from single organizations. For example, some people mistakenly view the national government as one organization when it consists of many organizations which provide many different services. Chandler demonstrates in *Strategy and Structure* that producing paints and nylon requires two separate organizations because different technologies are used.[10] The two organizations may share the name, Du Pont, but they are separate organizations.

The term "technology-product group" is used because some technologies have only a few products—for example, bulk steel, rubber tire, and cement manufacturers; other technologies produce a wide variety of products within a product group—for example, drugs, certain chemical products, and certain electrical products.[11] The same distinctions apply in the area of general services. Hospitals handle a wide variety of diseases, and thus clients, within the same broad "technology" of medicine which includes surgery, obstetrics-gynecology, pediatrics, and the like. In contrast, mental hospitals tend to serve one basic type of client. In the area of manufacturing we use seven-digit standard industrial classification codes to distinguish technology-product groups. In the public sector, there are no easy classification schemes. *The reason for making a distinction between technology-product groups is that widely disparate technology-product groups have to be housed in different organizations.*

The rule of thumb for deciding if a social collective is a single or a multiple organization is whether a worker can do easily the work in both collectives, a manager can handle easily issues in both, and the customers or clients of both are quite similar on the relevant dimensions. If the answers to these three questions are no, then the researcher has distinguished separate technology-product groups and thus separate organizations even if the pay source and chain of command are the same.

It is important to distinguish the category of technology-product groups from managerial functions or occupational categories. Only differences in the former require different organizations. For example, a hospital needs housekeepers, nurses, and lab technicians as well as the appropriate medical personnel. The hospital is a single organization with many occupations arranged in departments. The same is true in the industrial sector. Various manufacturers have many of the same managerial specialists but the specific *content* of marketing, purchasing, research, and the like is different because the product group or client group is different. Thus, a single organization has a division of labor organized around a single core technology and produces products or services in a common product/client group. When the range in the behaviors, skills, and knowledge in the technology/products is substantial, however, then separate organizations should be formed around the different technology-product groups. For example, the treatment of acute and chronic mentally ill patients is so different that they must be housed in separate organizations. They differ in the nature of their staffing ratios, the kinds of specific difficulties they encounter, and even the level of the qualifications of their employees. The occupations involved, however, are similar. It is not the mix of occupational skills or job titles but the specifics of what the personnel do that is the heart of the technology-client group distinction.

Normally, organizational elites learn the hard way what the limits of their managerial expertise are. McNamara's whiz kids, who did such an effective job with Ford, took on Philco and mismanaged it. Exxon has mismanaged most of the small, high-tech companies which it bought. Indeed, many of the conglomerates have not done well. Peters and Waterman observe that effective, large companies "stick close to their knitting," meaning that they stay close to their core technology.[12]

Why must different technology-product groups be housed and managed separately? The reason is that each kind of technology-product group has a whole series of specific skills which are not covered by general principles. In addition, there are limits to a person's cognition that prevent one from being a master of all trades. (Herbert Simon made this a cornerstone of his theory of administrative practice.)[13]

The last element of our definition is the specific outputs or goals of the organization. The specific goals are intrinsically linked to the organization's technology-product/client group. These are called instrumental goals or specific outputs because they are tangible and measurable, such as teaching, healing, making cars, making steel, and so on. When outputs are not clear or easily measured, success or failure is not demonstrable and performance tends to suffer. This is a problem for many public sector organizations.

In summary, our definition of an organization as one kind of social collective is complex and narrow, but this precision is absolutely necessary if organizational change strategies are to be applied properly. Making proper distinctions is a basic principle of science and we dishonor the organizational literature when we apply it to other kinds of social collectives. In fact, the literature on the sociology of organizations has a set of limits which we have tried to specify. As one moves farther and farther away from our definition, its applicability becomes less and less.

Performance and Output Gaps

A change effort must begin by specifying the change desired. Influential persons in the organization, or in a parent organization, must perceive a gap between the performances and outputs of the organization and acceptable levels of these performances and outputs. Otherwise, they will not change the organization. *A basic assumption of this monograph is that the motivation or pressure for change results from the identification of a performance or output gap that is valued by organizational decision makers.*[14] This assumption agrees with Leonard's remark: ". . . We know of no stronger impetus to administrative reform than clear, objective evidence of poor performance in a significant output area."[15]

No formula can be provided for identifying the performance or output gaps which will mobilize pressure for organizational change. The performances or outputs that are important to influentials vary with types of organizations and with cultural differences between societies. They even vary among organizations of the same type in the same society.[16] Nevertheless, change agents can begin their investigation by testing the assumption that the influentials are interested in increasing effectiveness, efficiency, and/or the volume of outputs, as long as other important interests or values are not sacrificed in the process. This assumption holds in almost all of the cases reviewed in this book.

Most change agents focus on increasing the volume of output, e.g., number of letters delivered, number of bridges built, number of adults who are taught to read and write. It is important to increase outputs but it is often more important to improve performances, especially efficiency or innovation.

Efficiency can be defined as the cost of delivering those letters, building those bridges, or providing those literacy campaigns. Many of the interventions in developing countries are in public sector organizations, but, as we can see, efficiency can be measured in these as well.[17] Innovation creates new products and services or new methods and processes. Innovation would develop new types of mail delivery services, new methods for building bridges, or new programs for educating adults. Innovation is also the addition of new services to the same organization.

Organizations have official objectives and top management can develop clear and detailed goal satements in guided discussion groups,[18] but these may not be the important objectives for the people with influence in the organization. The change agent, therefore, must find out who the influentials are and what their goals are for the organization. One method for discovering the real goals of the organization is to arrange discussions in unstructured groups. Another method is to examine the transactions between the organization and its environment (customers, suppliers, government agencies, and the like) and deduce the values which best explain these interactions. It is important to pay close attention to what organizations actually do and what they accomplish. Often the change agent will have to collect data on accomplishments to make performance or output gaps clear, because often organizations believe they are performing adequately when they are not. For example, recently, high schools in the United States have found out that they are graduating a shockingly large number of illiterates.

It is widely understood that interests influence the choice of goals. Usually the goals of an organization are determined by the interests of the decision makers. It is easy to overlook, therefore, the influence of ideas and ideologies on goals unless they are the ideas and values of decision makers. We draw attention, therefore, to five sources of ideas and ideologies that can influence critically the organization's goals, i.e., the performances and outputs that an organization emphasizes. These sources are the vision of a dominant person, the perspective of an occupational group, the strategy of the organization, the political ideology of the society, and the values of the society's culture. We give examples of these influences below.

There are many famous stories of the role founders of large corporations, such as Ford, Rockefeller, Vanderbilt, and Hughes have played in piloting their organizations, for better or for worse. They were leaders of vision, but sometimes performance or output gaps are created because the top person pursues one objective too relentlessly—using his position to stay on course even in the face of a performance gap. Consider the example of Eddie Rickenbacher, head of Eastern Airlines from 1935 to 1959, who constantly tried to reduce costs. Coffee and cookies were served instead of breakfast, seating was five abreast rather than four, and male flight attendants were hired to avoid pregnancy leaves. As the American public demanded more and better service, Eastern Airlines lost customers and profits. Although Rickenbacher retired in 1959, he remained on Eastern's board and continued to influence corporate policy. The airline did not recover until Floyd Hall took over in 1973 and bought new planes, emphasized customer service, and worked to change the image of Eastern Airlines to one of quality service. By 1975 profits were restored.[19] Eastern Airlines was an example of an organization which failed to change, even when faced with a performance gap for an extended period of time, because of the ideas of a single man.

Certain occupational groups can also dominate an organization, in which case their values will determine what is most critical. In *On a Clear Day You Can See General Motors* DeLorean describes how finance specialists gained and maintained control of General Motors.[20] Just as with Eastern Airlines, the consequence was a lack of innovation and too much concern with efficiency, which eventually led to GM's loss of market share to Japanese manufacturers who were more innovative.

Another influence on the choice of performances and outputs is the organization's selection of a strategy of success. The Ralston Purina Company provides an example.[21] When its competition reduced their prices, Ralston did not respond; instead, its strategy was to protect profit margins even if it lost business in the process. This strategy reflected its goals—to protect profit margins rather than to maintain a share of the market. Given this strategy, change is not possible until profit margins fall.

The development strategies of political elites can also influence the preferred outputs and performances of the organization. A society such as Korea's, which has set very ambitious goals of rapid economic growth, puts enormous pressure on managers to achieve constant gains in productivity. Political leaders in Tanzania, on the other hand, have chosen equality as their definition of development, a choice which creates other kinds of pressures on managers.

Finally, the larger values of the society and its culture help determine the relative importance of the various performances, outputs, and objectives of the organization. Corruption is defined in the West as a performance gap in government, but in LDCs it may simply reflect the positive cultural values of tribal or kinship loyalty. Efficiency has been a dominant value in the United States, but it is not valued everywhere. Presthus studied a Turkish organization filled with engineers which was inefficient by American standards. He discovered that their goal was to absorb unemployed professionals, a practice which he labeled "welfare bureaucracy."[22] By this criterion, the organization did not necessarily have a performance gap.

Strategies of Organizational Change

There are no satisfactory schemes for classifying organizational change strategies. However, there are three major literatures about organizations which provide analytical tools and practical guidelines for change agents. Each of these comes out of a different academic discipline. They are: (1) human relations and/or organizational development, (2) the sociology of organizations and/or organizational theory, and (3) management or organizational design. We use these three literatures to classify change strategies, using an analytical framework to compare them in a systematic way. Increasingly, each strategy of organizational change is borrowing ideas and techniques from the other strategies but most change agents generally employ only one of the three strategies.

A Framework for Analyzing Change Strategies

We define a strategy of organizational change as a plan for achieving a purpose. At minimum, the plan needs to indicate what the change should accomplish (the performance or output deficiencies which are to be corrected) and the change points (the components of the system which should be changed to increase performance and output). In addition, the plan should specify the change process, including the intervention level, the change tactics, the methods of data collection, and the resources needed. In other words, the change strategy involves three questions: why should the organization be changed, what changes should be made, and how should the changes be made? The framework that we propose is organized around these three questions, presented in Figure 1.1, and discussed briefly in the following paragraphs.

This is easily one of the most elaborate frameworks provided in the literature. We think an elaborate framework is necessary since many change efforts in the past have failed due to underestimating the complexity of the task. Often change agents worked with only one model of a good organization or proposed only one kind of change intervention, and were not sensitive to a different model or a different type of intervention being more appropriate. Furthermore, they often changed too few elements for lasting effects and/or utilized too few levels of intervention, tactics, resources, or methods of data collection. In particular, they did not emphasize sufficiently methods of data collection for demonstrating performance gaps.

Earlier we noted that there are optimists and pessimists when it comes to the possibilities for development in many Third World countries. We agree with the pessimists that development is a difficult task, but we agree with the optimists that it can be accomplished. The solution to this contradiction is that difficult tasks can only be accomplished with a complex approach. It is in this spirit that we offer Figure 1.1.

The three change strategies focus on different kinds of performance or output gaps (different reasons for changing the organization). The organizational development literature focuses on individual morale and motivation, clarity of goals and roles as a requisite of individual effectiveness, and team building. It looks at performances and outputs of individuals and groups which contribute to organizational performance and output. The other two strategies focus directly on performances and outputs at the organizational level but tend to emphasize different performances. Organizational theory emphasizes innovation while organizational design emphasizes efficiency.

Once the reasons for changing an organization are identified, the change agent must determine what component of the organizational system should be changed. The organizational system has five basic components: the culture-strategy, internal processes including managerial functions, structures, an environment, and inputs or resources. The causes of performance and output gaps can be traced to one or more of these variables. The three organizational change strategies identify the same components of the organizational system, but differ in the components which their interventions modify. Organizational development changes internal processes and inputs; it does the latter by changing the skills and attitudes of the personnel. Organizational theory mainly changes structures although structural changes will often require concomitant changes of processes and personnel. Organizational design changes culture and strategy, structures and processes.

The next question is how to change the organization. The change agent must determine the appropriate intervention level, tactics, resources for change, and methods of data collection. Most interventions occur at the micro- or organizational levels depending upon the strategy employed. Organizational development intervenes at the microlevel and works with individuals and groups, even though it may apply its microinterventions widely in the organization. Both organizational theory and organizational design generally intervene at the organizational level, although organizational design may also intervene at the departmental level. None of the strategies intervenes often at the environmental level, but both organizational theory and organizational design offer theories and analyses which can provide some guidance for environment-level interventions. *It is our assumption that change agents must be concerned about multiple levels and therefore draw upon several of these disciplines.*

Different levels of intervention involve change agents in different kinds of collectives. Because organizational development is a microstrategy, it can be used with work groups, voluntary associations, and small or embryonic organizations. While not as effective with these kinds of collectives, organizational theory and organizational design are relevant to changing the entire organization. One of the reasons organizational development can be effective with small organizations, voluntary associations, and task groups is that many of its major concepts, such as leadership and motivation, reflect the kinds of problems these collectives have. If one wants to upgrade the voluntary associations and task groups into organizations, however, then the two other strategies are more appropriate.

Figure 1.1   Basic Questions for Development Change Agents When Designing an Organizational Change Strategy

---

1. **Why change?**
   What are the performance and output *gaps*?

   a. Inadequate output of goods and services
   b. Low performance as measured by efficiency, innovation, or adaptiveness
   c. Inadequate utilization, support or maintenance
   d. Low motivation or insufficient rewards for individuals (job dissatisfaction)

2. **What change?**
   Which *component* of the system needs to be changed?

   a. Culture or strategy
   b. Structures
   c. Internal processes
   d. Resources or inputs
   e. Environment

3. **How to change?**
   At what *level* should the intervention be instituted?

   a. Microlevel, e.g., individuals and work groups
   b. Organizational level
   c. Environmental level, e.g. interorganizational, community or region

4. **How to change?**
   Which *tactics of change* or ways to introduce change in an organization are appropriate?

   a. Decree approach: New directions come from the top and are passed down through the organization with "one-way" communications.
   b. Replacement approach: To bring about organizational changes one or more individuals, usually in high-level positions, are replaced by others with different views or skills.
   c. Structural approach: The structure of the organization and the required relationships of subordinates are modified.
   d. Group decision approach: Group members participate in the selection and implementation of alternatives specified by others. (Others identify the problem, and the group agrees on a course of action from available alternatives.)
   e. Data collection and discussion approach: Information is obtained about the organization and feedback is given to the members by an internal or external change agent. Organization members then develop their own analysis of the data to identify problems and suggest solutions.
   f. Group problem-solving approach: The group gathers information, identifies problems, and designs and implements solutions.
   g. T-group approach: The group is trained to understand the processes of individual and group behavior and to relate more openly. As a result, work relationships improve and performance increases.
   h. Experimental approach: Trial and error is used to determine which change works best; sometimes these experiments are called pilots.
   i. Training: Members acquire new skills, concepts, and behaviors.

Figure 1.1 (continued)

---

5. **How to change?**
   What *resources* are needed for achieving change and what resources are available?

   a. Finances
   b. Power
   c. Knowledge
   d. Personnel
   e. Time

6. **How to change?**
   What *methods of data collection* are useful?

   a. Informant interviews
   b. Surveys of individuals
   c. Surveys of organizations
   d. Documents
   e. Observation

We suggest, however, that it is often better to combine several of these analytical levels even when focusing on one particular kind of social collective.

The first seven tactics of change presented in Figure 1.1 are derived from a classification scheme developed by Greiner.[23] To Greiner's list we have added experimentation and training, which are important because they tend to reduce resistance and encourage organizational learning. Each of the three strategies uses several of these tactics but varies in their mix. Organizational development emphasizes the tactics which involve groups: group data discussion, group decision making, group problem solving, T-groups, and sensitivity training. Organizational theory emphasizes restructuring, decree, data collection, and group discussion. Organizational design emphasizes restructuring, decree, and group problem solving.

Resources are an element in any change plan. In addition to financial resources, knowledge, and number and kinds of personnel, change agents need to take into account the time it takes to implement change and the power that can be marshalled in support of the change. All five of these resources are to a certain extent interchangeable, although the last two are frequently overlooked. When there is not enough money to pay for the requisite personnel, one can share power with beneficiaries in order to generate voluntary labor. Conversely, without much power one can use time to build support from key individuals, groups, and even coalitions. Both organizational theory and organizational design tend to be more concerned with nonpersonnel resource problems than is organizational development.

The change process often involves data collection. This is a frequently ignored but important aspect of any change strategy. Many organizations use information-feedback systems to trigger changes.[24] *Change agents may also use data-collection techniques to determine the existence of performance and output gaps and their causes.* Although all three strategies employ data collection, they differ in the ways in which they tend to collect and use their data. The organizational design strategy employs management consultants who conduct in-depth interviews with key informants. Organizational development research frequently relies on surveys of staff attitudes, while organizational theory researchers conduct surveys of organizations, using the organization as the unit of analysis and utilizing documents where possible.

In our following discussion of the three change strategies, we use the elements identified in Figure 1.1 and add the strategies' major assumptions and concepts. Intervention level, tactics, resources, and data collection are covered under the nature of the approach. This is a complex framework for analyzing organizational change strategies, but it provides an inventory of useful questions for development change agents to use as a diagnostic. In subsequent chapters, we use it to analyze the success of interventions.

Organizational Development

The best-known organizational change strategy is organizational development, usually called O.D., which focuses on tools and techniques for introducing change. Much of O.D. grew out of the human-relations approach to organizations.[25] In the beginning its famous T-groups developed some notoriety. Over time it has developed a wide variety of behavioral science techniques for identifying and attacking problems in organizations. It is well-grounded in a solid literature variously called "industrial psychology" or "organizational behavior." Figure 1.2 contains the major highlights of the O.D. strategy of change.

Assumptions and concepts.   Many of the crucial assumptions of O.D. involve motivation. O.D. change agents agree generally that most organizations stifle individual initiative and motivation.

Figure 1.2   Highlights of the Organizational Development Change Strategy

---

Fundamental Assumptions

1. Organizations should provide personal growth and development for its members.
2. Organizations should encourage openness and collaboration.
3. Organizations should encourage the expressions of feelings.
4. Organizations that improve human fulfillment also tend to be productive.

Major Concepts, Variables, and Ideas

1. Maslow's hierarchy of human needs
2. Skill variety, task significance, job autonomy, and feedback
3. Fiedler's contingency theory of leadership; Blake and Mouton's grid
4. Team building, laboratory training, and encounter groups
5. Groups, group problem solving, and risk taking
6. Intergroup relations, competition, and conflict
7. Climate and culture

Intervener Target: Closing Gaps in the Following Performances and Outputs

1. Clarity of goals and roles
2. Motivation and commitment
3. Collaboration and team building
4. Job satisfaction and employee attitudes

Change Points: Components of the System Usually Changed

1. Job design
2. Employees' attitudes
3. Group processes
4. Culture and climate
5. Role expectations

Nature of Approach

1. Usual intervention level: individuals and groups
2. Usual tactics of change: group decision making, T-group and sensitivity
   training, group problem solving, and data discussion groups
3. Usual method of data collection: surveys of individuals
4. Usual resources involved: low costs, influence rather than power, a few trainers
   in group processes, a few group facilitators, and short time frames

---

The basic thrust of the O.D. change strategy, therefore, is to improve motivation and morale, thereby increasing organizational productivity.[26] A major assumption of O.D. is that workers will be happier, harder working, and more productive if they are allowed to participate in group decisions and are given some authority.[27] The methods change agents use to increase motivation are improvements in job design, career opportunities, clarity of goals, and group processes, because problems in these areas are perceived to be the major causes of low morale and productivity. This approach has been very attractive to top management and O.D. change agents receive many requests to improve worker job satisfaction, motivation, and other work-related attitudes.

Unlike the other two strategies, O.D. does not assume that there is a rational order to the world or that people should be seen simply as rational calculators. In its variants of T-groups or encounter groups, O.D. places great emphasis on expressing feelings or increasing sensitivity, a concern not shared by the other two change literatures. It tries to deal with the whole person. For example, Beer and other O.D. change agents assume that workers desire personal growth and development. They urge organizations to encourage openness, collaboration, and the expression of feelings to motivate workers to work harder to achieve the goals of the organization.[28] The biases of social psychology and North American culture are evident in these assumptions. In our judgment the assumption about openness, collaboration, and expression of feelings may not fit many non-Western cultures, while that of the need for growth and development may.

Because it has grown out of an industrial and social psychology approach to the study of organizations, O.D. focuses on individual and group needs. There is a large literature on this subject, but we include in Figure 1.2 only a reference to the very influential theory of a hierarchy of needs developed by Maslow.[29]

One group of O.D. change agents is oriented to sociotechnical change and is guided by the research done at Travistock in England. Their purpose is to have the workers themselves, working in groups, redesign jobs so that they are more humane.[30] This approach makes a number of critical motivational assumptions. For example, it assumes that increasing skill variety, job autonomy, and job enrichment increases workers' happiness and motivation. Hackman and Suttle argue that skill variety plus task identity (i.e., the task makes an identifiable contribution) plus task significance times job autonomy and feedback on the results of one's work equals motivation potential.[31] These changes do not always increase productivity, but their goal is to pay for themselves in the long run by reducing turnover and absenteeism. A dramatic example of a successful use of this strategy is the redesign of the Volvo factory in Sweden around semiautonomous work groups. The rearrangement of the assembly line cost more, but the reduction in turnover paid for these costs.[32]

A major strength of the O.D. approach and, more generally, industrial psychology is the understanding of groups and how they function. A large body of research, usually entitled small-group research, has focused on the many advantages of groups over individuals working separately. Groups are better for working on complex, interdependent tasks which are too difficult for any one individual to perform, and for generating new ideas or creative solutions. They are also effective for creating liaisons and doing coordination, especially between departments which are different but interdependent.

Perhaps the most important asset of groups from our perspective is their ability to solve problems. Two famous examples of the use of groups for problem solving are quality work circles, used by the Japanese, and task forces as recommended in *In Search of Excellence*.[33] They are needed for problem solving in LDCs because development is a complex task requiring a great deal of creativity. For the same reasons they are usually needed for the critical function of implementing organizational change. Groups are also used effectively in some of the cases reported here in training, especially in new management technologies.

Intergroup relations are also a critical component of O.D. approaches to the study of organizations. A typical example of intergroup problems is the frequent conflict between sales and production. Beer reports the example of an intervention where the two groups were brought together in a motel to discuss their intergroup relations. Each group met separately, listed what bothered it, and listed what it thought bothered the other group. Reports were made to each other without opportunities to be defensive. The groups began to listen to each other's complaints and gradually better ways were found for resolving differences.[34]

The assumptions for the organizationwide version of O.D. are not uniform nor always clearly articulated. Frequently, O.D. change agents seem to view organizations as a collection of individual members (both organizational theory and organizational design strongly disagree with this view). Thus, when O.D. change agents attempt to improve the "climate" or "culture" of the organization, they clarify the goals and roles of individuals, usually through group discussion.[35]

Intervener targets: performance and output gaps. The major objectives of O.D. change agents are to clarify goals, make jobs more satisfying, improve motivation, build teams, and increase collaboration. The original T-group work started with the objective of increasing collaboration and was exemplified by an O.D. intervention in a company with bad union-management relations. The O.D. expert suggested that the union and management develop a new way of communicating with each other that stressed listening, constructive dialogue, and the expression of feelings. The new methods led to more trust and an improvement in labor-management relations.[36]

Usually, O.D. interventions address specific problems and directly involve only part of the organization. Occasionally, however, an O.D. intervention involves extensive changes. An interesting example of an intervention that changed the goals, roles, and culture of an organization was the attempt to transform the goals of a mental hospital from custodial to therapeutic.[37] This transformation required a fundamental shift in the values and behavior of all staff members. It was accomplished through extensive group discussions that built a consensus about the desirability of this change for improving the treatment of patients. There were extensive discussions among the staff about how to change their behavior to implement the new treatment successfully. In the process the power structure was altered from highly centralized to relatively decentralized.

Change points: components of the system usually changed. The major change point for O.D. is the internal process of the organization. This includes primarily group processes and job design. An example of a job redesign intervention occurred at the General Foods plant in Topeka, Kansas where O.D. change agents used the microstructural changes of job enlargement, job enrichment, and semiautonomous work groups to improve employee morale and productivity.[38]

Another change point in O.D. is role expectations. Social psychologists, such as Kahn, have demonstrated that conflicts in expectations lead to role conflict, role ambiguity, and role strain.[39] O.D. techniques, usually group discussions, have been developed to resolve such conflicts. One of these is the T-group which started as a way of improving communication between supervisor and subordinates. For example, a failing pajama plant was acquired by a competitor.[40] O.D. agents worked out a carefully sequenced organizational development plan. Supervisors were given sensitivity training to improve the collaboration of supervisors and subordinates; then they were taught to conduct problem-solving sessions with subordinates. Outside resources were also invested in the plant. The results were striking. Operator productivity improved 43 percent; turnover declined 90 percent and absenteeism 50 percent; errors in manufacturing were reduced by 39 percent; and profits moved from a loss of 15 percent to a gain of 17 percent in three years.

Group formation is a frequent change point in O.D. strategies to change organizations. The group may be created to diagnose the state of the organization and to identify performance or output gaps or it may be used to build communication between two groups which were antagonistic, as we saw in Beer's example of manufacturing and sales described earlier. In many of our cases groups are created to solve problems and to implement change, and in others they are used as effective tools for training. Group formation is an important part of most of the interventions which we review in Chapter 3.

Occasionally, the change point for an O.D. intervention is the culture or climate of an organization. We have already cited the mental hospital case in which an entire culture or climate of an organization was changed when its goal was changed. Although interventions at this level are rare in O.D., they may become more common in the future because of the current concern about culture in organizations. This concern is evidenced by the success of the book *Theory Z* and by the interest in the culture of Japanese organizations.[41]

Nature of the approach.   O.D. intervenes at two distinct levels. It usually intervenes at the microlevel, and changes individuals and groups. Sometimes it intervenes at the organizationwide level, and attempts to change the culture and climate of the organization by changing the values and beliefs of the members. O.D. tends to perceive inadequate organizational performances and outputs as due to inadequate individual efforts. O.D.'s solutions usually involve microchanges such as job redesign, training, or even group therapy.

Popular O.D. tactics are group decision making, T-groups, and problem-solving groups. Each has a slightly different objective. Group decision making or participation is used to build motivation, develop consensus on goals, clarify goals and roles, and modify the climate. T-groups and variations on them are used to create and improve communication and to build greater trust. The essence of T-groups is to heighten sensitivity. In contrast, problem-solving groups focus on solving problems rather than on morale and group relations. They attempt to determine the causes of certain difficulties and then work out solutions to them. For example, a small unionized plant had been losing money for two years. A new plant manager held a general meeting and presented data on the severity of the problem. Groups of managers and hourly employees were formed to discuss the causes of poor performance and thus to identify problems. Task forces were then formed by functional area to solve these problems. Solutions were recommended to the plant managers and the managers' decisions were communicated to the workers. Within three months the plant had reached a break-even point and commitment was very high.[42]

Generally, the resources needed for O.D. interventions are not large. O.D. change agents operate within a relatively short time frame because they usually work with only a part of the organization. One major exception is sociotechnical interventions which may extend over a considerable period of time and require a much larger investment of human and financial resources.

Surveys of individuals' attitudes are a very common technique for collecting data within the O.D. approach. They are used in studies of job design, job satisfaction, climate, motivation and to determine the extent of conflict in role expectations.

The above description of O.D. describes its major concerns in the past. Increasingly, however, O.D. is moving toward a systems perspective on organizations and trying to incorporate the concerns of organizational theory and organizational design.[43] Indeed, the term O.D. now covers such a variety of techniques that it has lost much of its previous distinctiveness. This expansion allows us to synthesize these three perspectives more easily into a comprehensive view of organizational change.

Organizational Theory

A second literature relevant to organizations is that of organizational theory (see Figure 1.3). The academic base for this change strategy is the sociology of organizations. While sociology identifies this field as "complex or formal organizations," business schools identify it as organizational theory (O.T.) Unlike O.D., there is no branch of O.T. that is expressly concerned with the applied issues of how to change organizations. One of its major re-

Figure 1.3   Highlights of the Organizational Theory Change Strategy

Fundamental Assumptions

1. How organizations are structured affects performances and outputs.
2. Values of dominant coalition also affect performances and outputs.
3. Environment sets limits on how organizations are structured.
4. People who lose status or power resist organizational changes.
5. The more exposure to change, the more acceptance of it.

Major Concepts, Variables, and Ideas

1. Division of labor, complexity, and concentration of specialists
2. Centralization, hierarchy of authority, and supervision
3. Communication and compliance
4. Technology, routineness, and task scope
5. Personnel size and budget size
6. Environmental complexity, uncertainty, and change
7. Environmental richness, leanness, and cooperation/competitiveness

Intervener Targets: Closing Gaps in the Following Performances and Outputs

1. Innovation in technology, services, or products
2. Effectiveness in terms of quantity and quality
3. Efficiency and productivity
4. Morale, absenteeism, and turnover

Change Points: Components of the System Usually Changed

1. Structure
2. Coordination/Control processes
3. Inputs
4. Environment

Nature of Approach

1. Usual intervention level: entire organization or environment including
   interorganizational relationships
2. Usual tactics of change: restructure, decree, data collection, and group discussion
3. Usual method of data collection: surveys of organizations rather than individuals,
   participant observation, and documents
4. Usual resources involved: personnel, money, and long time frame

---

search areas, however, is called "organizational change" and much of what follows is based on the organizational change literature.

Assumptions and concepts.   Organizational theory can be traced back to Weber. He perceived that a rational-legal bureaucracy was efficient because it had characteristics such as hierarchy of authority, rules, clearly defined responsibilities, files, careers, and so on. These provided more order, discipline, and predictability than was found in traditional or charismatic organizations.[44] This assumption differs considerably from the assumptions in O.D., which emphasize people rather than structure, and feelings rather than order or predictability. Although O.D. change agents now recognize the importance of structure, its proponents virtually ignored structure in the beginning.

The bureaucratic form, according to Weber, was superior to other organizational forms in achieving its goals. This assumption was disproved finally by empirical studies which found a second type of organization, the organic model, flourishing under certain circumstances. The organic model was designed to be innovative rather than efficient. Burns and Stalker found that the organic model has very different structural characteristics than the bureaucratic model. These characteristics—a network of communication, authority, and control; an absence of rules; an emphasis on careers; and continual redefinition of jobs—facilitated innovation in organizations.[45] The Burns and Stalker model gave birth to contingency theory, which can be reduced to the simple but profound notion that different models or structural characteristics are appropriate for different tasks or goals. The theoretical work of Perrow, Woodward, Thompson, Blau and his students, and Hage has been concerned with how tasks and environmental contingencies affect structure.[46] This work is reviewed in Chapter 2.

The term "contingency theory" comes from the famous work of Lawrence and Lorsch, two advocates of organizational design, who identified the impacts of environmental constraints on organizational structure.[47] Environmental contingencies—variables such as demand for the organization's outputs, technological change, product-mix, and the like—set limits on how the organization should be structured to survive and operate effectively. In some environments it should be structured bureaucratically with well-defined routines for producing large quantities of identical goods or services. In other environments it should be organically structured with few routines and many highly skilled professionals producing high-quality and relatively unique goods and services.

Although contingency theory is the dominant perspective in O.T., it is not the only one. The second most prevalent perspective is the political perspective, which emphasizes the influence of the dominant coalition's values on the organization's performances and outputs.[48] Even individual leaders can have a decisive influence on the way organizations perform and the outputs they produce. For example, a new superintendent introduced a series of bureaucratic controls in a high school district in Chicago.[49] Although the district had been one of the most innovative from 1959 to 1964, it became the least innovative after the introduction of PPBS (program, planning, and budget system). The new procedures not only caused a shift in goals from innovation to efficiency, but also a greater centralization of decision making. Teachers no longer had professional autonomy and the structure shifted from organic to mechanical (bureaucratic).

The motivational assumptions are fairly explicit in O.T. concerning organizational change. The most common assumption is that groups that have power, privilege, or pay are reluctant to share them—the vested interest argument. One demonstration of the power of vested interests is McCleery's study of the introduction of rehabilitation programs in a prison.[50] The guards resisted the change because it meant raising the power of the rehabilitators at the expense of that of the guards. The vested interest assumption is critical in organizational theory since structural changes usually upset the power arrangements.

Another assumption in O.T. is that experience with change develops a greater tolerance for change. It is a commonly observed fact that some organizations have a lot of change; clearly the members have developed coping mechanisms. In a study of a community hospital, Hage found that the doctors who were located in departments that had experienced a lot of change accepted a new program of medical education even when they lost power and status.[51] In contrast, doctors in stable departments resisted the change. The lesson for change agents is to introduce new programs first in a department or organization which has already experienced changes.

The major concepts in O.T. are listed in Figure 1.3. Complexity and centralization are perhaps the two most important structural properties of organizations in the O.T. literature. They are central to the organic and mechanical models and to discussions of innovation and size. Etzioni has established the importance of various compliance mechanisms for the structure and processes of organizations,[52] and communication patterns are central to the studies of innovation. Technology, size, and environmental factors define the contingencies in contingency theory and will be discussed throughout this monograph.

Intervener targets: performance and output gaps.   Typically, O.T. focuses on the performance dimensions of effectiveness, efficiency, morale, and innovation. Effectiveness is central to both O.T.

and organizational design. Some analysts, such as Price, define it as the summation of efficiency, morale, and innovation.[53] Others, such as Daft, distinguish between effectiveness and efficiency by defining effectiveness as the "degree to which an organization realizes its goals" and efficiency as "the amount of resources used to produce a unit of output."[54] Still others, noting the lack of conceptual agreement, argue that the concept should be dropped.[55] Nevertheless, every text contains a discussion of effectiveness and we find Daft's definitions distinguishing between efficiency and effectiveness acceptable and we judge it to be a useful concept for change agents.

The concept of effectiveness is central to this manuscript because performance and output gaps are usually classified as ineffectiveness. We recognize that effectiveness may be difficult to measure in certain cases, so we present an illustration of effectiveness measurement from the O.T. literature for a public sector organization. Hall and Clark studied youth-related welfare agencies in twelve large cities.[55] The organizations included juvenile courts, adolescent mental health centers, juvenile detention divisions, and school social work activities. To assess effectiveness, the research team visited each organization. Members and employees were asked to list the five most important tasks of the organization. From these responses the team developed a long list of goals. Respondents then indicated which were the key goals for the organization, and the final list of goals was approved by the organization's top administrator. This procedure was quite effective for identifying operational goals. The operative goals for one organization, the juvenile court, are as follows:

1. Determine the best disposition for each child who appears before the court
2. Protect the civil and legal rights of minors
3. Protect the community from those youths who are dangerous
4. Hear and justly dispose of cases before the court
5. Cooperate with other agencies who deal with problem youths
6. Remove children from family situations that are damaging to their welfare
7. Foster acceptance of an individualized rehabilitative treatment philosophy by the general public and other system agencies
8. Develop more resources and better methods of helping problem youth

Effectiveness would be the achievement of each of these goals. Failure in reaching any one of them creates an output gap and pressure for change. Therefore, a change agent would seek a rough consensus on indicators of success, adequate performance, and failure for these dimensions, and then measure and evaluate performance.

Organizational theory finds that both innovation and efficiency can not be pursued effectively at the same time because they require different structures. Organizations, therefore, must decide on the relative emphasis to place on each performance and then structure the organization accordingly. For example, while all welfare agencies produce services, some emphasize efficiency by servicing many clients with few workers while others emphasize the quality of services (more varied and innovative) with fewer clients per worker. Once one knows the relative importance of each performance—efficiency versus innovation, quantity versus quality of services or products, morale versus productivity—the appropriate structure can be specified.

Change points: components of the system usually changed. The main change point for the O.T. strategy is the structure of the organization. The major contribution of O.T. to the craft of improving organizational performances and outputs is its understanding of the structural arrangements which are the most effective in various contexts. When organizations are failing, or environmental conditions are changing, the structure should be changed according to O.T. to improve performances. The appropriate direction of structural change for the four most typical environmental circumstances is spelled out by contingency theory which is reviewed in the next chapter.

The structural variables which are changed by the O.T. strategy are listed under Major Concepts in Figure 1.3. Their influence on innovation has been identified by Hage and Aiken who have conducted a seven-year program of research on public sector organizations, such as welfare agencies, mental hospitals, residential treatment agencies, and sheltered workshops. They found that increases in the complexity of the division of labor, decentralization of the power structure, job autonomy and professional activity of the professionals, and equality among them in terms of pay correlated with higher rates of establishing new programs and services.[57] They also found that the above variables were related to a network pattern of communication which provided a much higher volume of communication, especially of a horizontal nature, than would a more hierarchically organized communication system.

Another major area of O.T. research concerns the structural determinants of morale, turnover, and absenteeism, concerns which are shared with O.D. From the O.T perspective, formalization of job descriptions, surveillance, centralization of decision making, and low job autonomy lead to low morale.[58] Also, Price found that in general the lower the status of the occupation, the higher the absenteeism.[59] The implication for change agents is that improving these variables should improve morale and reduce absenteeism.

O.T. also studies the role of coordination and control mechanisms and processes. Coordination is defined as the integration of programs to achieve the goals of the organization, while control refers to the conformity of individuals to job descriptions. Many scholars have studied these variables,[60] but the best-known contribution is a typology developed by Etzioni. He classifies organizations as normative, remunerative and coercive, on the basis of their compliance mechanisms. Some organizations motivate participants to act as the organization dictates through normative rewards, some through economic rewards, and some through coercion. It should be noted that most organization theory has been developed by researching remunerative organizations, and, therefore, applies most aptly to them. Most organizations, however, do not use only one type of compliance mechanism. The organic economic organization is based on remuneration but also uses some normative compliance mechanisms as well while mechanical organizations even use some coercive mechanisms in addition to remuneration.

Many theorists in O.T. have tried to determine the major contingencies that influence the choice of structure and coordination/control processes. A large program of research, initiated by Blau and his many students, has focused on size as a critical contingency.[61] The research shows that an increase in size leads to a more complex division of labor, especially more job titles, more departments and hierarchical levels, and, perhaps surprisingly, more decentralization.

Another line of O.T. research has focused on the effects of technology on organizational structure. Woodward demonstrated that small batch and process technologies are associated with organic organizational structures, while mass production and assembly-line technologies are associated with mechanical organizational structures.[62] Hage and Aiken found that routine technologies lead to greater centralization of power.[63] Technology and size, therefore, are input contingencies which affect the structure, control mechanisms, and performances of the organization.

Two new areas of research in O.T. are the environments of organizations[64] and interorganizational relationships.[65] An interesting line of research in the former area is on aspects of the environments that influence market interactions and the death rates of businesses. An example of the latter area is the work of Aiken *et al.*, which demonstrates how difficult it has been for change agents to construct interorganizational relationships in the area of mental retardation.[66]

Nature of the approach. Though few organizational theorists intervene in organizations, their ideas do constitute a strategy of organizational change. O.T. usually intervenes at the organizational level. More and more, however, O.T. analysts implicitly recommend intervening at the environmental level, but most environmental variables are difficult to manipulate.

O.T. change tactics emphasize structural changes, since so much of the theory deals with these variables. Nevertheless, O.T. is interested in other change tactics, especially decree and group decision making. In fact, one line of research compares the success of these two change tactics. The first style of organizational change which involves a broad participation via group decision making, is called "evolution" and the second style which involves decrees, is called "revolution."[67] Group decision making involves discussion and possibly also experimentation, resulting in slow and incremental changes. Decrees by top management usually produce structural changes resulting in quick and broad-ranging changes.

When is evolution or revolution the better tactic to use? The organizational change literature usually recommends evolution and widespread participation, but not always. The literature suggests that the greater the perceived crisis and the shorter the perceived time for change the more acceptable is change by decree. Also, if an organization is trying to emulate some other organization, then its members will accept decreed major changes.[68] The organizational change literature has also observed weaknesses in the evolutionary method. The major limitation of group decision making is that the change, especially if it is to be a structural one, will become emasculated by the group and only part of the needed change will become implemented.[69] The group will critique changes as being too costly, as being unnecessary, as being impractical and so forth. The more radical, and thus visionary, the change, the more likely this is to be the case. Change by decree, therefore, may be the most effective way in certain circumstances.

Organizational theorists do more research on organizations than interventions in organizations. They are expert, therefore, on data-collection methods. Their main research tool is a survey of a sample or population of organizations. The organizations are the units of analysis and are measured on structural, input, output, process, and environmental variables. The many indicators which they have developed are a major contribution of O.T. to the tool kit of change agents. O.T. research also uses participant observation and field studies of the process of implementing change.

Organizationwide changes tend to be expensive solutions to organizational problems, but they are likely to endure. The resources needed to make these kinds of changes are usually much greater than the microchanges of O.D. Also, organizationwide changes can provoke tremendous resistance if they are introduced in the wrong way. In dealing with resistance, O.T. tends to take a political science approach involving bargaining, cooptation, and mobilizing political support rather than a human relations or O.D. approach, but O.D. tactics can be very helpful.

In summary, O.T. has moved far beyond Weber to a contingency view of organizations. O.T. looks for contingencies in the inputs, nature of the task, and the environment, and identifies the structural patterns which are appropriate for these contingencies. O.T. is developing a more complex view of the organizational system, especially with its renewed interest in the role of elite values and strategies. In addition, O.T. is beginning to develop a contingency theory of change tactics. O.T. suggests that both decrees and group decision making have advantages and disadvantages depending on the situation.

Organizational Design

A third literature relevant to organizational change is called management science. One branch of management science is organizational behavior, which frequently overlaps with industrial psychology and organizational social psychology. Another branch is organizational design, outlined in Figure 1.4. Peters and Waterman's best-

Figure 1.4   Highlights of the Organizational Design Change Strategy

Fundamental Assumptions

    1. How organizations are structured determines performances and outputs.
    2. Strategy of dominant coalition also determines performances and outputs.
    3. Environment sets limits on how organizations are structured.
    4. The greater the differentiation, the more important is integration.

Major Concepts, Variables, and Ideas

    1. Strategic planning, culture, and goals
    2. Product, functional, and matrix departmentalization
    3. Span of control and managerial roles
    4. Conflict resolution techniques
    5. Control technologies: budgets, inventories, MBO, and PERT
    6. Environmental uncertainty, complexity, and volatility
    7. Galbraith's work on information handling

Intervener Targets: Closing Gaps in the Following Performances and Outputs

    1. Success and profits
    2. Efficiency and productivity
    3. Conflict reduction and integration
    4. Morale, absenteeism, and turnover

Change Points: Components of the System Usually Changed

    1. Divisional structure and departments
    2. Lines of authority and responsibility
    3. Managerial processes or functions and subsystems
    4. Managerial technologies

Nature of Approach

    1. Usual intervention level: organizationwide as in divisions and organizational
        departments
    2. Usual tactics of change: decree, restructure, and group problem solving
    3. Usual method of data collection: informant interviews and documents
    4. Usual resources involved: personnel, money, and long time frame

selling *In Search of Excellence,* uses this approach to explore effective organizations.[70] Organizational design is beginning to converge with O.T. by incorporating more and more of the findings of O.T. into the organizational design literature. A major contribution to this convergence is Lawrence and Lorsch's contingency theory.[71] It connects the variables emphasized in O.T. to the more nuts-and-bolts issues of organizational design, such as where to locate a new department. It also sensitizes organizational designers to environmental constraints. Although organizational design and O.T. are converging, it should be noted that several key concepts have quite different meanings in the two literatures.[72]

Assumptions and concepts. Organizational design shares many of its assumptions with O.T. It adopts the rationalistic premise that the structure of the organization affects performances and outputs; however, the meaning of "structure" is quite different for organizational design than for O.T. The former views structure mainly as the arrangements of departments and divisions, while the latter views structure in terms of variables such as complexity or centralization. O.T. uses abstract variables which affect performances and outputs, while organizational design describes how concrete organizational components should be put together. The two literatures inform each other because O.T. develops the more basic science while organizational design develops the more applied science. With time, the differences between these perspectives have gradually diminished as management texts have assimilated much of organizational theory. (Organizational theory, however, has not assimilated organizational design as readily.)[73]

Structural models that have become popular in organizational design include federal decentralization, matrix structure, and functional structure. Essentially, these models pose the same question: What is the best arrangement of divisions, departments, and positions to achieve the objectives of the organization? Organizational design does not always make explicit its criteria for choosing one or another structural arrangement, but generally the source of the greatest variation determines the most appropriate model. For example, if the greatest variation is in the technology, then organizational design recommends a functional model with divisions based on technologies.

One of the founders of management science is Fayol who identified the five functions of management: planning, organizing, commanding, coordinating, and controlling.[74] He argues that the functions form a logical sequence, with planning guiding the other functions. From Fayol, therefore, derives a basic organizational design assumption that planning, or the new term "strategy," is a major factor in the effectiveness of an organization. As a result, organizational design now includes a variety of managerial techniques to facilitate managers in planning. These include break-even analysis, capital budgeting, linear programming, program evaluation and review technique (PERT), management by objectives (MBO), critical path method, and forecasting technologies.

Organizational design, like organizational development, assumes that employee motivation is crucial to organizational success.[75] Organizational design, however, places more emphasis on money as a motivating reward and less on self-expression and feelings. Organizational design, therefore, might institute bonus plans, piece rates, and profit sharing to increase the commitment and productivity of employees.

A distinctive assumption in organizational design, proposed by Lawrence and Lorsch, is that increasing differentiation creates disintegrative forces. Separate divisions or departments develop different orientations and goals which create frictions and make coordination between departments more difficult. Therefore, more effort must go into integration as differentiation increases in order to maintain effective performance. Organizational design has developed conflict-resolving techniques including confrontation, intermediaries or boundary spanners, group meetings, negotiation, separation, and intergroup training to reduce occupational conflict.[76] It also researches the conditions under which each technique is the most effective.

Organizational design deals with the full range of management issues so that it employs a wide variety of concepts, variables, and ideas, many of which are associated with special managerial techniques and practices. We have already noted the importance for organizational design of the concepts of planning and strategies, and the types of departmental structures. Organizational design is also concerned about the optimal span of control for various types of work situations. First-line supervisors in mass production factories can handle nearly fifty subordinates, but in other types of industries they usually only have from one to two dozen subordinates. At higher levels, the ratio is more often one to four.

Organizational design looks at the organization from the point of view of the manager and it constitutes a body of knowledge which helps managers manage more effectively. It therefore deals with leadership, supervisory style, and managerial roles. It studies leadership in terms of the dimensions of "concern for production" and "concern for people."[77] It discusses the pros and cons of authoritarian and democratic supervisory styles. It also identifies the many roles managers perform, from figurehead and leader to resource allocator and disturbance handler.[78] Managers play an important role in reducing conflict and controlling and coordinating behavior, and organizational design provides a battery of managerial technologies for performing these and other managerial roles.

When organizational design employs contingency theory, it

examines the impacts of environmental complexity and uncertainty on organizational structure and performance, whereas O.T. considers the impacts of size and technology. Tosi and Carroll, in their organizational design management text, suggest that if both market and technology environments are certain or stable then a mechanical organization is the preferred model.[79] If both are uncertain or volatile, then an organic organization is preferred. When the certainty or uncertainty resides in technology but not in markets, mixed models are appropriate.

Organizational design includes Galbraith's strategies for handling information in organizations.[80] A major strategy for increasing information is to create teams and develop lateral relationships. This strategy is especially appropriate for organic organizations which have to process large amounts of information to handle the uncertainties. The structure which is generally proposed for this strategy is the matrix.

Intervener targets: performance and output gaps. Organizational design seeks to improve the performance of organizations and make them more successful. It is like O.T. in focusing on performance and utilizing contingency theory. It differs from O.T. in being much more concerned with success, profits, efficiency, and productivity, and much less concerned with innovation which may not be profitable in the short run. Organizational design's neglect of innovation is exemplified by Peters and Waterman's *In Search of Excellence,* which hardly mentions innovation.[81] The clientele for management science is usually top management; thus, organizational design's emphasis on profits and efficiency rather than innovation is understandable.

The major motivational assumption underlying organizational design is that performance gaps stimulate actions to close them. American businesses with their many accounting controls notice performance gaps quickly and, therefore, are prodded toward better designs and new technologies that improve efficiency and productivity. Organizations in trouble actively seek out management consultants to rectify some problem quickly. Detecting performance and output gaps is more complicated when performance measures and accounting controls do not exist, as is so often the case in the public sector. Performance measures can be created even in the public sector, however, as demonstrated by Philip Coulter who used several measures for effectiveness of fire departments, including fire prevention, fire suppression, total revenues expended, and efficiency.[82]

One of the more distinctive contributions of the organizational design literature has been its recognition of integration and conflict resolution as important objectives. Unlike O.T., which has tended to ignore conflict, contingency theory within organizational design made it a central problem. Lawrence and Lorsch focused on tactics for reducing interoccupational or departmental conflict.[83] Some examples are the use of confrontation, intermediaries, middle departments, group meetings, and the like. Organizational design, however, has not been interested in vertical conflict, such as strikes.

Another target for an organizational design intervention is morale, absenteeism, and turnover. Industrial psychology, which has been strong in business schools for decades, has produced an extensive literature on these issues which feeds into organizational design as well as into organizational development.

Change points: components of the system usually changed. The major change points for organizational design are divisional and departmental structures, lines of authority and responsibility, managerial roles, and managerial technologies. Organizational design management consultants will often modify the divisional or departmental structure of the organization and rearrange positions in order to improve performance. An example of how restructuring the organization can close performance gaps is the restructuring of the failing Ray-O-Vac Corporation.[84] A new president took over and spent the first few months visiting all three hundred managers to learn why the company was failing. He decided the problem was a lack of innovation and that the causes lay in the design of the structure. He restructured the organization by eliminating a layer of corporate vice-presidents and creating four product divisions, each with its own research, product-development, and marketing responsibilities. This reorganization led to considerable improvement in innovation and eventually in profits.

Typically, organizations are organized into divisions on the basis of widely disparate technology product groups. In our discussion of the definition of an organization, we observed that the divisional structure generally evolved when the staff, especially managers or administrators, could not be transferred easily among the components of the organization. For example, Du Pont bought a number of chemical companies after World War I that put out a variety of products.[85] Du Pont ran each line of business from central headquarters but discovered that this design was reducing profits. When Du Pont decentralized operations so that each division had the autonomy to make marketing, production, purchasing, and other decisions, profits quickly returned. Many large corporations decentralized following the pioneering example of Du Pont.

Once the multiorganization is arranged into divisions, then departments are organized along functional or product lines. Functional subdivision is by occupations, as in a university. Subdivision by product lines is necessitated by the differences in customers and their service needs. For example, IBM has one division for main frames and one for minicomputers. Within these divisions, there are departments for specific managerial functions. As noted earlier, the greatest sources of either variation or uncertainty should have the greatest influence on design.

Management principles often do not translate readily to the public sector because they are based on market control and competition. Daft presents an unusual example of an attempt to apply private sector-design to a public sector organization, Bakerfield University.[86] It was reorganized into profit centers, except for central services, with each school and division operating as an autonomous unit. Profit centers are a new and somewhat radical method for dividing large units; they involve even greater decentralization than the Du Pont decentralization into relatively autonomous divisions. The Bakerfield arrangement worked very well; indeed, so well that the central administration decided to do the same with the Computer Science Department. The latter, however, increased the costs of its services to other departments and recycled the money for the faculty's own research. This was possible because the Computer Science Department was the only provider of services to the other colleges and thus had a monopoly position. (It is worth noting that the report does not indicate what happens to unpopular areas like classics or how the booms and busts of student fashion are contained.)

Another change point for organizational designers is the relationship between authority and responsibility. One of its maxims is that authority and responsibility must go hand in hand. Management consultants often intervene to correct the chain of command, moving the locus of authority to the appropriate level so that effective action can be taken. A sign that authority and responsibility are not at the correct level can appear in excessive overhead costs. Too much centralization tends to produce an overly high administrative ratio.

The problem of incongruent lines of authority and responsibility is found in a study of Sears Roebuck.[87] The company has nine hundred stores, twelve thousand suppliers, and more than four hundred thousand employees. It is highly centralized with a swollen central headquarters which is symbolized by the largest building in the world, the Sears Tower of Chicago. Sears now needs a 50 percent markup to make a profit, while the average of the competitors need only 35 percent. More to the point, its overhead and administrative expenses absorb 30 percent of each sales dollar, whereas one competitor spends only 15.3 percent.

The growth of government and the creation of more and more levels in the bureaucracy are problems in many countries, but especially in Third World countries such as Egypt, and in developed countries such as Italy. As centralized governments grow in size, the government bureaucracy absorbs more and more of the resources in administration rather than services, and the lines of authority and responsibility become confused.

A third change point for organizational designers and a rapidly growing area of research is the appropriate role of managers for various contingencies. Mintzberg, a leader in this field, suggests that a manager performs many roles and he distinguishes three types of roles which subdivide into ten distinct roles. He distinguishes between interpersonal roles, such as figurehead, leader, and liaison; informational roles, such as monitor, disseminator, and spokesperson; and decisional roles, such as entrepreneur, disturbance handler, resource allocator, and negotiator.[88] He argues that contingencies determine which of these roles are to be emphasized by a manager at any one time.

A fourth change point for organizational designers is managerial practices. Many management texts present a vast array of managerial technologies that can be used to achieve each of the managerial functions.[89] For example, the techniques of forecasting, nominal groups, brainstorming, and delphi projections can be used in planning. Other managerial technologies deal with personnel practices and incentive systems that are supposed to make workers happier and more productive, an area that overlaps with O.D. We have already noted the tools and techniques for managing interdepartmental conflict, an area which is especially germaine to development administrators. Generally, the contingencies which determine the appropriateness of these tools and techniques are not specified, but the selection of techniques is left to the judgment of managers.

The nature of the approach. Like O.T., organizational design tends to intervene at the organizational level, though sometimes an organizational design management consultant will simply introduce new management technologies to specific subunits of the organization. The standard organizational design intervention consists of interviews with key actors, followed by diagnosis and then a proposed solution. It is likely that the diagnosis and solution will be biased in the direction of those solutions which are the specialties of the consultant or management consulting firm such as matrix structures or a set of managerial technologies. Many of these solutions have the best results when changes are made at both micro- and organizationwide levels. Increasingly, contingency theories are integrating the two levels by specifying the types of organizational contexts in which specific managerial techniques are most useful. This integration is most notable in the work of Mintzberg.[90]

A prominent tactic of organizational design is structural change. Whether one departmentalizes by function or product, employs federal decentalization or matrix structure, or employs a narrow or wide span of control, the prescribed solution for a performance gap is to change the structure. Often these changes are instituted by decree, a change tactic which naturally appeals to top management and its organizational design advisors.

Another important tactic of organizational design is problem-solving groups. Although these groups are also associated with O.D., they have probably had the greatest influence among organizational design change agents. Two kinds of problem-solving groups have become important in American business—task forces and quality work circles—both of which have been made part of the permanent structure of many organizations. Peters and Waterman view task forces as the essence of the modern succesful company.[91] For example, General Motors used such groups to decide to downsize cars and is now using them to deal with a number of organizational problems.

Organizational designers also use the tactic of replacement. Typically, management consultants who design organizations make recommendations about the replacement of key personnel. Design, therefore, is not just a question of arranging parts; it also deals with the people who fill the parts.

When data collection is involved, management consultants rely heavily upon informant interviews and the use of documents to identify performance and output gaps. The interviews deal with lines of authority, responsibility, communication, conflicts, and the like. They explore how key informants perceive the problem and its probable causes.

Organizational design interventions usually require considerable resources. Changing the design of an organization frequently takes a year or more and a considerable infusion of time and effort. It requires support from the top and can substantially alter the situation and/or behavior of many employees.

In summary, organizational design lies halfway between O.D. and O.T. Its treatment of such problems as leadership, motivation, and group processes is like O.D., but it shares contingency theory with O.T. Also, it places much more emphasis on managerial technologies and on motivation by material rewards than does O.D., and it differs from O.T. in a number of its emphases. First, it stresses the importance of strategy and planning for organizational performance and has developed many technologies for these activities. Second, organizational design views structure in terms of departments, divisions, lines of authority, and lines of responsibility. Third, there are subtle differences in the way organizational design and O.T. conceptualize the environment, although many of these are disappearing with time. Traditionally the concept of uncertainty was more critical to organizational design; now it is being replaced with O.T. ideas such as complexity and rate of technological change.

Synthesizing the Three Change Literatures

The three literatures are complementary and can be used by development change agents in bits and pieces as they wish. The purpose of Figures 1.2, 1.3, and 1.4. is to indicate to change agents where they might search for ideas. Our recommendation, however, is that the three literatures be used in combination because organizational intervention usually is very complex and needs a multi-level approach.

In this section we combine the three literatures in the analysis of why organizations fail; in other words, the causes of performance or output gaps (Figure 1.5).[92] A strategy of organizational change must begin with a causal analysis of the problem. The number of possible causes, however, is very large, so we identify in Figure 1.5 the major groupings of these causes as portrayed in the three literatures we have reviewed. Each literature emphasizes certain sets of causes over the others but increasingly they are borrowing from each other's lists.

The five components of the organizational system identified in Figure 1.1, and discussed under Change Points in Figures 1.2, 1.3, and 1.4, are used to categorize the list of causes of organizational underperformance. The five components of the system are:

1. The strategy of the organization including the dominant coalition's values, leadership style, and climate or culture
2. The processes of the organization including managerial technologies, group processes, and coordination mechanisms
3. The structures of the organization including micro- and macrolevels
4. The inputs or resources including the personnel and their skills
5. The environmental context

Figures 1.2, 1.3, and 1.4 list the major concepts, variables, and ideas associated with these parts of the system, and the overviews of the three literatures provide the concrete references which change agents need.

The model in Figure 1.5 starts with the environmental context, which influences three groups of variables. It limits the outputs and performances, determines what strategies are appropriate, and sets limits on resources, i.e., technology, resources and workers. Next, strategy affects processes and resources affect structures. Next, structures affect processes. Finally, strategy, processes, structures, and resources affect performances and outputs.

Within each variable group the organizational development approach focuses on behavioral processes and human outputs at the microlevel. Organizational theory, on the other hand, focuses on the organizational level and on the impact of the environment on the organization. Organizational design looks at both the micro-level and the organizational level.

Figure 1.5   An Arrangement of the Concepts for Analyzing the Causes of Performance and Output Gaps

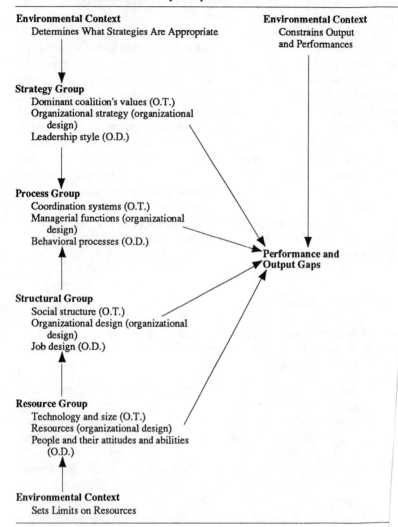

Environmental Context
Determines What Strategies Are Appropriate

Environmental Context
Constrains Output
and Performances

Strategy Group
Dominant coalition's values (O.T.)
Organizational strategy (organizational
design)
Leadership style (O.D.)

Process Group
Coordination systems (O.T.)
Managerial functions (organizational
design)
Behavioral processes (O.D.)

Performance and
Output Gaps

Structural Group
Social structure (O.T.)
Organizational design (organizational
design)
Job design (O.D.)

Resource Group
Technology and size (O.T.)
Resources (organizational design)
People and their attitudes and abilities
(O.D.)

Environmental Context
Sets Limits on Resources

There are, then, five major groups of factors that affect perf
mance. Except for the environmental variables, each group h
three elements which correspond to the three major literatu
that form the basis of our discussion. In the strategy gro
sociologists tend to emphasize the values of the dominant coaliti
management emphasizes strategy and planning, and industi

psychologists emphasize leadership style. In the process group, these three literatures use, respectively, the terms "coordination systems," "managerial functions," and "behavioral processes." Similar differentiation occurs for the two other groups of variables.

This schematic presents a checklist with which to explore each concrete situation. The list also sensitizes the change agent to the potential necessity of having to change several parts of the system at once to have a significant impact. As Beer notes, changing people and behavioral processes but not structure usually does not give permanent results.[93] The changes will erode. The reverse is also true. Davis and Lawrence observe that introducing the matrix design in an organization requires considerable training and other O.D. tactics to achieve congruence between workers' values and behaviors and the new structure.[94] In summary, many organizational interventions require both micro- and organizational-level changes. In fact we suggest that the failure of many decentralization efforts by Third World governments is due to the neglect of microlevel changes.

Summary and Conclusion

This chapter has set forth the major strategies for changing organizations to make them more effective. When one changes an organization, it is important to recognize:

1. Not all social collectives are organizations and exemplify organizational theories.
2. The literature on organizations has three major segments: organizational development, organizational theory, and organizational design.
3. The main branch of organizational theory is contingency theory, but there are several other relevant perspectives including political theory. (In the next chapter we present a contingency theory of organizations that uses the many parts of Figure 1.5.)

Most organizational changes result from the perception of *performance or output gaps* by organizational decision makers. Then the strategy of change must identify what *component of the organizational system* is to be changed and *how* the change is to be implemented. The strategy must select the intervention level, tactics,

data-collection methods, and the resources required in implementing the change. Figures 1.2, 1.3, and 1.4 provide a summary of the change strategies presented in each of these change literatures, and Figure 1.5 provides an overall summary. The framework for understanding organizational change presented in this chapter is employed in Chapters 3 and 4 in the analysis of a number of cases of organizational change in LDCs; but first we develop contingency theory more fully in Chapter 2.

Notes

1. For a review of the history of USAID policy relevant to administration, *see* Dennis Rondinelli, 1987, *Development Administration and U.S. Foreign Aid Policy* (Boulder, Colo.: Lynne Rienner).

2. David Korten and Norman T. Uphoff, 1986, "Bureaucratic Reorientation for Participatory Rural Development" (NASPAA Working Paper No. 1, Washington, D.C.); and Theodore Thomas, 1986, "Reorienting Bureaucratic Performance: A Social Learning Approach to Development Action" (NASPAA, Washington, D.C.)

3. *See* John Cohen, May Hebert, David Lewis, and Jon Swanson, 1981, "Development from Below: Local Development Association in the Yemen Arab Republic," *World Development,* vol. 9, no. 11/12, pp. 1039–1061.

4. Examples are found in Dennis Rondinelli, 1983, "Implementing Decentralization Programs in Asia: A Comparative Analysis," *Public Administration and Development,* vol. 3, pp. 181–207; and his 1981 "Government Decentralization: Theory and Practice in Developing Countries," *International Review of Administrative Sciences,* vol. 47, no. 2, pp. 133–145; and finally his 1981 "Administrative Decentralization and Economic Development: The Sudan's Experiment with Devolution," *Journal of Modern African Studies,* vol. 19, no. 4, pp. 595–624.

5. For examples of this complexity, *see* Michael Beer, 1980, *Organizational Change and Development: A Systems View* (Glenview, Ill.: Scott, Foresman), p. 38; and Koya Azumi and Jerald Hage (eds.), 1972, *Organizational Systems: A Text-Reader* (Lexington, Mass.: D. C. Heath), Chapter 6; Jerald Hage, 1980, *Theories of Organizations: Form, Process and Transformation* (New York: Wiley Interscience); Henry Mintzberg, 1979, *Structuring Organizations*

(Englewood Cliffs, N.J.: Prentice-Hall); and even popular paperbacks such as Thomas Peters and Robert Waterman, Jr., 1982, *In Search of Excellence: Lessons from America's Best-Run Companies* (New York: Warner).

6. Paul R. Lawrence and Jay W. Lorsch, 1967, *Organizations and Environments,* (Cambridge, Mass.: Harvard) is the first work to make this assumption explicit.

7. Some authors list properties of organizations. *See,* for example, Pradip N. Khandwalla, 1977, *The Design of Organizations* (New York: Harcourt Brace Jovanovich), pp. 2–7, who lists hierarchy of authority, roles, techniques, formality of communication, specialization of functions and division of labor, employment of skilled personnel, and specificity of persons. He also discusses how these properties vary among organizations, families, groups, and communities.

Since paid employment is one of our defining characteristics for organizations, our narrow definition is largely confined to "utilitarian organizations" in Etzioni's terms. *See* Amitai Etzioni, 1975, *A Comparative Analysis of Complex Organizations* (New York: Free Press). Most organizations defined by Etzioni as normative or coercive would be excluded by our definition of organizations.

Another concept that is close to our narrow definition of organizations is "formal organizations." Some formal organizations would not fit our definition, however, because they have few paid employees (e.g., a small church).

8. *See* Khandwalla, 1977, *op. cit.,* p. 5; and Richard L. Daft, 1983, *Organizational Theory and Design* (St. Paul, Minn.: West), p. 8. The bulk of these definitions rests on Talcott Parsons, 1960, *Structure and Processes in Modern Societies* (New York: Free Press), which contains the reprint of his 1956 article "Suggestions for a Sociological Approach to the Theory of Organizations," *Administrative Science Quarterly* (June), pp. 63–85.

9. *See* Hage, 1980, *op. cit.,* p. 68.

10. Alfred Chandler, Jr., 1962, *Strategy and Structure: Chapters in the History of Industrial Enterprise* (Cambridge, Mass.: M.I.T. Press).

11. A number of texts in both organizational theory and organizational design build their work around the issue of core technology; *see* James Thompson, 1967, *Organizations in Action* (New York: McGraw-Hill); Lawrence and Lorsch, 1967, *op. cit.;* Khandwalla, *op. cit.;* Hage, *op. cit.*

12. Peters and Waterman, 1982, *op. cit.*

13. *See* James March and Herbert Simon, 1958, *Organizations* (New York: Wiley).

14. Gerald Zaltman, Robert Duncan, and Jonny Holbek, 1973, *Innovations and Organizations* (New York: Wiley), pp. 55–58.

15. David K. Leonard, 1977, *Reaching the Peasant Farmer: Organization Theory and Practice in Kenya* (Chicago: University of Chicago Press), p. 22.

16. The classic example is of course Robert Presthus, 1961, "Weberian vs. Welfare Bureaucracy in Traditional Society," *Administrative Science Quarterly,* vol. 6 (June), pp. 1–24.

17. For discussions of how to measure efficiency in the public sector, *see* Richard Scott, 1979, "Measuring Outputs in Hospitals in National Research Council," *Measuring and Interpretation of Productivity* (Washington, D.C.: National Academy of Sciences), pp. 255–275; and Jerald Hage, 1983, "Organizational Theory and the Concept of Productivity," in Arthur Brief (ed.), *Productivity Research in the Behavioral and Social Sciences* (New York: Praeger), pp. 91–126.

18. For example, the Plankton School District in the Chicago Metropolitan area developed a list of eight goals, including developing intellectual curiosity and a positive attitude toward the structure and processes of the American Free Enterprise System. *See* Daft, 1983, *op. cit.,* p. 84.

19. *Ibid,* p. 90.

20. J. Patrick Wright, 1979, *On a Clear Day You Can See General Motors,* based on interviews with John Z. DeLorean (New York: Avon).

21. Daft, *op. cit.,* p. 80.

22. Presthus, 1961, *op. cit.*

23. Larry E. Greiner, 1967, "Patterns of Organizational Change," *Harvard Business Review,* vol. 45, no. 3, (May/June), pp. 119–130.

24. Jay Galbraith, 1973, *Designing Complex Organizations* (Reading, Mass.: Addison-Wesley); Hage, 1980, *op. cit.,* Chapter 7.

25. Galbraith, 1973, *op.cit.*

26. Beer, 1980, *op. cit.,* pp. 28–29; Huse, 1975, *op. cit.*

27. Beer, *op. cit,* p. 42; Huse, *op. cit.* p. 35.

28. Beer, *op. cit.,* pp. 28–31; Huse, *op. cit.*

29. Abraham H. Maslow, 1954, *Motivation and Personality* (New York: Harper and Row); and Frank L. Herzberg, 1966, *Work*

and the Nature of Man (Cleveland, Ill.: World).

30. E. J. Miller and A. K. Rise, 1963, *Systems in Organizations: The Control of Task and Sentiment Boundaries* (London: Travistock); Fred Emory and Einar Thorsrud, 1964, *Form and Content in Industrial Democracy* (Oslo: Oslo University) and their 1976 *Democracy at Work: The Report of the Norwegian Industrial Democracy Program* (Canberra: Australian National University, mimeograph). For an application in a Third World setting, *see* Lyman Ketcham, 1984, "Sociotechnical Design in a Third World Country: The Railway Maintenance Depot at Sennar in the Sudan," *Human Relations,* vol. 37, no. 2, pp. 135–154.

31. J. R. Hackman and J. L. Suttle, 1977, *Improving Life at Work: Behavioral Science Approaches to Organizational Change* (Santa Monica, Calif.: Goodyear), p. 13.

32. Pierre Morin, 1976, *Le Développement des organizations* (2nd ed.), (Paris: Dunod).

33. Peters and Waterman, *op. cit.*

34. Beer, *op. cit.*

35. *See Ibid.*, pp. 33–35 for a definition of "culture."

36. *Ibid.*, p. 51.

37. *See* Morris Greenblatt, R. H. York, and Esther Brown, 1955, *From Custodial to Therapeutic Patient Care in a Mental Hospital* (New York: Russell Sage).

38. Beer, *op. cit.,* p. 169.

39. Robert Kahn *et al.,* 1964, *Organizational Stress: Studies in Role Conflict and Ambiguity* (New York: Wiley).

40. Beer, *op. cit.,* p. 213.

41. William Ouchi, 1981, *Theory Z* (Reading, Mass.: Addison-Wesley); and also the September 1983 issue of the *Administrative Science Quarterly,* vol. 28.

42. Beer, *op. cit.,* p. 63.

43. *Ibid.*, pp. 245–264.

44. For a review *see* Hage, 1980, *op. cit.,* Chapter 2.

45. Thomas Burns and G. M. Stalker, 1961, *The Management of Innovation* (London: Travistock).

46. James Thompson, 1967, *Organizations in Action* (New York: McGraw-Hill); Charles Perrow, 1967, "A Framework for the Comparative Analysis of Organizations," *American Sociological Review,* vol. 32 (April), pp. 194–204; Peter Blau, 1970, "A Formal Theory of Differentiation in Organizations," *American Sociological Review,* vol. 35 (April), pp. 210–218; Joanne Woodward, 1965, *In-*

dustrial Organization (London: Cambridge); Derek Pugh, David Hickson, and C. Robin Hennings, 1969, "An Empirical Taxonomy of Structures of Work Organizations," *Administrative Science Quarterly,* vol. 14 (March), pp. 115–126; and Hage, 1980, *op. cit.,* Chapters 12 and 13.

47. Lawrence and Lorsch, *op. cit.*

48. Jeffrey Pfeffer and Gerald Salancik, 1978, *The External Control of Organizations: A Resource Dependence Perspective* (New York: Harper & Row); Jerald Hage and Robert Dewar, 1973, "Elite Values Versus Organizational Structures in Predicting Innovation," *Administrative Science Quarterly,* vol. 18 (September), pp. 279–290; Lucien Karpick, 1972, "Les Politiques et les logics d'action de la grande entreprize industrielle," *Sociologie du Travail,* vol. 13 (April-June), pp. 82–105.

49. Daft, *op. cit.,* pp. 274, 275.

50. Richard McCleery, 1957, *Policy Change in Prison Management* (East Lansing: Government Research Bureau, Michigan State University).

51. Jerald Hage, 1974, *Communication and Organizational Control: A Cybernetics Perspective in Health and Welfare Systems* (New York: Wiley-Interscience), Part One.

52. Etzioni, *op. cit.*

53. The initial starting point was Parson's famous AGIL scheme, but it was made operational in the work of Hage. *See* Jerald Hage, 1965, "An Axiomatic Theory of Organizations," *Administrative Science Quarterly,* vol. 10 (December), pp. 289–320; James Price, 1968, *Organizational Effectiveness: An Inventory of Propositions* (Homewood, Ill.: Irwin); and Perrow, 1967, *op. cit.*

54. Daft, 1983, *op. cit.,* p. 92; *see also* Amitai Etzioni, 1964, *Modern Organizations* (Englewood Cliffs, N.J.: Prentice-Hall), p. 6.

55. *See* Paul S. Goodman and Johannes Pennings, 1977, "Toward a Workable Framework," in Goodman and Pennings (eds.), *New Perspectives on Organizational Effectiveness* (San Franciso: Jossey Bass), pp. 146–184.

56. Richard H. Hall and John P. Clark, 1980, "An Ineffective Effectiveness Study and Some Suggestions for Future Rsearch," *The Sociological Quaterly,* vol. 21, pp. 119–134.

57. Hage, 1980, *op. cit.,* Chapters 3, 6, and 9. This research has now been extended to the private sector; *see* Frank Hull and Jerald Hage, 1982, "Organizing for Innovation: Beyond Burns and Stalker," *Sociology,* vol. 16, no. 4, pp. 564–577.

58. Hage, *op. cit.,* Chapter 9.

59. James Price, 1977, *A Study of Organizational Turnover* (Ames, Iowa: University of Iowa).

60. Basil Georgopoulos and Floyd Mann, 1962, *The Community General Hospital* (New York: Macmillan); Thompson, 1967, *op. cit.*; Etzioni, 1975, *op. cit.*; Lawrence and Lorsch, *op. cit.,* Hage, 1974, *op. cit.*

61. Blau, 1970, *op. cit.*; Peter Blau and Richard Schoenherr, 1971, *The Structure of Organizations* (New York: Basic Books); Peter Blau, Wolf Hydebrand, and Robert Stauffer, 1966, "The Structure of Small Bureaucracies," *American Sociological Review,* vol. 31, (April), pp. 179–191; Peter Blau *et al.,* 1976, "Technology and Organization in Manufacturing," *Administrative Science Quarterly,* vol. 21 (March), pp. 20–40; Peter Blau, 1972, "Interdependence and Hierarchy in Organizations," *Social Science Research,* vol. 1 (April), pp. 1–24.

62. Woodward, 1965, *op. cit.*

63. Jerald Hage and Michael Aiken, 1969, "Routine Technology, Social Structure, and Organizational Goals," *Administrative Science Quarterly,* vol. 14 (September), pp. 366–377.

64. Howard Aldrich, 1979, *Organizations and Environments* (Englewood Cliffs, N.J.: Prentice-Hall).

65. *See* Richard Hall *et al.,* 1977, "Patterns of Interorganizational Relationships," *Administrative Science Quarterly,* vol. 22, no. 3 (September), pp. 457–474.

66. Michael Aiken *et al.,* 1975, *Coordinating Human Services* (San Francisco: Jossey-Bass).

67. Hage, 1980, *op. cit.,* Chapter 7.

68. *Ibid.,* Chapter 6.

69. Jerald Hage and Michael Aiken, 1970, *Social Change and Complex Organizations* (New York: Random House), Chapter 4.

70. Peters and Waterman, *op. cit.*

71. Lawrence and Lorsch, *op. cit.*

72. Even the concept of centralization means different things in the two literatures. For example, compare Hall, 1983, *op. cit.,* Chapter 6; or Hage, 1980, *op. cit.,* Chapter 4 with Pradip N. Khandwalla, 1977, *op. cit.,* pp. 508–510; and Martin Gannon, Jr., 1982, *Organizational Behavior* (Boston, Mass.: Little Brown and Co.) For an exception *see* Henry Mintzberg, 1979, *The Structure of Organizations: A Synthesis of the Research* (Englewood Cliffs, N.J.: Prentice-Hall), Chapter 11.

73. In particular, *see* Mintzberg, 1979, *op. cit.*; Khandwalla, 1977, *op. cit.*; and Jay Galbraith, 1973, *op. cit.* They tend to cite various organizational theorists such as Peter Blau, Jerald Hage, Charles Perrow, etc.; the reverse is less true. The best examples of contingent approaches are Galbraith, 1973, *op. cit.*; Khandwalla, 1977, *op. cit.*; Mintzberg, 1979, *op. cit.*; and Henry Tosi and Stephen Carroll, 1982, *Management* (2nd ed.), (New York: Wiley).

74. Fayol, 1916, *General Industrial Management,* translated by Constance Storrs (London: Pitman, 1949).

75. Daft, *op. cit.,* pp. 101–102.

76. Lawrence and Lorsch, *op. cit.*; but also *see* Richard Walton and John Dutton, 1969, "The Management of Interdepartmental Conflict: A Model and Reviw," *Administrative Science Quarterly,* vol. 14 (March), pp. 73–90; Richard Walton, John Dutton, and Thomas Cafferty, 1969, "Organizational Context and Interdepartmental Conflict," *Administrative Science Quarterly,* vol. 14 (December), pp. 522–543; Eric H. Neilsen, 1972, "Understanding and Managing Intergroup Conflict," in Jay W. Lorsch and Paul R. Lawrence (eds.), *Managing Group and Intergroup Relations* (Homewood, IL: Irwin and Dorsey Press), pp. 329–343.

77. Robert R. Blake and Jane S. Mouton, 1964, *The Managerial Grid* (Houston: Gulf Publishing); and their 1969 *Building a Dynamic Corporation Through Grid Organization Development* (Reading, Mass.: Addison-Wesley).

78. Henry Mintzberg, 1980, *The Nature of Managerial Work* (Englewood Cliffs: Prentice-Hall).

79. Tosi and Carrol, 1982, *op. cit.* Also see Robert Duncan, 1972, "Characteristics of Organizational Environments and Perceived Environmental Uncertainty," *Administrative Science Quarterly,* vol. 17 (September), pp. 313–327.

80. Galbraith, *op. cit.*

81. Peters and Waterman, *op. cit.*

82. Daft, *op. cit.,* pp. 80–81.

83. Lawrence and Lorsch, *op. cit; See also* Walton, Dutton, and Cafferty, 1969, *op. cit.*

84. Daft, *op. cit.*

85. Alfred Chandler, Jr., 1962, *Strategy and Structure: Chapters in the History of Industrial Enterprise* (Cambridge, Mass.: M.I.T. Press).

86. Daft, *op. cit.*

87. Daft, *op. cit.,* pp. 133–134.

88. Mintzberg, 1980, *op. cit.*

89. These managerial functions are a major gap in organizational theory.

90. *See* Mintzberg, 1979, *op. cit.,* and especially his concept of coordination as the way of seeing how different organizations are structured.

91. Peters and Waterman, *op. cit.*

92. This schematic of potential causes of performance gaps is very similar to the framework developed by Samuel Paul, 1982, *Managing Development Programs: The Lessons of Success* (Boulder, Colo.: Westview). He uses environment, strategy, structure, and implementation process. We add to his scheme the resource group, which has been very important in recent organizational theory. Resources, however, are implied in Paul's analysis.

93. Beer, *op. cit.*

94. Stanley M. Davis and Paul R. Lawrence, 1977, *Matrix* (Reading, Mass.: Addison-Wesley).

2

A Contingency Theory
of Organizations

Organizations are changed because they are failing to perform at expected and desirable levels. Sometimes organizational leaders can figure out what changes will improve the deficient performance of the organization but sometimes they need guidance. In this chapter we provide guidelines on the direction of organizational change which is appropriate for different situations. We employ the contingency theory of organizations which identifies four organizational models that are effective in four different sets of contingencies. The change agent then can use the contingency theory to determine the type of change which is needed for improving the performance of specific organizations.

The four models of organizations presented in this chapter are: mechanical, organic, craft, and mechanical-organic. The first is the rational-legal bureaucracy, which we call the mechanical form; the second is the professional organization, which we call the organic form. The mechanical form is desirable when the production or provision system is standardized, most jobs require low levels of skill, and the demand for the product or service is sizable and constant. Since the human capital needs are low and frequently the technologies are easy to borrow, this model can be applied by development change agents in LDCs. The organic form is desirable when the production system is nonstandardized, many jobs require high levels of skill, and the demand is small and changing. In this model, human capital needs are large, which mitigates against its use in some LDCs. However, it is the form most able to create the new or more appropriate technologies needed in LDCs to develop a competitive edge in international competition and to satisfy increasing demands at home, thus reducing imports. The third model is the traditional-craft form, which meets local needs and produces products or services in small batches. Many community interventions and rural or urban development programs build this kind of organizational form. It has been underappreciated as a successful organizational type. The fourth is the mixed mechanical-organic form, which usually attempts to do both large-scale research and mass production. This type is useful in large countries interested in developing expensive and complex technologies such as military equipment, energy production, nuclear bombs, main-frame computers, and the like.

What is the origin of these four models? They evolved in three steps in comparative classifications. First, Weber compared bureaucracies with traditional organizations. Second, both Burns and Stalker and Lawrence and Lorsch distinguished organic organizations from bureaucracies. Third, both Hage and Perrow identified a fourth model which mixes characteristics of both the organic and the mechanical model.

Development administration has long emphasized the bureaucratic model. The model was developed by Max Weber while he worked in an Austrian military hospital in Vienna and derives from his historical studies of the Prussian government.[1] It was originally proposed as the most rational and efficient way to structure an organization regardless of differences in outputs, technological tasks, markets, or societal contexts. During the last two decades, both organizational theory and organizational design have moved to a contingency theory of structure and process. Their literatures argue that bureaucracy is appropriate for certain contingencies and not appropriate for others.

Two major works during the 1960s developed the contingency approach. The first, by Burns and Stalker, looked at companies in the Scottish electronics industry.[2] They found that companies which successfully engaged in mass production of such goods as television sets were bureaucratically organized, and they designated this pattern as a mechanical organization. In contrast, companies successfully producing small batches of special design products were organized in a much more flexible and adaptable way, and they designated this pattern as an organic organization. Each type of organization is effective for different kinds of customers and markets. The mechanical-bureaucratic model is highly successful in producing mass products efficiently at low cost. The organic-professional model can be highly innovative in producing new products and services. Both approaches are relevant to development in LDCs, but the need for the organic model is not widely understood. It is commonly known that LDCs need to increase the productivity and technical efficiency of their economic organizations. It is not commonly known that they also need to increase the innovativeness of at least some of their economic organizations in order to create appropriate technologies and new products or services. Economic development requires not only productivity but also breaking the cycle of technological dependency. Furthermore, variations on the organic form can be useful when developmental programs share power with beneficiaries and tailor services to a variety of local conditions.

The second work which developed the contingency approach was Lawrence and Lorsch's study of two container manufacturers, two food processing companies, and six plastics companies.[3] They found that when the environment became more complex or uncertain, more specialties were required to deal with it, the structure of the organization had to become more complex, communication had to increase, and conflict between specialties had to be managed. When integration was low in a complex environment, the firm was less successful. This study provides rich insights for development change agents. When development agencies sponsor institutional development programs, according to Brinkerhoff, they must intervene in complex systems characterized by high levels of uncertainty and low levels of control by the development agency.[4] We would go further and suggest that most development activities in LDCs are inherently complex tasks, because problems are more difficult and intractable in Third World contexts than in First World contexts. Third World countries, therefore, need complex organizations. This is a challenge, however, which they usually can not meet and is often responsible for disappointing results.

Perrow focused on technology as a basic contingency.[5] He classifies technologies by the degree to which they are analyzable and the number of exceptions to their rules. These two dimensions provide a fourfold classification of organizations. On the main diagonal is included the mechanical (problems are analyzable and there are few exceptions) and the organic (problems are analyzable and there are many exceptions). Perrow labels this dimension routine versus nonroutine technology. Off the main diagonal are two other types of organizations which he labels craft and mixed mechanical-organic. Associated with these four organizational types are large numbers of characteristics, including the power structure, system and product goals, coordination mechanisms, and managerial ideology.

Later, Blau demonstrated that size was another critical contingency which affected a large number of different properties of an organization.[6] Building on Blau, Perrow, and microeconomics, Hage combined the size dimension with the concept of economies of scale, and observed that organizations with economies of scale produced mass products with routine technologies. In these cases the markets are governed by price considerations until size reaches oligopolistic or monopolistic levels. There are also small-batch markets, however, where customization is critical. When these markets involve low technology they are served by craft organizations; when high technology, they are served by organic organizations. While Perrow focuses on the routineness of the technology, Hage focuses on the sophistication of the technology. Sophistication is measured by the educational level of the employees and the type of machines used in production. Hage crossed the two dimensions of the complexity of technology and the economies of scale inherent in small versus large markets and created a fourfold typology of contingencies for organizations: small market/low tech, small market/high tech, large market/low tech, and large market/high tech. Each set of contingencies is conducive to a certain organizational form: craft, organic, mechanical, and mixed mechanical-organic, respectively. Hage's specification of these four organizational models draws upon the works of Perrow, Blau, organizational design, and the microeconomic theory of the firm.

Four Organizational Models

Although the four models derive from the crosscutting of two contingencies (simple-complex technologies and small-large markets), the single dimension of the mechanical-organic continuum dominates the fourfold classification of organizations. The mechanical and the organic organizations are at the poles of this continuum and the other two models are toward the middle. The mechanical-organic continuum provides the major basis for discussing structural changes in organizations in this monograph. It is therefore featured in the discussion of the four organizational models which follows. We also look at the components of the system indicated in Figure 1.5: performances, culture, processes, structure, and inputs. In each area, however, space limitations prevent us from going into much detail, and our focus is on the most basic variables. (For more detail, the reader is referred to Daft, Etzioni, Hage, Mintzberg, Paul, and Perrow.[7])

The Mechanical-Bureaucratic Model

Figure 2.1 outlines the basic characteristics of the mechanical-bureaucratic model. It is the appropriate model for production with simple technologies for large markets. It emphasizes productivity,

Figure 2.1   The Causes of Performance Level in the Mechanical-Bureaucratic Model

Performances	Environmental Contingencies
Large quantity of outputs	Large demand for services
Efficiency: low cost per unit of output	Standardized service
	Economies of scale
Productivity: minimum labor per unit of output	Simple technologies

Structure	Culture
Small variety of specialists	Vertical and horizontal integration strategy
Generalists as administrators	
Highly centralized	Rationalization is a value
Authority based on position	Values of inner circle dominate
Fixed leader	
Highly stratified	
Clear roles and responsibilities, high formalization	

Resources	Process
Unskilled labor	Vertical downward communication
Machine technology (where appropriate)	Few committees
	Communications as orders
Capital intensive	Control by rewards and punishments
Large size	

Weaknesses

Can not serve variable demand
Inflexible, slow changing
Low morale
Not highest quality of goods
   and services

efficiency, and capital-intensive mass production. It is routinized, hierarchical, and centralized. It is far more productive than craft organizations and is very important for the economic development of LDCs.

Bureaucracy or the mechanical model of Burns and Stalker is most effective when the demand for its service or products is large and the level of skills which are needed to provide it is low. The last part of this statement conflicts with popular opinion because many bureaucracies are staffed with educated people. In many cases, however, the work is largely clerical, most of the expertise is learned on the job, and the individuals are overtrained. Europe ran some of its most successful public bureaucracies in the nineteenth century—the postal service and the railroads—with grade school and high school graduates. Credentialism, a problem in both developed countries and LDCs,[8] raises the educational level of employees in bureaucracies higher than required by the functional tasks.

Mechanical organizations are best designed to produce a standardized service or product which is provided throughout a country. They emphasize the specialization, rationalization, and routinization of work and cost cutting so that the system is quite efficient and productive. The mechanical organization has several weaknesses, however. It produces only medium-quality goods and services and, by definition, it is insensitive to individual tastes or local needs and customs. Its formalization and routinization lead to rigidity and inertia so that it can become inefficient over the long haul. We see this in the complaints about red tape in bureaucracies and the present-day problems of many large companies in the United States. It is not a popular organizational model because workers have little discretion or control over the work process. They have low morale and high turnover, except where they have high incomes relative to their skills. These weaknesses are related to the economies of scale which the mechanical-bureaucratic organization achieves. Economies of scale are obtained by breaking complex tasks into simple ones that do not require much training and are performed by low-skilled personnel. Control is maintained via programs, rules, procedures, and the supervisory chain of command. These controls are especially important as the organization gets larger and larger in size. Salaries are hierarchically ordered and many LDC bureaucracies do not pay their clerical employees very much. When these employees are underpaid, they are not very responsive to the close supervision and tight controls of bureaucratic organizations—control breaks down and performance suffers.

Mechanical organization is effective in producing certain services such as insurance and banking; mass production products such as paper, steel, rubber tires, and toys; and public services such as post offices, railroads, telephones, and telegraphs. (The first large bureaucracy was the Pennsylvania Railroad in the United States, where the mechanical form was invented. The army and the post office were parallel developments.) These are mass products or mass services. They involve millions of transactions, telephone calls, letters, passengers, or units of products. The mechanical form excels in producing a single output, especially if it is an economic one.[9] It also produces a uniform output which may be desirable in certain cases. Montgomery observes that it has been effective in land reform, where the same law is applied everywhere and the program may bog down if it is sensitive to local needs.[10]

Organization design excels in developing techniques for making organizations more mechanical. A collection of these techniques has been fashioned into a program for increasing the effectiveness of organizations in LDCs. Brinkerhoff calls it the "performance improvement approach."[11] It emphasizes realistic plans, budgets, and schedules; the establishment of clear roles and responsibilities; and the creation of rewards or sanctions that support the goals of the organization. It also uses new managerial technologies such as PERT, MBO, and so forth, which help make bureaucracies rationally directed toward their objectives and therefore more efficient.

The main tactics for changing mechanical organizations are decree and training. Change is usually initiated at the top and communicated down through the organization. Many changes, however, are too complicated to be conducted in this way. Often problem-solving groups, learning by doing, or action training are needed to improve the performance of mechanical organizations. These nonbureaucratic tactics often are used successfully in bureaucracies, but in the process the bureaucracy is temporarily made less mechanical (unless the team's task is to define more rules).

The Organic-Professional Model

Figure 2.2 outlines the basic characteristics of the organic-professional model. It is the appropriate model for production with

Figure 2.2   The Causes of Performance Level in the Organic-Professional Model

Performances	Environmental Contingencies
Custom-made products/services Innovation High quality Adaptable to changing conditions	Small, but rational demand Nonstandardized service No economies of scale Complex technologies

Structure	Culture
Large variety of specialists Professionals as administrators Highly decentralized Authority based on skill Shifting leader Highly egalitarian Nondefined roles and shifting responsibilities	Research is the strategy Technical progress is a value Shifting coalitions

Resources	Process

Professionals
High technology
Venture capital
Small size
	Horizontal communication
	Many committees
	Communication as advice
	Control by commitment to
	    larger goals and professional
	    norms

Weaknesses

Expensive
Low productivity
Slow production

---

complex technologies for small markets. It emphasizes innovation and quality products and services which are tailored to customer needs. It has low routinization, hierarchy, and centralization. It involves a large variety of highly skilled or professional specialists who are coordinated more through horizontal communication than vertical control. Its high-skill requirements restrict its use in LDCs, but it is needed to achieve very complex tasks such as integrating rural development or innovating new technologies.

The professional organization or the organic model of Burns and Stalker is most effective when the need is for unique, high technology products such as a space shuttle, or unique, high technology services such as a technology assessment. It is also the ideal organizational form for small-batch, high-technology goods and services.

In general, the contingencies for the organic model are the exact opposite of the previous form: small demand, high-skill levels required for tasks, nonstandardized services, and few economies of scale. Organic organizations are designed to produce highly complicated services that are adapted to specific customer/client specifications/needs. Its emphasis is on quality and innovation in the production of relatively unique outputs. The organic model is particularly suitable for research organizations that produce technological innovations. It is the ideal form for universities, therapeutic mental hospitals, agricultural research centers, university hospitals, and the like. Normally these organizations produce multiple outputs in small quantities.

USAID policy has neglected organic organizations except for agricultural research centers. They are relatively scarce in LDCs but they are essential to the development of technologies which are appropriate to the LDC context. Also, many LDCs face complex problems in many sectors and they need organic organizations to solve them. Of course, the need for organic organizations does not automatically produce them. In fact, they are very difficult to create in LDCs because of resource limitations, especially the limited availability of highly skilled personnel in many areas.

The organic form involves a great diversity of occupational specialists who participate jointly in decision making and work in teams. The power structure is decentralized and there is considerable equality of rewards. The organizations remain small, which facilitates an informal atmosphere. Similarly, authority and control are based on networks rather than hierarchies because there are many decisions to be made and they require the inputs of many people. Innovation is increased by job diversity, group problem solving, and a large amount of informal communication. When the members attend conferences elsewhere, the diffusion and circulation of ideas increases. These dialectics stimulate more creativity; the development of new and more appropriate technologies, services, or products; and the solutions to complex problems.

Control is maintained via peer pressure and the informal norms of group processes. Also, individuals who work in these kinds of organizations have high self-control resulting from professional training and they tend to be highly motivated. In fact the morale problem, if there is one, tends to be burnout rather than apathy.

The organic model is much praised in the United States as adaptive, high tech, humane for workers, and the wave of the future, but it, like all other models, has weaknesses. It is neither efficient, productive, nor fast producing; rather, it is slow, expensive, and requires highly skilled personnel. In fact, there is constant pressure to replace highly educated professionals with paraprofessionals working with guidelines, formulas, and routines in order to reduce costs and serve more clients. We predict, therefore, that the pure organic form will always be relatively rare. Many organizations, however, are and will move in the organic direction to deal with complex tasks and to increase innovation.

How are mechanical and craft organizations made more organic? The first step is to increase the level of skills by replacement or training and by adding new occupational specialties. Second, the organization must be restructured to be less hierarchical and centralized and to increase the complexity of the division of labor (because of the new specialties). Third, specialists must work together in teams and expand horizontal communication and networks. Finally, innovation and quality must be emphasized in organizational strategy and policy, and must be more highly rewarded.

The above changes can enable the organization to articulate more closely with customers and clients and to become more flexible and capable of learning. The increase in the complexity of the division of labor and the decentralization of power internally will greatly increase information feedback and self-criticism, and therefore, organizational learning. These structural characteristics break down groupthink and assumptions about one-way causation. The organic organization institutionalizes the learning process and is the essence of the flexible structure.

The Traditional-Craft Model

Figure 2.3 outlines the basic characteristics of the traditional-craft model. It is the appropriate organizational model for production with simple technologies for small markets. If the market is too small and the technology too simple, however, production will be by individual craftspeople or by families rather than by hired labor in craft organizations. It is well suited for providing local services and craft products such as art objects and handmade rugs which cater to specific tastes. The critical dimensions of this form are both its small size and the artisan quality of most of the work. There is little need for a bureaucratic staff to do the administration and the workers are given considerable autonomy in their work. The owner or director has a lot of power over strategic decisions. The small size

Figure 2.3   The Causes of Performance Level in the Traditional-Craft Model

Performances	Environmental Contingencies
Adapted to local needs, tastes	Moderate, but local demand
Mixture of quantity/quality	Partially standardized services
Easy to start up	No economies of scale
	Simple technologies

Structure	Culture
Crafts, semiprofessions	No strategy for growth
Centralized, but job autonomy	Individualism as a value
Small administrative component	Domination by founder
Low formalization	

Resources	Process
Crafts, artisans	Few meetings
Simple technology	Upward and downward
"Family capital"	communications
Small size	Mixture of formal and informal
	controls

Weaknesses

Low productivity
Low efficiency
High failure rate

and craft quality of the work result in few motivational problems and few needs for control. These organizations, however, are frequently plagued by poor management. In the private sector many go under, while in the public sector many remain inefficient and ineffective. At the same time, if there are many of these organizations (e.g., family farms), the inefficiency of some is not as much of a problem.

Traditional-craft is the dominant form of organization in LDCs because it requires little capital, highly educated manpower, sophisticated technology, or administrative capacity, and can be started as a family enterprise. Its minimal requirements are an advantage in low-income countries, but there also are disadvantages. Its minimal requirements mean that craft organizations do not have the benefits of economies of scale, more productive machinery and other technologies, and higher skilled workers. Often their performance can be greatly improved if they can upgrade their factors of production. One way for governments or donor agencies to stimulate economic growth is to provide credit, technologies, information, or training to improve craft organizations. Training in accounting and other management procedures is especially important.

Since most LDCs have multiple ethnic, racial, religious, and even linguistic groups, they have a variety of cultures and therefore tastes. Topographic diversity further increases this cultural diversity since topography has profound impacts on work and life-styles in traditional societies. These environmental conditions are poorly suited to most mechanical organizations but are well suited to small organizations that are adaptive to community needs and tastes and can be staffed and run by local owners and workers. These organizations do not require skilled personnel; instead they require people who are trained for relatively short periods or who received training informally via apprenticeships. For this reason the model is called the craft model. Its output is more standardized and much less complicated than the output of organic organizations, but is more varied and less standardized than the output of mechanical organizations.

Most services associated with local government, especially in the early stages of development, are best arranged in this traditional-craft form of organization. Small farms and cottage industries are other examples; although technically many of these organizations do not fit our standard of at least ten employees, they fit the traditional-craft model on most of the dimensions discussed in this section. Since the output is singular, simple, and easily measured, craft organizations are natural vehicles for entrepreneurs and flourish whenever both entrepreneurial attitudes and modest opportunities exist together. It is in this environmental niche where the laws of competition work the best. Small businesses, which usually start out as family businesses, tap enormous wells of motivation that are absent in large bureaucracies and many compete with larger, better endowed organizations simply on the basis of hard work.

The Mixed Mechanical-Organic Model

The fourth major model in contingency theory is the mixed mechanical-organic model and its basic characteristics are presented in Figure 2.4. It is the appropriate model for production with complex technologies for large markets. It tries to emphasize both efficiency and innovation, both quantity and quality, and both service to a variety of customer/clients and productivity. It does this by

Figure 2.4   The Causes of Performance Level in the Mixed Mechanical-Organic Model

Performances	Environmental Contingencies
Quality and quantity	Moderate to large demand
Moderate innovation	Multiple products from same
Moderate efficiency	technology
Productivity and adaptability	Economies of scale
	Complex technologies

Structure	Culture
Engineers, specialists	Diversification as a strategy
Professional field agents	Long-term employment a value
Centralized and decentralized	Domination by committees
Some components mechanically structured and some components organically structured	

Resources	Process
Skilled workers	Committees
Sophisticated technology	Mixture of vertical and
Capital intensive	horizontal communication
Large size	

Weaknesses

Potential for value conflicts
High start-up costs
Instability of mechanical-organic
balance

structuring part of the organization mechanically and part of the organization organically. One common mechanical-organic organization pattern is to have the production component of the organization structured mechanically, with the research and development component of the organization structured organically. Many large manufacturing corporations in the United States are structured in this way. Another common mechanical-organic organization pattern is to have field teams organically structured and working in many communities or locations, supported by a mechanically structured central organization. When USAID sends out organically structured project teams it fits this model, as do some high-tech military operations.

The mixed mechanical-organic organization can provide standardized services in relatively large quantities and considerable variety by balancing productivity with adaptation to customer/

community needs. One set of contingencies which favors mechanical-organic organizations is economies of scale combined with a technology which can produce a variety of products. Examples are electrical companies, which produce many electrical appliances and products from a common electrical technology, and drug companies, which produce many drugs from a common pharmaceutical technology. The mechanical-organic structure involves a specialized division of labor, the combination of both mechanical and organic components as pointed out earlier, and both centralized and decentralized organization. The organization is managed via an elaborate committee structure and communication is both horizontal and vertical.

At first glance the mixed form would appear to be the best of all possible worlds because it provides a balance between innovation and efficiency, but it has an Achilles heel. There is a tendency for this organization to evolve towards too much centralization at central headquarters and not enough autonomy for the widely dispersed field teams. Then the integration between national and local levels declines and the organization becomes too insensitive to customer or community needs. Another tendency is for the emphasis on efficient production to dwarf the emphasis on innovation; in other words, for it to become more mechanical. Often the emphasis on short-term profits over long-term market position accounts for the trend toward the mechanical. Nevertheless, when this form balances the mechanical and organic patterns well, it can be highly successful. For example, most successful American firms now use this model rather than the mechanical-bureaucratic form, and Peters and Waterman claim that this model is the secret to success in American businesses.[12] The development literature, however, largely ignores this model even though it is basic to the centralization-versus-decentralization debate.

This type of organization has other weaknesses, which make it impractical for many industries and services in LDCs. It is very expensive in capital, technology, and skilled personnel; in other words, it has high start-up costs. This model, however, can be used to reorient existing mechanical organizations in the direction of more adaptiveness, flexibility, and/or innovation.

We have outlined four organizational models. Under certain conditions, which we have identified, each model is more effective than the other models. As we have said several times, there is no single best model, but several "best" models depending upon the circumstances. The models that we have presented are ideal types.

They are presented in a relatively pure form, but very few real organizations exemplify these pure forms. Many craft organizations are dominated by family principles and personal ideosyncracies. Many mechanical and organic organizations are mechanical-organic hybrids of a million varieties, and most mixed mechanical-organic organizations have hybrid instead of pure components. Nevertheless, the four models are important analytical constructs which serve as guides for change agents as to the direction which restructuring should take in order to make organizations more effective in their particular environments.

Contingencies and Choice

In the previous section we described four organizational models that are appropriate for four sets of conditions based on the size of market demand and the sophistication of the technologies. In this section we discuss the role of choice or strategy in determining these two types of contingencies. We also discuss political contingencies that affect organizational structure. An important point to recognize is that in most cases the contingencies are not simply predetermined but are chosen by political processes. They may be predetermined from the perspective of the change agent who tries to restructure the organization in the direction of the organizational model which fits the contingencies, but not from the perspective of policy makers.

Choice of Market Contingencies

When governments provide services, they can often choose the *type of demand* they will serve. We illustrate this principle by discussing alternative ways for LDCs to provide for primary education (although similar choices are made for the servicing of other basic needs). One possible way is to provide a fixed and uniform curriculum. This is based on the assumption (choice) that everyone should learn exactly the same language, math, history, and cultural reference points. Many European countries used this approach to ensure a single spoken language and national culture. This choice of a standardized subject matter is served most effectively by a bureaucratic organization organized along the lines of the mechanical model.

In contrast, policy makers might prefer a system of education whereby each city or town would decide its educational policy and curriculum for primary education. Each school district would be allowed to adapt to local conditions and values in deciding what should be taught. This system is decentralized and produces a greater amount of variation among school districts and among various regions of the country in curriculum and quality. This was the pathway chosen by the United States when it created its system of education.

Thus, *one fundamental contingency is whether the organization seeks to provide a standard service or to provide a nonstandardized service that is adapted to local needs and ethnic tastes.* Standardizing the service will lower costs because of economies of scale; however, standardized services are very insensitive to local needs and interests. Nonstandardized services allow for greater community participation but they are more costly. Here is a clear dilemma or policy choice.

A related market contingency which results from policy choices is the *level* at which a service is provided or organized. Many LDC governments prefer to provide services at the local level, while others prefer the national level. Centralization versus decentralization continues to be a major debate in the development literature.[13] The debate would be more easily resolved if people would recognize that some services are provided best at the local level while others are provided best at the national level. Contingency theory provides suggestions about when to take each course.

Most countries have chosen the level-of-service provision on the basis of cultural values rather than on the basis of contingency theory. For example, the tradition of local control of education is quite strong in Anglo-Saxon countries and some LDCs (frequently those associated with British rule), while the tradition of centralized control is equally strong in France, Germany, and many other LDCs.

The level at which services are provided is not always optional. Sometimes the efficiencies for the two levels are so different that the choice is practically predetermined. For example, some government services are almost always organized at the local level: fire, police, sewage, water, urban housing, and health clinics. It does not make sense to centralize these services because they capture only local economies of scale, require local knowledge, and the public demands that they be adapted to their needs and interests. The advantage of using local knowledge is illustrated in the study of the

National Irrigation Administration in the Philippines discussed in greater detail later. The rice farmers understood which arrangements of irrigation canals would work socially and which would not work, and while the engineers could design irrigation systems that were hydraulically efficient, these inevitably would fail for social reasons.[14] Similarly, the study in Yemen, discussed in Chapter 4, indicates that there are services and needs which are best handled at the local level. Many of the basic necessities, such as food, clothing, and shelter, are subject to wide variations in local conditions and tastes. Ultimately, topography and climate shape these needs and people's perceptions of them. Nevertheless, local tastes are very powerful. For example, Brazil produces soybeans and cheese, but the Brazilians will not eat them. As a consequence, Brazil has to export these products. When demands are governed by specific tastes which vary across regions, then the products are best produced locally.

On the other hand, some services are best standardized over wide areas and therefore best provided nationally. Postal service is a good example, for it would be chaos if each town used different stamps. The same holds true for other uniform services, such as telephone and telegraph, and for national transportation systems, such as railroads and airlines. These services also involve economies of scale and heavy capital investments; thus, their provision is best done at the national level. In contrast, there are no economies of scale for chauffeured limousines or singing-messenger companies; they are local and small. Although we do not think of the military as providing a service, it does offer a collective good called national security. It too involves economies of scale and heavy capital investments, and thus should be centrally organized. There are many consumer and industrial products that are wanted in standardized form, such as cement, glass, steel, paper, and cigarettes. Again, the production of these products tends to involve economies of scale and heavy capital investments, which encourages centralization.

Another market contingency that affects structure is the *supply/demand ratio,* the result of both consumer choices and policy choices. Typically in LDC public agencies, demand and supply are out of balance. Sometimes there is too much demand and very little supply because the government uses its limited resources in other ways. An example of this is credit for small farmers. Sometimes there is too much supply and very little demand, as is the case with birth control clinics. Even education is not necessarily in high demand; dual-end vocational tracks have been resisted in many countries.[15] Indeed, many government agencies have to worry about generating demand for their services. Whether the agency is overwhelmed by demand or has to mobilize it affects how it should be structured.

Trade areas and the size of potential demand are other market contingencies which are affected by public policies. Normally, free trade is allowed within a nation and tariffs are raised at the borders to limit competition. The larger the trading area and market demand, the greater the potential for economies of scale and the larger the plants if mass production technologies exist. For example, in the United States and Western Europe, industrial companies with large volumes built very large plants because they were more efficient. Sometimes the scale of production is large even for batch production, if the product or service is very expensive and the buyers are large, such as that for airplanes or ships. Most batch production, however, occurs when trade areas and market demand are small because mass production and economies of scale do not exist or are not accepted by consumers. For example, up to now it has been more efficient or more acceptable to consumers to construct houses on-site rather than construct them in factories and deliver them to the sites. (This may be changing today.)

The standardization of a service and its volume tend to go together. As volume increases, managers are encouraged to rationalize the production process and they do this by standardizing and mechanizing what is done.[16] Central bureaucracies that handle services tend to use standardized forms, procedures, and rules as methods for handling large volumes of services.

In our discussion we have used market demand for free public services as well as for purchased goods and services. This is an uncommon usage for the concept of market demand, but a justifiable one. Some public services must conform to local tastes and therefore serve small markets; others can be the same for all users and serve large markets. The latter kind of public service can be centralized and bureaucratized, e.g., postal service and tax collecting. Administrators seek economies of scale and capital investments, which increase efficiency, and they can achieve savings by standardizing and rationalizing the production process.

Technological Contingencies

Choice has a smaller role in technological contingencies than in market contingencies, but one choice which often must be made explicitly or implicitly is whether to utilize or ignore local knowledge. Too often it is ignored, with detrimental results, and often the fault is the blind arrogance of the professionals. We do not present many examples of this problem because we focus on successful cases. Failures, however, are plagued with this problem.

Technological contingencies are largely a matter of the skill level needed to provide the service and the amount of training required to attain these skills. For example, health services might require simple or complex technologies. The technological requirements for providing smallpox vaccine shots are minimal; in a short period of time, people can be trained easily to give them. In contrast, the technological requirement for open-heart surgery is very high. It requires a highly specialized team with the most sophisticated health equipment available. Policy choices determine the types of services to be provided but after that, the technological contingencies are relatively fixed.

The major factor that influences the level of skill required is the sheer difficulty of the task. As difficulty increases, one must rely more and more on highly trained individuals who have demonstrated their competency. Perhaps this is an obvious point; nevertheless, it is a critical one in the design of any organization. As the task becomes simplified and less difficult, then one can downgrade the level of training rquired; but, when the technology becomes more sophisticated, tasks become more complex and higher levels of skill are required. It is hard to do effective neurological research without a CAT scanner—not only does this technology require highly trained physician-researchers, but also quite specialized paramedical personnel.

Another factor that affects the level of skills required to provide services is the rate of technological change. When new techniques are created, all other things being equal, the organization requires both more skilled personnel and more sophisticated machinery. Many research institutes require both highly skilled personnel and the most up-to-date equipment because of the fast pace of technological change. One illustration is agricultural research, an activity in which most LDCs invest. If the technology is changing slowly, then fewer skilled researchers are adequate. Thus, the pace of technological change partly determines the need for highly skilled human capital.

Another technological contingency determining the choice of an organizational model is the number of different specialists required. Complex tasks such as planning or organizational change require a variety of specialists who can work together. This presents a major problem since different specialists do not work together naturally. They have conflicting values and trouble communicating with each other. *Teams are the best solution to the problem of integrating a variety of specialists working on a common task.* Relatively egalitarian, open communication and cooperation in task groups, called teams, is the most effective way to elicit the contributions of all specialists and coordinate them. This is the reason why teams are so essential in organizational change interventions. (Examples of this are given in Chapters 3 and 4.) Many change agents know that teams are effective but we have seldom found explanations for their effectiveness in the development administration literature.

Another factor which affects technological contingencies is the complexity of the environment. Complex environments generally require complex technologies and these are best handled in organic organizations. This connection of environmental complexity with organizational structure is a major theme in Paul's analysis.[17] He argues that the strategy, structure and processes of an organization must be appropriate for the level of complexity of the environment. Although he neglects the role of the level of technology, which we emphasize, his analysis is fully compatible with ours. He defines complexity in terms of the scope, diversity, and uncertainty of the environment. Scope involves the geographic range and number of relevant economic sectors in which the organization functions. Diversity refers to the heterogeneity among key external actors, such as beneficiaries, and thus includes diversity of demand. Uncertainty is largely a matter of the degree of stability/instability. Finally, *Paul argues that broad scope and diverse and uncertain environments generally require flexible, nonstandardized, and decentralized organizations [organic].*

Paul does not specify how specific types of environments determine the scope of services provided. We believe that as the level of technology increases, services become more specific and their combined scope increases. As knowledge develops there is a tendency for specific clients to become more recognizable. Concrete examples of this would be the movement of primary education to include more special education and the proliferation of curable disease entities in medicine. The growth in knowledge, therefore, leads to a greater scope of services than was previously offered.

It is important to consider that many services can be provided at several different skill levels, thus making policy choices possible. For example, health care for a variety of the most common problems can be provided either by paramedics in clinics or by skilled physicians in well-equipped hospitals. These service delivery systems involve very different levels of skills and very different costs. Many LDCs have tended to invest heavily in education, often raising skill levels of service personnel unnecessarily high. For example, Leonard reports that agricultural extension agents in Kenya were overtrained.[18] He argues that high school education rather than college education would have been more appropriate for the role they played and the kind of knowledge which they diffused. Primary schoolteachers may also be overtrained in many LDCs. While Europe eliminated illiteracy by giving primary schoolteachers only a few years of training beyond primary school, many LDCs are providing higher levels of training than this. The wisdom of their choice can be questioned when resources are so scarce.

Another choice made when providing services is the level of machine technology used. Again, LDCs often choose the high-tech option even though the low-tech option would employ resources more effectively. Many LDCs are investing in sophisticated machines that reduce the work force rather than buying older machines which are more labor intensive. In some markets the high-tech option may be the only way in which companies can compete; with services, however, it may be an unwise choice.

We thus see that the choices made in human capital and technology have implications for the choice of organizational form, and vice-versa. Thus, a coherent development strategy should include not only the choice of organizational forms for different contingencies but also the choice of technological and skill levels for the goods and services which are provided. (We deal with this briefly in the Epilogue.)

Political Contingencies

Political contingencies are especially important for organizations in LDCs. A major contingency is the relative power of particular tribal, ethnic, and racial groups. Their power and presence frequently make governments decentralize their services to meet the special needs of these groups. Paradoxically, the principle of decentralization to meet specific needs comes from organizational design. Its purpose is to compete more effectively in separate markets, based on the theory that the greater the geographic variation in tastes, the more the provision of services needs to be geographically decentralized.

A different political consideration causes an opposite reaction. For example, Sudan decentralized its many ministries into regional governments in order to break up the power of national elites that were entrenched in central government bureaucracies.[19] Thus, while decentralization usually is used to cater to special interests, at times it may be used to nullify their control.

Another important political contingency is the government's policy on the relative importance of meeting basic human needs versus rapid economic growth. As is well known, donor agencies have shifted some emphasis from the latter goal to the former. At the same time, many LDCs modified their basic development strategy to providing more services to the poor. This political goal has consequences for organizing the public sector. Meeting basic needs requires highly responsive organizations and some form of local control and/or participation. In contrast, the pursuit of economic growth creates a force in the opposite direction, toward national planning and centralization of the economy. Potentially, as in Korea and Malaysia, both forces could coexist, but the choice of national developmental goals tends to tip a society one way or another.

We have not exhausted all of the possible contingencies, and we have not emphasized one in particular—uncertainty—which is quite common in the organizational design literature, on the grounds that it is too subjective.[20] Efforts to operationalize uncertainty have usually failed. Some have tried to define it as changes in market demand, technology, the availability of raw materials, or even as changes in the rate of change itself. The problem with all of these measures is that different managers experience different uncertainty levels under the same objective circumstances.

Specifying the contingencies described above should make it easier for change agents to diagnose the situation and select the most appropriate organizational form. This, in turn, specifies the appropriate direction of organizational change.

Contingency Theory and Development Administration

For a long time, development administration has emphasized the bureaucratic model and has trained many public servants in its principles. More recently, a variety of new approaches has been advocated in the literature on public administration in LDCs. We briefly review these here and compare them to our contingency theory.

First, we outline three current perspectives in the development administration literature and, later, we review Samuel Paul's contingency theory. We follow Brinkerhoff in our selection of current approaches to review—learning process, performance improvement, and rural development capacity building—and accept his claim that these three are ". . . elaborated to the point of providing practitioners with proposals or guidelines for action."[21]

Brinkerhoff describes *the learning process approach* as combining the external resources of the development agency with local needs and knowledge in order to solve mutually determined problems. The assumptions are that blueprints for projects and programs do not work and that the development agency together with its clients must learn from trial and error. The inputs from local peoples who can contribute local understanding is essential to successful agency learning and adapting. This process requires that local peoples be empowered, making the learning process approach a strong champion of decentralization of power in the organization and participation by local peoples in the design and implementation of projects. One of the most successful examples of this approach, the National Irrigation Administration of the Philippines, is described in the next chapter.

The distinctive features of this approach are its experimentation and the creation of new coalitions for mobilizing power in the organization. Experimentation and pilot studies provide the basis of learning. Coalitions are built which cut across normal hierarchical lines of authority in order to facilitate the processes of learning and of protecting the experiment during the critical initial stages of learning.

Korten and Uphoff have argued that it is necessary to reorient bureaucracy in the following ways:

1. Strategic management: getting decision makers to see their organization and its objectives strategically and proactively
2. Organizational incentives: providing rewards (such as salaries, promotions, postings) to members based on success in strengthening local development capacity, setting clear targets, and so on

3. Planning systems: simplifying planning requirements to permit project experimentation and evolution during implementation
4. Monitoring and evaluation: designing a focus on results with explicit attention to building beneficiary capacity
5. Personnel policies: promoting long-term staff placements, emphasizing local knowledge and experience, and using multidisciplinary teams
6. Financial systems: providing multiyear, stable funding levels with lowered emphasis on procedural accountability and more on outcomes
7. Organizational structure: designing flexible structures to adjust to particular client needs and to permit efficient coalition building
8. Training: teaching organization members learning process skills and a participatory orientation
9. Outside resources: using applied social science to gather data, analyze experience, and provide feedback and guidance[22]

We point out that this list emphasizes managerial processes and says little about the structural arrangement which facilitates these processes. The list does suggest that the structure is to be more flexible and use multidisciplinary teams, and Korten and Uphoff's text indicates that it becomes more flexible by developing specialized units and services to serve different client groups. Elsewhere, Korten argues that bureaucracies must be transformed from static change-resisting organizations to "strategic organizations," the latter involving strategic action throughout the organization. "The most important task of top management in a strategic organization is not the making of strategic decisions, but rather the development and maintenance of a total institutional capacity for strategic action."[23] The strategic organization is an organic organization which provides services tailored to specific client or community needs. Korten's discussion of the strategic organization begins to identify structural features of learning organizations, but more elaboration is needed.

Brinkerhoff notes that the learning process approach has been criticized as more ideological than practical and that it ignores the constraints of the funding procedures of donor organizations which require that objectives and activities of projects must be specified before funds will be approved.[24] He also observes that the emphasis on empowerment scares both developing country political elites and donor agencies.

In summary, the learning process approach is committed to building beneficiaries' capacities; thus it advocates modifying organizational structures and processes to improve the agency's articulation with local participants. The emphasis of this approach is on improving managerial processes to facilitate experimentation and learning and to motivate workers toward the community development goals. This approach discusses structural changes less thoroughly and clearly than it does learning processes, but it does advocate decentralized structures with participation by beneficiaries. Recent writings advocate a variation on the organic model as the structural form which is the most conducive to organizational learning and building beneficiary capacity.

The performance improvement approach is built on the managerial functions discussed briefly in Chapter 1. According to Brinkerhoff, "The generic management functions include clear and shared objectives, consensus on strategies and means for attaining objectives, agreed-on and delineated roles and responsibilities, incentives and sanctions supporting goal-directed behaviors and action, and feedback, guidance, and adaptation mechanisms."[25]

The performance improvement approach depends heavily upon teams to implement performance improvement changes in the organization. Members' support is seen as critical to the successful institutionalization of changes, so their changes are not decreed but devised by teams with broad representation in the organization. Outside change agents work as members of the performance improvement team and guide the team's problem-solving activity in the beginning until the inside members have learned the process. The objective of the team is to improve the performance of the organization; this usually means increasing outputs. Implicitly, therefore, the focus is usually on the performance of efficiency or productivity.

Rather than experimentation and pilot studies, training is employed. The particular training approach used is called action training, a form of learning by doing. We will look at several examples of this in Chapter 3; generally, however, managerial technologies associated with the basic managerial functions are taught. In particular, much attention is paid to planning, budgeting, and designing roles and rewards to implement the plan.

Another distinctive feature of the performance improvement approach is the emphasis on facilitative conditions, including felt need for change, commitment to change, multilevel involvement, openness to learning, and continuity of effort. It advises against implementing changes until these conditions are present, making the first job of the development change agent to develop these conditions.

The performance improvement approach says little about organizational structure. Its major structural interest is in roles which encompass microstructures but not macrostructure. It does not explicitly use a contingency approach because it uses a single formula for improving all organizations. Its formula is a set of managerial technologies for creating consensus on goals and means; realistic plans, budgets, and schedules; clear roles and responsibilities; rewards and sanctions for goal achievement; and feedback mechanisms. These technologies are implemented through teams and a process of learning by doing. The structure is left alone unless the problem-solving teams propose and implement structural changes. Such changes may conform to the prescriptions of contingency theory, but, if they do, it is not because contingency theory was explicitly followed but because such was the obvious direction for change.

We also point out that any structural changes are likely to be only incremental. Brinkerhoff notes that this approach involves much less change than the learning process approach and, therefore, it does not confront the larger issues of power, community control, and the like. He also observes that the approach is vulnerable to derailment or cooptation.[26]

In summary, the performance improvement approach generally seeks improvement within the given organizational structure and environmental conditions. Since it normally seeks to improve productivity and efficiency, it fits well into the mechanical model of organizations. It endeavors to clarify objectives and to better relate all activities to these objectives; this increases the fit of means to ends. Therefore, it is an ideal approach to use when organizations should be mechanical but are plagued by inefficiencies due to confusion of goals, unexamined traditions and routines, and primitive managerial technologies. It can improve the performance of these organizations by making them more truly mechanical.

It is important to note, however, that the process of changing organizations is not a routine task and usually, therefore, it can not be conducted in a mechanical manner. It is a complex task and must be conducted in an organic manner. Hence the task force or problem-solving groups which design and implement these improvements operate in an organic manner and temporarily make the organization more organic. If the task force is institutionalized as a permanent department within the organization which is responsible for strategic planning or training in new managerial technologies, then the organization is transformed from a mechanical to a mechanical-organic organization.

The rural development capacity-building approach is a hybrid of the previous two and is especially appropriate for agencies serving rural communities. Like the learning process approach it tries to involve clients in the design and implementation of the projects to increase their stake in the projects. Like the performance improvement approach it uses many new management technologies, task forces, and action training. Its seven elements are:

1. Risk sharing between clients and service providers
2. Involvement of actors at multiple levels
3. Demonstrated success/utility of new technologies/behaviors over old ones
4. Collaborative operating style and joint action
5. Emphasis on learning
6. Appropriate incentives
7. Use of an existing resource base[27]

Again, the emphasis is on process factors and little attention is given to changing the macrostructure of the relevant agencies. It seeks to improve their design and implementation capacities through managerial technologies, task forces, and microstructural changes. Its main structural concern is with linkages, both interorganizational linkages and those to local groups. The seventh element refers to the local linkage and proposes that ". . . sustained benefit flows depend upon some amount of autonomous control over resources by beneficiary groups."[28] In Chapter 4 we review cases which demonstrate the importance of this principle.

Brinkerhoff questions whether the rural development capacity-building approach is a unified approach since it combines elements of both previous models and includes, perhaps, too many factors to be pursued in an integrated way. Any specific action is likely to entail only a subset of its prescriptions. We would also point out that this approach is likely to have difficulty pursuing its two objectives simultaneously, i.e., improving the capabilities of the agency (without significant structural change) and building community capacity. It tries to serve two masters—the action agency and the rural communities—but can the two masters be served equally?

In summary, all three recent development administration approaches emphasize managerial processes rather than organizational structure. References to structure refer usually to microstructures or general calls for decentralization, and contingencies are not specified. In contrast, the contingency theory of organizations specifies what structures are appropriate for various conditions and various purposes.

One work stands out as closest to our own work, conceptually and methodologically, and that is Samuel Paul's *Managing Development Programs: The Lessons of Success*.[29] Paul describes and analyzes six cases of successful development programs and explains their successful performance in terms of the congruence of strategy, structure, processes, and environment. Our framework presented in Figures 2.1 through 2.4 utilizes these four factors, and both Paul's and our definitions of them are similar. Paul's theoretical perspective is also similar to ours. He uses a contingency theory that assumes that organizational structures must be appropriate for the environment. He selects the sectoral and geographic scope of the program, diversity of the services, and uncertainty as the contingencies of the environment which determine the appropriate organizational structure. We select different but related contingencies. According to research findings, the level of the core technology and market size are the dimensions of the environment that have the most effect on organizational structure. The two sets of contingencies are distinct but almost equivalent in that diversity and certainty generally translate into sophisticated technology, and scope is roughly allied with market size. Paul's key structural dimensions are centralization/decentralization, functional/matrix form, and organizational autonomy. These dimensions do not translate readily into the structural dimensions of the four organizational models in our contingency theory so that, in this regard, the two contingency theories are distinct. They are similar in approach but different in focus: Paul's derives largely from organizational design and ours derives largely from organizational theory.

One feature of Paul's work that deserves special attention because it represents a significant advance in contingency theory is his differentiation between the degree of centralization of various functions within organizations. He shows that ". . . functional areas dominated by scale economies (e.g., decisions on purchases, technology choices, processing)"[30] are centralized in all six of the successful cases he presents, but service delivery is decentralized in them all. The four other functions which he examines, i.e., allocation and control of funds, supervision and control of field activities, resource generations, and design of service, were decentralized in some cases and centralized or mostly centralized in other cases. His study demonstrates the fact that different contingencies operate for different functions.

Summary and Conclusion

Contingency theory argues that different organizational structures are required for different organizational contexts. The specific contingency theory utilized in this monograph argues that the traditional/craft model is suited to low-tech small markets, the mechanical model is suited to low-tech large markets, the organic model is suited to high-tech small markets, and the mechanical/organic model is suited to high-tech large markets. This fourfold model of contingency theory is the major perspective currently in organizational theory and is a major analytical tool for development change agents.

Can these models based on Western business firms be applied to organizations in the LDCs? Do they apply to public bureaucracies? We argue that the same problems occur in LDCs and in public bureaucracies; therefore, the theories do apply. However, LDCs have other problems which occur much less frequently in DCs, such as scarcities of the factors of production and patrimonial bureaucracies, so that these theories need to be supplemented with models and theories which are suited to these conditions. In Chapter 5, therefore, we supplement the four contingency theory models with two additional models which are applicable to some of these special conditions.

Although the range, number, and variety of organizations vary according to the level of socioeconomic development, the same four kinds of organizations found in developed countries are found in both the public and the private sector in LDCs. *In fact, the problem of development from an organizational perspective is to stimulate the growth of a variety of organizations, each of which is needed to achieve certain performances.*

We find that the four models of contingency theory are very helpful in analyzing the cases of organizational change presented in Chapters 3 and 4, with the mechanical-organic continuum being especially useful. There has been a great deal of discussion about the need to reorient bureaucracy, and most commentators think that bureaucracies in LDCs should become less mechanical and more organic. We will see examples of this in Chapters 3 and 4. Mechanical bureaucracies, however, are effective for some tasks, such as land reform, and in such cases it would be inappropriate to move from a mechanical to an organic model. For example, the Training and Visit Agricultural Extension model is a mechanical organization that has been effective in certain contexts.[31] There are a variety of tasks that are best done with this kind of organization. Indeed, some recent organizational change efforts are making certain organizations *more,* not less, bureaucratic. Chapter 3 will describe several examples in which teams introduced mechanical managerial technologies that proved to be effective. (Note that sometimes the term bureaucracy is used to denote a mechanical organization. However, not all government bureaucracies are structured in a mechanical way. To avoid this confusion we use the term mechanical organization rather than bureaucracy.)

Although we disagree with the tendency to malign mechanical organizations, since they are appropriate for certain contexts, we agree that many organizations in LDCs should become more organic. For example, some development administrators are trying to implement integrated rural development, which is a very complex task. According to Lawrence and Lorsch this complexity is best handled by an organic type of organization involving the use of teams. Jamaica, Guyana, Colombia, and the Philippines provide cases in which complex tasks were accomplished with interdisciplinary teams, which in turn made the organizations more organic.

Although we have argued that contingency theory based on the contingencies of technology and markets can be usefully applied to organizational development in LDCs, we also discussed political contingencies because they often play such an important role in developing countries. These too must be borne in mind by change agents. Political theory does not provide managerial technologies but an alternative theoretical perspective to contingency theory. Both theories can be used together by change agents, however, because contingency theory prescribes how organizations should be structured to be effective in four types of market/technology conditions and political theory helps explain why organizations are not structured appropriately and why they operate ineffectively.

Finally, we have related the contingency theory of organizations to three existing approaches in development administration and to Paul's version of contingency theory. We began with the learning process approach to development administration which tends to make agencies more organic. It endeavors to reorient bureaucracies to increase their flexibility and this requires change in the organic direction. The organic and mixed mechanical-organic models are relevant to this reorientation and suggest the ways that structural, cultural, and resource variables have to be changed. The organic model thus provides a clear prescription for development change agents who want to create learning organizations.

The performance improvement approach to development administration fits well with the mechanical model. Although we do not normally think of public bureaucracies as needing reorientation to make them more efficient, this is frequently the case, and the mechanical model indicates how structural, cultural, and resource variables have to be changed. The performance improvement approach seeks to institutionalize a number of modern managerial technologies which are necessary for efficient, and therefore mechanical, operation.

The rural development capacity-building approach involves both mechanical and organic tendencies. It uses new managerial technologies which make organizations more mechanical. It also involves clients in the design and implementation of projects which increases the complexity of these processes and the decentralization of power.

The final approach which change agents in LDCs should draw upon is Paul's congruence theory which is a contingency theory based upon organizational design rather than on organizational theory. He argues that the key to high performance for agencies is the congruence of strategy, structure, processes, and environment. Achieving this congruence is the responsibility of top management. As with much of the development administration literature, Paul focuses on the issue of centralization versus decentralization. One of his major contributions is his thesis that centralized organizations are effective in some situations and decentralized in others, and another is his demonstration that successful organizations have some functions centralized and others decentralized.

Notes

1. Max Weber, 1947, *The Theory of Social and Economic Organization* (New York: Oxford University Press).

2. Thomas Burns and G. M. Stalker, 1961, *The Management of Innovation* (London: Travistock).

3. Paul R. Lawrence and Jay W. Lorsch, 1967, *Organization and Environment: Managing Differentiation and Integration* (Cambridge, Mass.: Harvard Graduate School of Business Administration).

4. Derick W. Brinkerhoff, 1986, "The Evolution of Current Perspectives on Institutional Development: An Organizational Focus" in Derick W. Brinkerhoff and Jean-Claude Garcia-Zamar (eds.), *Politics, Projects, and People: Institutional Development in Haiti* (New York: Praeger), pp. 11–59.

5. Charles Perrow, 1967, "A Framework for the Comparative Analysis of Organizations," *American Sociological Review,* vol. 32 (April), pp. 194–209. *See also* James Thompson, 1967, *Organizations in Action* (New York: McGraw-Hill); Joanne Woodward, 1965, *Industrial Organization* (London: Cambridge); Derek Pugh, David Hickson, and C. Robin Hennings, 1969, "An Empirical Taxonomy of Structures of Work Organizations," *Administrative Science Quarterly,* vol. 14 (March), pp. 115–126; and Jerald Hage, 1980, *Theories of Organizations: Form, Process, and Transformation* (New York: Wiley-Interscience), Chapters 12 and 13.

6. Peter Blau and Richard Schoenherr, 1971, *The Structure of Organizations* (New York: Basic Books); Peter Blau, Wolf Hydebrand, and Robert Stauffer, 1966, "The Structure of Small Bureaucracies," *American Sociological Review,* vol. 31 (April), pp. 179–191; Peter Blau et al., "Technology and Organization in Manufacturing," *Administrative Science Quarterly,* vol. 21 (March), pp. 20–40; Peter Blau, 1972, "Interdependence and Hierarchy in Organizations," *Social Science Research,* vol. 1 (April), pp. 1–24; Peter Blau, 1970, "A Formal Theory of Differentiation in Organizations," *American Sociological Review,* vol. 35 (April), pp. 210–218.

7. Richard L. Daft, 1983, *Organizational Theory and Design* (St. Paul, Minn.: West), Chapter 5; Amitai Etzioni, 1975, *A Comparative Analysis of Complex Organizations* (New York: Free Press); Hage, 1980, *op. cit.;* Henry Mintzberg, 1979, *The Structuring of Organizations* (Englewood Cliffs, N.J.: Prentice-Hall); Samuel Paul, 1982, *Managing Development Programs: The Les-*

sons of Success (Boulder, Colo.: Westview); and Charles Perrow, 1967, *op. cit.*

8. Randall Collins, 1979, *The Credentialist Society* (New York: Academic Press).

9. Alfred Chandler, Jr., 1962, *Strategy and Structure: Chapters in the History of Industrial Enterprise* (Cambridge, Mass.: M.I.T. Press).

10. John Montgomery, 1979, "The Populist Front in Rural Development: Or Shall We Eliminate the Bureaucrats and Get on with the Job," *Public Administration Review* (January-February) pp. 588–565.

11. Brinkerhoff, 1986, *op. cit.*, p. 13.

12. Thomas J. Peters and Robert H. Waterman, Jr., 1982, *In Search of Excellence: Lessons from America's Best-Run Companies* (New York: Harper & Row).

13. Examples are found in Dennis Rondinelli, 1983, "Implementing Decentralization Programs in Asia: A Comparative Analysis," *Public Administration and Development,* vol. 3, pp. 181–207; Dennis Rondinelli, 1981, "Government Decentralization: Theory and Practice in Developing Countries," *International Review of Administrative Sciences,* vol. 47, no. 7, pp. 133–145; and Dennis Rondinelli, 1981, "Administrative Decentralization and Economic Development: The Sudan's Experiment with Devolution," *Journal of Modern African Studies,* vol. 19, no. 4, pp. 595–624.

14. David Korten, 1980, "Community Organization and Rural Development: A Learning Process Approach," *Public Administration Review,* vol. 40, no. 5 (September-October), pp. 480–511.

15. George Psacharopulos and William Loxley, 1984, *Diversified Secondary Education and Development: A Report on the Diversified Secondary Curriculum Study* (draft report for the World Bank, Washington, D.C.)

16. Chandler, 1962, *op. cit.*

17. Paul, 1982, *op. cit.*

18. David Leonard, 1977, *Reaching the Peasant Farmer: Organization Theory and Practice in Kenya* (Chicago: University of Chicago Press).

19. Dennis A. Rondinelli, 1981, "Administrative Decentralization and Economic Development: The Sudan's Experiment with Devolution," *The Journal of Modern African Studies,* vol. 19, no. 4, pp. 595–624.

20. Howard Aldrich, 1979, *Organizations and Environments* (Englewood Cliffs, N.J.: Prentice-Hall); Robert Duncan, 1972, "Characteristics of Organizational Environments and Perceived Environmental Uncertainty," *Administrative Science Quarterly,* vol. 17 (September), pp. 313–327.

21. Brinkerhoff, *op. cit.,* p. 22. We rely heavily on this useful summary of the three approaches in the following sections.

22. *Ibid.,* p. 24; and David Korten and Norman T. Uphoff, 1981, "Bureaucratic Reorientation for Participatory Rural Development" (NASPAA Working Paper No. 1, Washington, D. C., November), pp. 18–20.

23. David C. Korten, 1984, "Strategic Management for People-Centered Development" (mimeo, March 21), p. 6.

24. Brinkerhoff, *op. cit.,* p. 26.

25. *Ibid.,* p. 30.

26. *Ibid.,* p. 31.

27. *Ibid.,* p. 33.

28. *Ibid.*

29. Paul, *op. cit.*

30. *Ibid.,* p. 186.

31. Michael Cernea, 1981, "Sociological Dimensions of Extension Organization: The Introduction of T and V System in India" in Bruce Crouch and Shankariah Chanda (eds.), *Extension Education and Rural Development,* vol. 2 (Chichester: John Wiley and Sons), pp. 221–235.

3

Organizational Change Strategies: Development Interventions

This chapter and the next one combine the theories and strategies of organizational change, which were presented in Chapters 1 and 2, with case materials from developing countries. In this chapter we present six model cases in some detail, using the framework developed in Chapter I. The first three cases involve significant structural changes and the last three cases emphasize work groups, managerial technologies, and training. The chapter concludes with an analysis of the implications of all six cases for change agents. The cases in this chapter represent explicit efforts to change an organization to improve its performance. The cases in chapter 4 represent efforts to improve services to communities and strengthen community associations, while changing the service organization in the process. The line between these two sets of cases, however, is admittedly not as clear as these statements imply.

We use an analytical framework derived from the conceptual schemata of Chapter 1 to guide our analysis of the six cases of changing organizations in LDCs. The elements of the framework are:

1. Synopsis of the case
2. Performance and output gaps
3. Environmental context: opportunities and constraints
4. Structural, design, and environmental changes
5. Nature of the approach
6. Results
7. Conclusion

Each case study begins with a brief synopsis of the organizational change episode. Since our emphasis is on analysis, our synopsis is only a bare sketch but references are provided which give the more complete story. Next we discuss the performance or output gaps and how they are perceived to determine the degree of pressure for change.

The environment enters the analysis in two ways, as context and as impact area. As context the environment presents constraints and opportunities, and the results achieved by the intervention should be evaluated relative to these. As impact area the environment encompasses organizations or community associations that are changed by the intervention. In Chapter 3 we look at the effect of the change on the organization itself and at its impacts on organizations in the environment. One environmental impact is the development of linkages between organizations, as in integrated rural development, and another is the creation of a performance improvement team which works with a number of other organizations. Throughout this chapter, however, the accent is on structural and design changes within a single organization or within some system of organizations. In Chapter 4 the accent is on changes in the environment, especially the creation of stronger instrumental voluntary associations within the community. Usually the structural and design changes of the service organizations in these cases are for the purpose of strengthening the community voluntary associations.

The nature of the approach delves into intervention levels, tactics, methods of data collection, and resources. Tactics range from decree, which is rather authoritarian, to problem-solving groups, a nonauthoritarian tactic. We also look at the methods of data collection, the use of data in the process of change, and the resources involved. Finally, we conclude our case analysis with a discussion of results and the presentation of our conclusions.

We noted in Chapter 1 that there has been an increasing overlap in the three organizational change literatures. One consequence of this overlap is that actual interventions in the field are seldom pure or ideal types, but usually mixtures. It is not easy to classify one case as O.D., another as O.T., and still a third as organizational design. Most change agents do not work explicitly out of one of these strategies. As change agents cope, they "invent" solutions—frequently not realizing that these inventions have occurred elsewhere. Interventions result in continual reinventions of various tactics or approaches. In this chapter our concern is to see what works and to learn this inductively from some cases at hand. As one focuses on both the how and what of change, more than one of these strategies is likely to be involved. Typically, the more successful cases of intervention involve the best elements of more than one strategy.

There are surprisingly few well-documented cases of organizational change (using the narrow definition of organizations) in the development literature. In a relatively short time, we canvassed a large literature but found relatively few cases documented well enough to be included here. There are many reasons for this. First, change agents seldom report their inventions in either the developed world or in LDCs. Action and reflection are seldom combined in the same person. Second, some of the most interesting organizational change stories—the invention of new organizational forms—are the products of men and women of vision. Often the only record of these critical changes is a biography (e.g., that of Elliot and the transformation of Harvard) or autobiography (e.g., that by Slone of General Motors). In this respect, Chandler has done a major service in reconstructing from documents some of the major organizational changes in large American corporations.[1]

The application of the framework of Chapter 1 to the case materials in this and the next chapter presents some problems. We have not always found the information we wanted. In some instances we have interviewed the change agents themselves; in others we have sought out additional documents. Even this extra effort has failed to answer all the questions we posed in Chapter 1. We are, therefore, forced to speculate on some of the dimensions in the framework.[2]

SIX CASE STUDIES

The Organizational Change of the National Irrigation Administration (Philippines)

The change of the National Irrigation Administration (NIA) in the Philippines has received a great deal of attention.[3] Most of what has been written about this organizational change intervention has focused on the success of NIA in strengthening instrumental voluntary associations, i.e., building effective local irrigation associations. In our judgment, however, the most interesting aspect of this intervention for organizational change agents is the considerable alteration of the design and structure of NIA. It became more organic by adding a new specialty (community organizers), using problem-solving teams for planning and implementation, and producing irrigation systems which are more tailor-made for the individual communities.

Synopsis

NIA has thirty thousand employees working in twelve regions on two types of irrigation systems: nationals which are large and are operated and maintained by NIA, and communals which are small and operated and maintained by farmers. In 1976 NIA started a project to improve its Communal Irrigation Program. Previously, NIA had installed facilities for many small, gravity-fed, communal irrigation systems, but many of these were not being used properly nor being adequately maintained. The problem was due more to social factors than to engineering deficiencies. Typically, NIA would call a meeting of farmers and have them elect officers for an irrigation association, to operate and maintain the communal system, shortly before turning the system over to them. Many of these associations then performed inadequately. NIA took two new actions to correct the problem. First, it contracted with the Farm Systems Development Corporation to provide community organizers to mobilize farmers into the irrigation associations. In contrast to the past, the community organizers worked with a nine-month lead time and in most cases were able to develop effective associations to take over the irrigation systems.

The second action that NIA took was to develop gradually the capacity in NIA itself to organize users. It started with a pilot project that used NIA community organizers in two communities. This project tried to develop community associations and integrate their inputs with the engineering procedures. When the farmers organized they expressed their concerns about the location of diversions and canals, the timing of construction, and the choice of laborers for construction work. These concerns were fed back to the technical staff by the community organizers within NIA whose main purpose was to facilitate the interaction between the farmers and the technical staff. Since the farmers gained some influence in the design of the communal irrigation systems, they were more committed to the systems and their associations functioned more effectively. The pilot project, however, was plagued with problems that caused delays, and it required more adjustments in NIA's operating procedures than was expected. Nevertheless, the pilot project proved the value of integrating social and technical approaches, provided learning laboratories that identified problems, provided engineers and organizers with valuable experience in working together, and experimented with solutions.

A top-level National Communal Irrigation Committee was formed to guide the integration of the community development capacity into NIA. In addition, research support was provided by several outside institutions, including the Asian Institute of Management, the Institute of Philippine Culture, and the International Rice Research Institute. They not only studied what was happening, but also developed guidelines, training programs, and evaluations, and contributed to planning.

Once a satisfactory program model was developed and tested, one communal project was selected as a pilot in each of NIA's twelve regions for implementation of the community organizer approach. "Each region, thus, would be 'seeded' with its own learning laboratory through which regional personnel could gain experience with the new methods and adapt them to their needs."[4] By 1983, the new program was diffused throughout NIA and had become the standard operating procedure on all of its communal irrigation projects. The basic participatory approach was also tried on one national system in 1981 and expanded to twelve in 1982.

Performance and Output Gaps

We have suggested that a key element in organizational change is the recognition of a performance or output gap. Top management of NIA recognized that the organization was failing to create successful communal irrigation systems (i.e., it had recognized an output gap).[5] It also diagnosed the problem as the result of ineffective irrigation associations, which were not correctable without adding new components to the organization. This perception of failure led to experimentation with a participatory approach. The first experiment made use of the Farm Systems Development Corporation for articulating with communities, but it had many problems (i.e., there was a perceived performance gap). These difficulties increased the pressure to internalize the community development capacity within NIA. Therefore, this case demonstrates that when an organization wants to improve itself, basic changes are possible.

NIA's objectives, which included constructing and maintaining effective communal irrigation systems, were fairly measurable and failure was obvious. Unmaintained canals were encumbered with vegetation, filled with silt, or even leaking through rifts. Furthermore, there was a widespread concern within NIA over the poor performance of many irrigation associations. More critically, a government law required the communities to pay for the irrigation systems by contributing 10 percent of construction costs in the form of materials or labor and paying back a loan for the other 90 percent over time. This law gave the communities a big stake in the design and operation of the systems and it made the success of NIA depend more heavily on the effectiveness of the irrigation associations. The gap in their performance, therefore, became even more visible and created considerable pressure for change.

Environmental Context: Opportunities and Constraints

We argue that performance must always be evaluated relative to the difficulty of the task. The results of a change effort, therefore, should be evaluated relative to the opportunities or constraints imposed upon the organization. In other words, the environmental context must be taken into account in evaluating the success or failure of an intervention. The environmental context must also be taken into account by change agents when they design and implement a program of change. The main reasons for the dismal record of failures in program and structural changes in LDCs are unrealistic ambitions which underestimate the difficulties, i.e., the environmental constraints. Therefore, the environment is a crucial factor in our analytical framework.

The NIA organizational change had an unusually favorable environmental context for an LDC. The first favorable condition for change was the crop which was involved in most of the irrigated areas. Wet rice cultivation creates a community of relative equals and equality is conducive to cooperative voluntary associations. It is hard to be a big landowner with a crop that is labor intensive and has not been mechanized. Rice culture is associated with greater than normal social, political, and economic equality. We suggest, therefore, that the nature of the crop and the topography led to much greater cooperative behavior, the indigenous development of cooperatives, and a sense of interdependence. This hypothesis is based on the research on cooperative behavior in the developed world which finds the strongest cooperative movements in vineyards, fishing, hunting, corn farming, and other crops that engender similar social structures of relative equality and interdependence.[6] Another literature which supports the above hypothesis is the development literature which demonstrates how frequently rural development projects fail when they are conducted through community elites. In this connection, the Yemen study reported in the next chapter is informative because it suggests an upper limit for participatory programs of an income ratio of six to one between the upper and lower 20 percent groups.[7]

The second favorable aspect of the environment was the new policy directives in both donor agencies and the host country favoring basic human needs and greater local participation in projects. It is very difficult to estimate the weight of these values for the policy makers in NIA but they do provide a real opportunity for changing development organizations in the participatory direction. In fact, we have noticed that a large number of LDCs have been experimenting with decentralization or devolution, as well as with various forms of community participation. These experiments imply that there may be a relatively widespread support for change in the participatory direction, at least on an experimental basis.

The third favorable condition was the educational level in the Philippines. It is an unusual country in many ways. Because it was a former American colony, it has much larger investments in education than many comparable Third World societies have, and participation tends to work better with better-educated people. Furthermore, some of the professional and managerial personnel earned degrees in the United States which should have made them more open to change and to participatory programs.

The fourth favorable condition or opportunity was the fact that NIA is not a normal bureaucracy. Typically, engineers are quite different from civil servants who work in ministries. They are more open to data collection and the use of data to solve problems. Their problem solving and performance orientation should make them more open to change efforts and to measures of performance gaps. The work of the Asian Institute of Management with NIA would be another factor predisposing NIA managers to be open to change.

The most fascinating aspect of NIA is its apparent lack of many of the problems that continually plague most LDC organizations.

For example, NIA seems to have experienced little or no corruption, ethnic conflict, political interference, bureaucratic rigidity, or poor morale. If these problems were, in fact, absent, NIA had substantial advantages over most LDC organizations.

Structural, Design, and Environmental Changes

The changes in NIA were quite widespread and more profound than is perhaps appreciated. It was changed in two basic and related ways. It became more organic structurally in a variety of ways and its design became more decentralized. It was made more organic by adding an occupational specialty (thus becoming more complex), greater use of problem-solving groups, decentralization of strategic decision making, increasing communications, and making communication flows more horizontal.

The main structural change in NIA was the addition and integration of a new occupational speciality. The NIA started to experiment on a small scale in 1976 when it hired six community organizers for its pilot project for enhancing community participation in the design, implementation, operation, and maintenance of communal irrigation systems. The use of community organizers expanded next to a pilot project in each of twelve regions and later diffused throughout the organization. By 1983 NIA employed four hundred community organizers. The addition of a new occupational specialty throughout NIA increased its structural diversity, which, when accompanied by successful integration of several occupational specialties, improves the adaptiveness of the organization to its environment, increases its flexibility, and stimulates a higher rate of innovation. From an organizational theory perspective, adding an occupational specialty and integrating it with other specialties is a major structural change in the organic direction.

Another major structural alteration of NIA in the organic direction was decentralization of some of its strategic decisions by the creation of the Communal Irrigation Committee as a problem-solving group at the top level of the organization. This committee planned the implementation of the community organizing program throughout the organization and thereby broadened the participation in strategic decisions.[8] Peters and Waterman in *In Search of Excellence* discuss the importance of this type of problem-solving group in designing and guiding organizational changes. They document a number of cases where ad hoc task forces are especially useful in solving basic, organizationwide problems.[9] Planning the implementation of a structural change of an organization is usually a very complex task which is best tackled by a multispecialist task force which represents a variety of perspectives within the organization. The Communal Irrigation Committee demonstrated these organizational principles and seemed to contribute greatly to the success of the organizational change effort.

As experienced managers know and organizational theory predicts, organizational changes generally, and structural differentiation specifically (adding a new occupational specialty), cause some initial conflict. The greater participation of farmers in the design of irrigation systems and in implementation decisions infringes on the job autonomy of the engineers. They are required to share their work decisions with nonprofessionals and they must share control over the project process with the community organizers. The addition of one occupational specialty changes the power or, at minimum, job autonomy of another. In this case the conflicts were minimized by wise planning of the organizational change and by the role of the Communal Irrigation Committee. The change was implemented slowly in stages, using pilot projects. The first pilot project had numerous problems which caused considerable delays, but it helped to work the bugs out of the program and gradually to build wider support for the participatory approach. Then a pilot project was started in each region served by NIA, which allowed regional adaptations and gradual learning of innovations. Since many problems were worked out during the gradual diffusion process, conflicts were minimized. Conflicts were also contained by passing the major ones up to the Communal Irrigation Committee for resolution.

There also appears to have been a considerable increase in the amount of lateral or horizontal communication and in the amount of both upward and downward communication. As pointed out in Chapter 2, high levels of horizontal communication and high levels of total communication are characteristic of organic organizations and are conducive to problem solving, adaptability, and organizational change. This increase occurred for a number of reasons. The community organizers met with the village associations, helped them develop and articulate group decisions, arranged meetings with engineers, and communicated the needs and desires of farmers to NIA technicians and administrators. Committees were created within NIA to deal with new inputs and new problems. A

major data-collection effort was started during the pilot projects
which became a communication tool and encouraged the committees to become problem-solving groups. A report prepared by de las
Reyes documented some of the activities and problems which
emerged from the data collection efforts.[10] These included the community's desire for NIA to hire more local personnel for the project,
confusion over the equity requirements, the community's need for
engineers' assistance in obtaining rights of way, and unclear
guidelines on legal requirements. Dealing with these matters generated a considerable volume of communication.

Another important structural change was the reformulation
and strengthening of the linkage between NIA and the village associations. Previously, NIA and the irrigation associations worked
mostly sequentially with minimal interaction—the system would
be built and then turned over to the associations. The new policy
was to bring the associations into the designing and construction
activities and not confine them to operation and maintenance activities. This change in the nature of the linkage required some
internal restructuring of NIA as pointed out previously.

Many of the changes involved participation, and we distinguish three types of participation in this case. First is the breadth
of participation by members within an organization in the decisions of the organization. Second is the degree to which the clients
of an organization can participate in the decisions which affect
them. (For example, the extent to which students can influence
course requirements or the rules of a university.) Third is the
breadth of participation by clients or beneficiaries in articulation
of client interests to the organization, i.e., is it basically articulation by leaders, or by all? If the clients are organized to represent
themselves, are they democratically organized or hierarchically organized? In the NIA case the task forces broadened participation
within NIA, farmers' inputs into NIA decisions increased, and the
farmers became better and more democratically organized.

A common theme to the structural changes that occurred in
NIA was that they made the organization less bureaucratic and
more organic. *According to the social science literature, the change
from a bureaucratic organization to an organic one, or those changes
that make organizations less hierarchical and more flexible, increase innovation and responsiveness to the needs of the clients.* Korten calls this structural change "reorienting bureaucracy in the direction of the 'learning process approach.'"[11] His analysis is helpful

because it identifies some key processual changes which should accompany the structural changes in the organic direction. Obviously we prefer to use the terminology of contingency theory and describe these changes in terms of the organic model. The advantage is that contingency theory links to a large literature that would specify what changes were needed to make NIA more organic.

The design changes that were made had the effect of increasing decentralization. The first change was the creation of a task force at the top of the organization. The second was the creation of work groups, which were essentially quality work circles or problem-solving groups, within both NIA and the user associations. Earlier we stressed that these changes decentralized strategic decisions and created a network of communication, characteristics of organic structures. Here we point out that these are managerial technologies which are practiced widely in organizational design.

Nature of the Approach

The intervention occurred on several levels and within the environment as well. At the top of NIA a task force was created; at the bottom a new occupational specialty was added and committees were instituted. Eventually the village associations were considerably strengthened. Thus, the intervention was truly systemic and affected all levels.

The available documents indicate that at least six tactics of change were used, all of which contributed to the success of the organizational change. They were:

1. Restructure
2. Data collection
3. Data discussion
4. Group decision making
5. Group problem solving
6. Experimentation

NIA was restructured by the creation of the high-level task force, the addition of the new occupational specialty, and the creation of problem-solving groups at low levels. We have already noted how the collection and discussion of data facilitated the volume of communication. The group decision making and group problem solving improved morale and reduced resistance to change, both within NIA and in the voluntary associations.

Two distinctive features of this case, both keys to NIA's success, were the extensive use of experimentation or pilot projects as a way of learning how best to implement the new policy direction and the extraordinary data-collection activities. In addition to its teaching function, experimentation reduces resistance to change and allows, when used with group problem solving and group decision making, the development of more complex and appropriate solutions. While the usual organizational data-collection methods were used, social scientists also studied the new participatory programs using a variety of data-collection methods. Their research demonstrated performance and output gaps, created pressure for change, and helped work out solutions.

The NIA intervention enjoyed high motivation and strong commitment. The Communal Irrigation Program had strong, high-level support, as evidenced by the fact that the community development program was expanded even though the pilot projects had considerable problems. Normally, high-level support for an intervention is a strong motivating factor. Another is the normative appeal of the participatory approach as democratic, humane, avant-garde, and creative. Also, the NIA innovation drew positive public and professional attention which served as a motivating factor. In addition, the increased interactions proved to be intrinsically rewarding; for example, the engineers found their interactions with farmers to be very fruitful even though frustrating at times.

The NIA intervention was also blessed with a richness of resources. The Ford Foundation provided funds to help pay the costs of instituting structural changes and its contribution proved to be critical. Many organizational change efforts fail because the process of change—especially when the bureaucracy is being reoriented towards an organic model, as was true in this case—requires an *extra* infusion of funds. The funds are needed to pay for hiring community organizers, conducting experiments, and creating task and problem-solving groups. In LDCs there are no slack resources for these purposes. The availability to NIA of money to cover these costs was an enormous inducement to change and facilitated the process. We also note that the demonstration of performance gaps can be used by LDCs to obtain resources from donors and to pressure for resources internally.

Another resource which was used lavishly in the NIA intervention was time. It has spanned more than eight years. This length of time was desirable because of the magnitude of change that was being attempted. The tactics of experimentation and pilot projects require considerable time, especially when they include elaborate data-collection methods.

The intervention approach used in NIA combines many of the techniques found in all three organizational change literatures. While most of them are associated with O.D., we point out that a number of major structural changes were made in the organic direction, which fits the principle of contingency theory.

Results

We are not provided with systematic, comparative before/after data on the performances of the communal irrigation systems, but the changes are described as highly successful. The communal irrigation systems were better designed, operated, and maintained. Perhaps the most interesting result was the reduction in construction costs as a consequence of farmers' suggestions. In about one-third of the irrigation systems, substantial changes were made after the farmers' input, and in another quarter of the cases, irrigation channels were deleted.

Another major result was greater organization and mobilization of the irrigation associations. As a consequence, the associations contributed more labor to and paid for more of the costs of construction and more effectively maintained the systems than previously. A cost-benefit analysis suggests that these gains were enough to pay for the cost of the addition of the community organizers.

One of the most important results of the change effort was an increase in organizational innovation. Several examples are mentioned in the reports and some others can be inferred. NIA developed new data files which focused on social needs as well as technical ones. The addition of an occupational specialty changes the way organizations define problems. Another fundamental innovation was the change in orientation of NIA towards postconstruction issues. As the task force began to focus on this problem, the organization became more concerned about the long-term functioning of the systems, not an unusual pattern for an organization as it becomes more organic. Other innovations are inferred from the report of the adoption of new procedures, policies, manuals, and guidelines, and from the fact that NIA became much more open to ideas.

Perhaps the best measure of success of the changes is that they continue today. The experiment has been institutionalized and the methodology is being employed across the country.

Conclusion

The intervention in NIA illustrates aspects of all three organizational change efforts. The structure was altered to make it more organic, and group problem solving was added to the design. A wide variety of change tactics was employed, many from the O.D. perspective. The intervention can be judged a success although a number of favorable conditions made success easier to achieve.

The Training and Visit System [India]

Synopsis

The Training and Visit (T and V) Agricultural Extension System in India is a case in which a successful pilot study became a successful state program.[12] It is also a case in which a somewhat organic or undisciplined organization was changed in the mechanical direction, the opposite direction from the NIA change. T and V reoriented the extension service to become a model of a mechanical bureaucracy!

Although the Training and Visit Agricultural Extension System was first tried in Turkey and is used presently in various countries both in Africa and Asia, we concentrate our attention on its application in India because most of the available information reflects its use there. In particular, we have a very careful evaluation of the impact of the T and V system on farm visits and farmer knowledge of various agricultural production technologies, done by Feder and Slade for the World Bank.[13]

In T and V the extension agent's activities are scheduled on a two-week basis. The agent visits different contact farmers and farmers' groups daily, Monday through Thursday, for two consecutive weeks. On alternate Fridays, the agent receives a day of training from either a subject-matter specialist or an agricultural extension officer. The subject-matter specialist, together with the supervisor, teaches the agent what to tell the farmers for that period and supervises the agent's work. Saturday is a make-up day used for office work, extra field visits, and the like, and Sunday is the agent's holiday. Then this two-week schedule is repeated. Since the agent visits the same farmers' group on the same day every two weeks, the farmers expect him and this helps regulate the agent's behavior.

The organizational structure of T and V is more centralized than the traditional extension service. The two-week standardized program is ratified at the top and instituted throughout the organization with only relatively minor variations for regional and local conditions. The organization becomes more hierarchical as the span of control is narrowed to between six and eight subordinates or agents, and supervision is tightened. Agents have relatively little discretion and control over what they do and how they do it. However, they do receive more training than extension agents in other extension systems and have more technology to offer farmers, which gives them some sense of greater power even as their autonomy is reduced.

T and V has been introduced into India on a very large scale. At first it was introduced only in three "command areas" and the following year in six districts in West Bengal. It was such an improvement over the traditional extension service that West Bengal extended T and V throughout the state, and five other states followed suit. Thus it suddenly grew to gigantic proportions. T and V is projected to cover 22 million farm families, including 2.3 million contact farmers, and to involve 38,230 extension staff.

Performance and Output Gaps

The T and V system derives from ideas developed by Daniel Benor[14] and was first tested in several limited areas in Turkey and India. The impetus for these ideas came from the widespread recognition of the failure of agricultural extension services in many LDCs. A number of studies indicated problems with the traditional model of extension, which had largely been developed in Western Europe and the United States during the nineteenth century. Part of the recognition of failure occurred because of the cost-benefit studies of the World Bank, which showed very poor returns to investment.

Benor felt that certain difficulties existed with the typical agricultural extension system. Agents were asked to do too many things, with the result that they performed poorly in all areas.

Typically, agents had multiple supervisors and, as a consequence, had little real supervision and little monitoring of their perform- ance. (Field agents are difficult to monitor and supervise in most organizations, but extension agents in some countries have un- believably poor records of accomplishments.) Finally, most exten- sion systems involved inadequate and ineffective links with ag- ricultural research. Most of these problems were well documented in India, along with poor morale and frequent absenteeism. Thus, there was a widely perceived and sizable performance gap, making experimentation possible.

Environmental Context: Opportunities and Constraints

The key to the success of an extension program is the quality of the information passed on to its farmers. Some have complained that the subject-matter specialists working with T and V extension agents in India are often appointed for reasons other than compe- tence. When this is the case, T and V does not work. It may be a well-designed vehicle of communication but it can be no better than the information it communicates. Despite these problems, however, empirical evaluations of T and V in India so far are, on the average, positive.

The major constraint on the extension of the T and V system into new areas was resistance from the old bureaucracies. Previously, the field agents were community development agents with a vari- ety of tasks to perform, including oversight of the supply of inputs and credit to farmers. Under T and V, field agents provide only ag- ricultural information, following its philosophy of improving pro- ductivity through improved farm management and technology rather than by increasing inputs. Generally, the agents regretted losing control over the provision of inputs and the power that this control gave them, and in some places the interest of farmers in the program declined when it no longer provided them with inputs. Thus, motivation became a major problem.

The major constraints or opportunities for an agricultural ex- tension service are the features of the natural environment, crops grown and their variability by area, the farmers' resources and characteristics, and the degree farmers are organized. Topography partially determines population densities and accessibility, and low densities and accessibility hamper extension efforts. Since the density/accessibility issue would be similar for both the old and new extension system, it should not be a major factor in the success of the change. (Low densities lengthen the distance and therefore the link to research inputs for T and V extension agents but would also make it more difficult to supply farm inputs through the traditional extension agent.) Another feature of topography which affects extension efforts is its variability. The T and V system is highly routinized and works best when the same technology package can be delivered to many farmers over a wide area. It is not well suited to a wide range of soils, rainfall, elevation, and ecological systems, which require different technological packages. The type of crops covered by extension agents also affects the degree to which standard or special knowledge is required. We speculate that this is one reason why T and V has been especially successful with wheat, which tends to cover wide areas with relatively constant environmental conditions. Finally, the characteristics, resources, and degree of organization of farmers affect the appropriateness of standard versus special knowledge. The degree of association among farmers also multiplies the effectiveness of extension agents. New technologies generally diffuse rapidly when farmers have dense networks.

Structural and Design Changes

The T and V system involves the following structural changes. First, the job of the agent is restricted to a single goal or output, namely increasing agricultural production through technology transfers. Second, the duties are highly programmed to include two visits per month to the contact farmers. Third, the ratio of agent to contact farmer is fixed for each major crop or farm production system. Fourth, the organization is centralized and the agents are closely supervised. Basic decisions and the design of the extension program are made at the top and the extension agent follows a prescribed course. Visibility of poor performance is relatively high because of the very specific focus and description of job duties; thus, control is relatively high for the dispersed field agents. Motivation has been maintained by continual training in new farm technologies appropriate to the specific area and through continuous interaction with a supervisor.

The organizational design is a very tall structure because the span of control is kept between six and eight agents or subordinates. This limitation ensures that supervisors can offer the necessary training and supervision. Subject-matter specialists and supervisors get information from research centers and then package it into a series of specific recommendations for farmers.

Although Benor should be credited with being an organizational visionary, it is worth observing that his model is very similar to the one used with Forest Rangers in the United States as reported by Kaufman.[15] Its most distinctive feature is the formalization of the linkage with research centers at the level of middle management.

Nature of the Approach

The intervention level for T and V was the organization and the change was organizationwide. The organization was radically restructured from top to bottom, becoming more centralized and hierarchical, with the span of control narrowed at all levels, the outputs of the organization changed (from provision of inputs to farmers to teaching them new technologies), the internal and external processes altered, and the job descriptions radically revised. Change was extensive throughout the organization, but the greatest change occurred in the job description of the extension agents and in their relations to their supervisors and subject-matter specialists. The agents lost considerable discretion and job autonomy.

The major tactic was decree. The decision was made by the head of the extension system and his superiors, and was decreed upon the organization. The reports do not describe the process of change so that our analysis of the way tactics were employed to effect the change is incomplete. Nevertheless, we are told that this case of organizational change heavily employed five tactics:

1. Decree
2. Restructure
3. Data collection
4. Experimentation
5. Training

What is unclear is the extent to which problem-solving groups were employed. We would expect that the implementation of a change of this magnitude would require problem-solving groups at several levels, but the reports do not tell how the decree was implemented.

This case is a major example of restructuring. The gap to be closed was low productivity; thus, the restructuring was in the mechanical direction. Mechanical organizations are very efficient and productive if the technology is simple or modest and markets are large for standardized goods or services. Are these conditions found in agricultural extension? The demand for better agricultural technologies is very large in LDCs, but the problem for mechanical extension services is whether the technology of delivering the service can be made simple enough and whether the standardized technologies being delivered are appropriate. Benor worked out a simple routinized technology for delivering information to farmers based largely on a rigid schedule of activities, which solved the first problem. He devised a system for delivering timely information to farmers to try and solve the second problem. In the old system agents mostly had preservice training which, as the years passed, became seriously eroded. In contrast, T and V agents have twice monthly training in technologies relevant for use in that month. Thus, the technology provided by T and V is much more relevant than that provided by the old system. In this way Benor has created a much more mechanical structure than the old system for delivering relatively standard but timely information to farmers. The organization is more efficient and more productive and has made farmers more productive.

Experimentation and data collection are also prominent tactics in T and V. The T and V system was first introduced on a small scale in Seyhan, Turkey and was evaluated as successful. It was introduced in three limited areas in two states of India and in six districts in West Bengal, and its results were evaluated and found to be impressive. It was extended to other areas of India very rapidly and, through the World Bank, it was introduced into Thailand, Indonesia, Bangladesh, Malaysia, and Sri Lanka. T and V ended up being diffused very rapidly, thereby having a very short experimental stage, but experimentation was basic to the approach. In fact, the reason it diffused so rapidly was because data was collected on the pilot project which demonstrated that T and V was vastly superior to the traditional extension service. The demonstrated performance gap was so great that the push for change was strong and the change was swift. Perhaps the diffusion was too swift. The purpose of experimentation is not only to demonstrate the virtues of the new system but also to work out problems and adapt the system to the realities of the regional or local conditions.

The institutionalization of T and V may have had more problems because it occurred so rapidly, but the reports are silent on this issue.

Data collection figures prominently in this organizational change in another way, also. The increase in hierarchy widened the distance between top and bottom levels of the organization and reduced and slowed the communications between them. To offset this problem it was necessary to set up evaluation units to provide to the top additional information on the activities and performance of the bottom.

Training is another tactic which is widely used in T and V. The agents are constantly being trained in the technologies which they provide farmers, and managers are trained in new managerial procedures. The reports, however, do not describe the management training which is provided.

The two resources which were used lavishly in the transformation to T and V were power and money. Top ministers decided to institute T and V and the decision makers had sufficient power to decree the changes. The widespread perception of the failure of the old system and the demonstration of the superiority of T and V undercut the opposition to the changes and mobilized widespread support for it. The money for the changeover was made available by the World Bank, which had taken on T and V as one of its major missions. Free extra resources not only made the transformation possible, but also provided an incentive for change. Finally, we should mention that the World Bank as a major source of funds was able to create considerable pressure for countries to change to T and V.

Results

The results of the intervention appear to be highly successful so far. The new system achieves much more contact between extension agents and farmers, and greater amounts of technology transfer. It also has increased the amount of contact with poor farmers even though it, like most extension systems, is biased toward the better-off farmers. However, because the system focuses only on agricultural technology, the program does not provide credit, fertilizer, and other components of rural development.

T and V is very successful, according to Benor and Harrison:

> The Training and Visit System of Agricultural Extension has helped increase agricultural productivity impressively in several areas. In the Seyhan project in Turkey, farmers increased cotton

yields from 1.7 to over 3 tons per hectare in three years. In Chambal, Rajasthan (India), farmers increased paddy yields from about 2.1 tons to over 3 tons per hectare in two years. Combined irrigated and unirrigated wheat yields in Chambal, Madhya Pradesh (India), rose from 1.3 tons to nearly 2 tons per hectare after one season and have since risen higher. The area under high-yielding paddy and wheat varieties in the entire state of West Bengal increased substantially in a single year.[16]

Not all observers agree with this glowing praise for T and V, but overall it seems to be an improvement on previous ways of organizing agricultural extension.[17] Contingency theory, suggests, however, that T and V will be less effective when local conditions vary considerably. T and V is a standardized process for communicating relatively standardized technical information to farmers; high variation in local conditions, however, calls for nonstandardized information. Perhaps in the future T and V will have to become more organic.

The increase in size created some special organizational problems for T and V, including a heightened hierarchical pyramid, which in turn led to slower vertical communication. It had acquired some of the disadvantages of the bureaucratic form of organization. On the other hand, it also added "a strong statewide monitoring and evaluation capability" to compensate for some loss of supervisory oversight in the expanded system and to improve the vertical communication.[18]

Conclusion

Together, T and V and NIA illustrate the value of a contingency theory of organizational change to help determine when an organization should become more mechanical or more organic, more standardized or more adaptive to specific client needs, more efficient or more innovative. T and V demonstrates that at times clients can be better served when an agency becomes more mechanical and efficient; sometimes a centralized bureaucracy is desirable.

Health Management Appraisal Methods Project in a Ministry of Health (Jordan)

The intervention in the Jordanian Ministry of Health (MOH) is a case of decentralization and management improvement.[19] Originally, the Ministry was very centralized: Most decisions were made at the national level and few decisions were made at the regional or district levels. The intervention created a regional health care system. It introduced processual changes and provided considerable training to accompany the structural decentralization. Managers were taught new managerial technologies and supervisory styles, and they were trained to be much more goal oriented. The change agents had a formal set of steps for problem solving, which they employed systematically throughout the intervention, and they often created task forces to solve problems and increase the problem-solving capacity of the Ministry.

Decentralization of government is a current concern in development administration,[20] and this intervention is almost a textbook case of how to decentralize a ministry successfully. Many factors contributed to its success, but training managers for their new responsibilities seems to be key.

Synopsis

In 1980, at the urging of USAID, the Jordanian Minister of Health requested that the Association of University Programs in Health Administration (AUPHA) study the agency and recommend improvements. The Minister was committed to change because he was convinced that the organizational structure of MOH was out of date. His primary interest was to decentralize the ministry and secondarily to improve various management functions. A one-year consultancy was established, involving six two-week visits, paid for by USAID. The consultancy was renewed for a second year, and eighteen months were completed at the time of the report on this case.

The Ministry of Health served a population of almost one million people. It provided medical care to those who were not served by the private sector or the military health facilities. It had six thousand employees, ran thirteen hospitals and over five hundred health centers and clinics, and conducted a variety of programs in preventive health care including malaria control, vaccinations, supplemental feeding programs, and health education. It also monitored food, air, and water quality, inspected and licensed health facilities, licensed practitioners, and tested pharmaceutical products. Most of these services were concentrated around the capital city of Amman and, although it had eleven health districts, they had few administrative functions. Despite MOH's size and the range of its activities, it was highly centralized. "The Minister of Health still authorized the absence of the lowest employee and passed judgment on most hirings."[21] This degree of centralization placed a heavy burden on the Minister, slowed operations, and frustrated the personnel. In addition, the minister had too broad a span of control since twenty-three officials reported directly to him.

The first step in the intervention was to assess the problems of MOH and recommend changes. In two weeks the AUPHA International Director and a management professor produced a lengthy report on MOH that identified its problems. The report was thorough and well researched, and established the need for change. The quality of the report established the credibility of the consultants and the Minister directed them to work out solutions. They devised a reorganization of MOH and presented it to MOH's top officials, after explaining the principles involved. They proposed the transfer of line responsibilities from Amman to five regions that were being created, as well as the creation of four divisions—curative medicine, basic health care, administration, and planning and training. The proposal was accepted with some minor additions. The major device for designing the implementation of the reorganization was the preparation of a job description manual, which included approval and decision responsibilities of various positions. Approval levels were set far lower than previously. The major device used for implementing the changes was workshops to train individuals in their new responsibilities. The team of consultants focused the training on the regional directors who acquired many new responsibilities and on central office staff who would have to provide more field supervision.

The decentralization was the change that was spotlighted, but the consultancy was also committed to making management more goal oriented and improving specific management functions. MOH had been very lax throughout its organization in defining goals and in evaluating activities in terms of goals. For example, while one-third of Jordan's deaths occurred to children under five years of age, only 8 percent of the budget was devoted to maternal and child health care and other primary care programs. Obviously, services were not being provided in proportion to needs. To stimulate goal orientation among managers, the team of consultants conducted three seminars. The first had managers analyze existing health service statistics for their utility to the managers' needs; this exercise demonstrated that existing data was a gold mine of useful information for managers if they learned to interpret and use it. The second seminar used an in-basket exercise to teach some data-based decision tools and to examine the decision-making style of the directors. The third seminar focused on the use of financial data in decision making. "The common thread in all three seminars weighed the costs of a present activity against its demonstrated benefits."[22] In addition the consultancy developed a goal- and priority-setting exercise and used it with a management group, which later distributed it to others in the ministry. A heavy agenda of activities for a brief consultancy did not allow much additional training in goal orientation but a definite change in agency practice was observed anyway.

A change which received considerable attention was the development of an information system for management. Top management needed more and better operating information for monitoring field activities in the decentralized structure and for use in goal-setting activities. The data was being generated but not being used. The information system had to be put under the control of the manager-users, and managers had to be trained in its use. A workshop on information systems was conducted for managers; subsequently, some of these managers were constituted into a task force which defined the data needs of managers and worked with providers and outside experts in developing a functional information system.

In a similar vein the consultancy sought to institute a new system of financial control. The old system was extraordinarily lax and was not being used to evaluate and monitor programs. The consultancy collected considerable data on the capacities of the personnel and the functioning of the current system. It trained sixty clerks in simple accounting systems and provided two weeks of intensive in-service training to the districts' head accountants on the Ministry's procedures. At the same time, the district and regional directors were trained in the use of financial data for managing. Finally, the accountants and directors were formed into a task force which designed a financial control system for the decentralized structure. The new system had been instituted for too brief a period to have been evaluated by the time of the report.

A major area of focus of the consultancy was supervision. It sought to increase substantially central office supervision and to separate monitoring supervision from teaching and motivating supervision. It used workshops and task forces to achieve these ends. The first workshop used a role-playing experiment to contrast authoritarian, supportive, and results-oriented styles of supervision. The authoritarian supervision had the poorest results in all circumstances, the supportive supervision had the best results in the single work-group situation, and the results-oriented supervision had the best results in the multiple work-group situation. These results were thoroughly discussed and central office supervision went up markedly because ". . . the officials were quite willing to supervise once they were confident that they were doing the right thing."[23]

The second workshop used role playing to demonstrate the three supervisory functions of monitoring, teaching and motivating. The work group also discussed how to keep the monitoring function separated from the others in practice. Subsequently, three work groups were established to prepare guides, checklists, and goals for supervisors to use. Inspection checklists and indicators of performance were developed for each operating unit and training objectives were created for practitioners. The process of adopting these materials was beginning when the report was written.

The consultancy also sought to teach programming skills and institute regional programming, whereas the only programming previously had been at the facility level. The consultancy team devised a programming exercise which several individuals worked through. At the time of the report, one person had become a proficient programmer and was assigned the task of assisting each regional office in operational planning.

Over eighteen months and through seven team visits of two weeks each in duration, the consultancy worked on these and several other problems. It accomplished a lot in a short period of time and for the modest cost of only $75 thousand. The team of consultants was efficient because they used a standard change approach involving the following seven steps:

1. Make client aware of the magnitude of the problem.
2. Help client specify where changes need to be made.
3. Create the ability in the organization to design solutions through training or recruitment.
4. Design solutions.
5. Make client aware of implementation practices.
6. Implement the solutions.
7. Evaluate the new system.

Performance and Output Gaps

Having come in with a mandate to revitalize the Ministry, the new Minister of Health recognized that the administration needed upgrading. Since he had received training in the United States, he was aware of American management practices and open to their introduction in MOH. The Minister was also aware of the gap recorded by available statistics between MOH services and the civil population's health needs. Health care is one public sector area where there are some relatively clear-cut output measures in mortality; morbidity statistics are well developed and provide an assessment of which illnesses and diseases are the major problems. Such statistics demonstrated clearly that women and children were underserved by MOH because they had relatively high rates of mortality. Epidemiology is also available as a methodology for locating possible causes of diseases.

The prominent occupation in MOH is that of the physician and physicians generally are more open to change than are civil servants. Physicians, like engineers and unlike civil servants, are trained to think in problem-solving terms and to recognize problems. The report on the intervention pointed out that the physicians had already recognized many of the organizational and procedural problems of MOH. Surprisingly, the physicians also had recognized that they did not have much competence as managers and were open to a management improvement intervention. Their awareness of performance gaps had been heightened by a task force of physicians and administrators that had tried for eighteen months to redesign MOH, but had not achieved sufficient consensus on a plan to implement. They were highly motivated to change the Ministry and became allies of the management consultant team.

The final cause of the widespread perception of performance and output gaps was the consultancy team's detailed report which identified these gaps and analyzed their causes. The team's analysis was accepted with little revision and the team was asked to design solutions.

Environmental Context: Opportunities and Constraints

The major opportunity was the strong support for change at the top and among the physicians. Another favorable circumstance was the willingness of physicians to problem solve and to participate in changes. However, it is important to note that the tactics of change maintained the motivation and interest of the Minister and the physicians by keeping them involved in problem solving.

As we will note in several interventions, high levels of education and exposure to other countries make people more open to change. Jordan has a higher education level than many former British colonies and the physicians and managers in MOH are relatively highly educated. Since Jordan lacked a major medical college, most of the physicians were trained abroad and gained a comparative perspective that should have made them relatively open to change. The Minister had some training in the United States and appreciated American management practices.

Many change interventions are hindered by conflict between the donor agency and the host country. This was not an issue in the present intervention. Both MOH and USAID were supportive of the intervention and worked in tandem. In particular, the USAID health officer was a positive force in the intervention. Another favorable condition was adequate finances. MOH had an expanding budget and was relatively well-endowed in comparison to many other LDCs. It had twenty dollars per capita to spend.

No special constraints were reported.

Structural and Design Changes

This intervention made an extraordinary number of changes. It instituted major structural and design changes. It introduced many processual changes and it trained managers and technicians in managerial and technical skills. Since the Minister's top priority was the restructuring of the agency, the consulting team related many of the other changes to the restructuring.

The first major change was the decentralization of MOH and the reduction of the span of control of the Minister of Health. This change was part of a broader decentralization movement in the country, which was committed to building up administrative capacity in five regions while reducing the dependence on Amman. Previously there was no regional level between the national and district levels of MOH. A whole new administrative/geographic level was being created in MOH quite apart from the consultancy, but the consulting team was asked to design the new structure and train people in their new roles and responsibilities. The team's restructuring plan was approved with slight modifications. The occupants of the new positions then worked as a task force on a job description manual for the new regional design and this provided the basis for the restructuring activities.

The second major change was the introduction of "management by objectives." The team conducted three seminars for managers that taught them to evaluate activities in terms of their costs relative to their accomplishments. The team also created an exercise for setting priorities that was used by a number of managers.

The third major change was the institutionalization of an information retrieval system. One administrative problem was the underutilization of reports on diseases and other information. Thus training was designed to indicate how to use what was available. There was also a need to create a new data system. A task force of managers identified the information needs of MOH's managers and worked with Westinghouse Health Systems, a technical assistance team that was expert in data-collection methods, in creating a new information system.

The fourth major change was to increase supervision and train supervisors in supportive and goal-oriented styles of supervision. Despite the previous centralized structure not much supervision was actually performed, the reason being mainly a lack of knowledge about how to supervise. The consulting team used role-playing exercises in several workshops to improve the supervisory skills of managers. This not only increased the amount of supervision but also changed the style from monitoring or surveillance to teaching and motivating.

The fifth major change was the introduction of a financial control system. Unlike the above changes, this change was not previously perceived as a problem by the agency. One member of the AUPHA team was an expert in public sector accounting and she found tremendous weaknesses in the existing system. Most people involved in it did not understand the overall process. No records of costs for types of activities were kept at hospitals or regional offices—the system kept track of fees but not much else. The system was totally inadequate for an agency of the size of MOH. A decentralized financial control system for the new regional structure of MOH was designed by both the regional directors and the clerk accountants in a workshop. The clerks were trained in how to operate the new system and the directors were trained in the management use of the financial data.

Other changes included the creation of an inventory of resources, both human and otherwise, and training in programming.

When these and other management activities were introduced or improved, the consultancy team used workshops and seminars not only to teach the new skills required but also to develop in MOH a capacity to create, modify, and evaluate methods and programs without outside assistance. Since many of the changes were in the process of being implemented, the report could not evaluate how well they will work out and how long they will be sustained. However, the results which they were able to observe were impressive.

The Nature of the Approach

This intervention originated at the top levels and affected the entire Ministry, with changes occurring literally at every level. The Minister was continuously and directly involved; reports on performance gaps were made to him and he was asked to participate in the analysis of problems. The head of the organization played a larger role in this intervention than in our other cases. This is an example of an ideal management consultation.

A variety of tactics was employed but the emphasis was on training, problem-solving groups, and restructuring. The main tactic was training. The training was done in a wide variety of different skills and at many levels, from the Minister to very low-level clerks in the system. In many of the training sessions staff at various levels of MOH were taught how to design solutions. Then, task forces would work on problems or develop new management systems.

We review several examples to indicate the many ways that training facilitated the change process. In one workshop the trainees ran through an exercise that emphasized how managers could use information that was available. In another, managers identified their information requirements. Another workshop taught the design principles of management. Several workshops sought to improve supervision. One used a role-playing exercise to demonstrate three styles of supervision and evaluate their relative effectiveness. The results revealed the weaknesses of authoritarian supervision and the superiority of democratic supervision and results-oriented supervision depending on the circumstances. Another workshop on supervision taught managers through role playing and discussion to separate the function of monitoring from the functions of teaching and motivating. Several workshops trained clerks, accountants, and managers in the new financial control system. A large seminar was held for the clerks. The head accountants from each district were given two weeks of in-service training. The district and regional directors were given a workshop on the management uses of financial data. One other workshop was provided for some managers on programming.

The second major tactic was problem-solving groups, which generally were used in tandem with training. Problem-solving groups are not effective unless the group members have the required substantive knowledge and process skills. Experts have the former and educated persons usually have the latter. In MOH some members of problem-solving groups needed more technical knowledge, while other needed more experience with problem-solving group processes, and the consulting team provided the appropriate training.

Problem-solving groups worked on designing or implementing the new regional structure, new financial control system, and new information system. With the backing of the Minister these changes could have been designed by the consultants and implemented by decree with minimal participation by the staff. The consulting team, however, was careful to involve staff participation and build up their ownership of the new systems and other changes.

The third major tactic was restructuring. Regional administrative centers were created and considerable authority devolved from Amman to the regions. Although this change was decreed the reorganization design was discussed, modified, and approved by high-level managers and implemented by task forces. The major device used for implementing the reorganization was a job description manual that was based on job descriptions drafted by occupants of the positions in the reorganized structure and coordinated and synthesized by task forces.

Three other tactics were also important: data collection and discussion, experiments, and decree. One of the purposes of the intervention was to better fit the services of MOH to the health needs of the civilian population. This necessitated a reordering of priorities that had to be based on information on needs and services. The documentation of the high death rates of women and small children increased the priority of basic health care programs. Data collection was less crucial to perceptions of performance and output gaps than in our other cases, but it helped sharpen these perceptions and indicate areas which most needed attention. Data collection and discussion figured heavily in the many redesign activities of the intervention. In some cases the data were already available but were not being utilized. Managers had to learn what information existed and how to use it in managing their programs.

Experiments were not emphasized in this intervention but an experimental approach was employed. No pilot project was conducted but new systems were tested and revised in the process of implementation. Some of the products of the workshops were utilized on a trial basis.

The initiation of the intervention by the Minister meant that the tactic of decree could have been employed widely, but it was not. Instead, the consulting team would gently lead the staff through seven steps for each set of changes:

1. Problem awareness
2. Problem specification
3. Ability to design solutions
4. Design of solution
5. Knowledge of implementation practices
6. Implementation of the solution
7. Evaluation of the system

Even when the consultants designed a change they always presented solutions in formats in which they would be discussed, criticized, and altered by the staff. Nevertheless, decree was also operating in this intervention. The decentralization to regional administrative centers had been decreed, and then widespread participation was obtained in implementing the decree.

The intervention team wisely recognized the difference between the adoption of structural changes and managerial technologies, and their utilization. It encouraged utilization by involving managers in the design of many of the changes, training staff in the necessary skills, leading staff to discover the reasons for the changes through workshops, and not drawing attention to poor past performances. In most instances, the team attempted to use an exercise that led the officials, step by step, through the design of a particular management system or through the solution of a given problem. This process enabled the participating officials to learn both how to do things and why they are done.

The main resources used in this intervention were power and knowledge. The interveners had unusually great power because of the support of the Minister but they worked hard for credibility and the support of both the Minister and the staff. They used knowledge to attain this credibility and support, and all of the changes were based on knowledge. The financial resources were small for the consultancy, but they were adequate. This is one of the few studies which reported the total cost of the intervention: $75 thousand. The good financial condition of MOH, however, helped make the many changes possible. The time span was only eighteen months, making time the scarcest resource.

Results

The report does not identify results in the areas of the performance and output gaps. It does not report that death rates were lowered or demonstrate that services were improved, for example. Instead, it reports on the many changes noted above that were made, and, in a sense, these are the concrete results of the intervention. It claims that new systems and practices were instituted and skills were learned, but it does not trace the consequences of these changes on the quality and quantity of health care services provided by MOH. Nor does the report evaluate the degree to which the changes were institutionalized, since the report was written at the end of only eighteen months and before many of the changes were completed.

Conclusion

This intervention is almost a model case of an organizational design change strategy. It decentralized MOH, redesigned jobs, and trained staff in their new responsibilities. It also employed many O.D. tactics in addition to training. The changes were successfully implemented as far as we can tell. The most interesting finding of this case is that regional decentralization requires many other changes to be effective.

Management-Improvement Teams in the Ministry of Agriculture and an Electrical Utility (Guyana)

A number of organizational design interventions are performed every year, either by the LDCs themselves or by management consultant firms. Unfortunately, they are seldom described in the literature on development. Here, we describe the first of three cases featuring management improvement. This intervention emphasizes the creation of management-improvement teams, while the next two cases emphasize the development of managerial technologies. This change involved the installation of management-improvement teams in two agencies to identify problems and create and train a task force for solving the problems. The intervention in Guyana was made by Larry Cooley,[24] a management consultant, and has great potential for use in other countries.

There are several noteworthy features of this management-improvement intervention. First, it was relatively successful in making a public bureaucracy more adaptive and flexible, demonstrating one method for reorienting a public bureaucracy to become more organic. This is the type of change that is often championed in the current development literature. Second, the book *In Search of Excellence* has popularized the use of task forces as a characteristic of the more successful American corporations. We wanted to know, however, whether task forces would also be effective in Third World contexts. The NIA and MOH interventions used task forces effectively, and their use in Guyana provides two additional test cases on this issue. Third, this project introduced the same intervention in two different organizations at the same time, thus making a comparative research analysis possible. Comparative analyses are much more powerful in determining general causes of success or failure than are single cases. Unique conditions, personalities, and events can dominate the outcomes of single interventions and provide faulty guidance for someone intervening in another case. In a multiple-case analysis, if the cases are similar enough for useful comparison, as we find in Cooley's study, the unique factors fade somewhat from view and the general causes emerge more clearly.

Although the final report calls the intervention a matrix management approach, in many senses it is not. Matrix management indicates that all managerial and technical personnel, if not all employees, are placed simultaneously into two departments, one functional or occupational and the other based on project-area or client type.[25] This structure works best when these two sources of variation are almost equally important. The two interventions reported here are not sufficiently extensive to be classified as matrix management. Only one team was created in the electrical utility and two in the Ministry of Agriculture. Nevertheless, as in matrix management each team draws people from different areas and they report to two managers: the project leader and the department head.

On the other hand, the teams differ from matrix management teams in their tasks: the project teams are essentially trouble-shooting and problem-solving teams. They are like quality work circles except that they tackle management problems. Matrix management teams, in contrast, conduct the normal business of the department, agency, or firm which has the matrix structure.

In the following discussion, the usual set of topics are followed, but in a somewhat different pattern, than we used for the other cases of this chapter. We accent the differences between the two situations in Guyana where approximately the same intervention was made. These comparisons can be extremely valuable to change agents in allowing them to choose their interventions more judiciously and to alter their tactics to fit specific circumstances.

Synopsis

The Management-Improvement Teams Project began in 1979 when three American management consultants trained seven Guyanese management consultants of the Public Service Ministry and the Guyanan Management and Training Center in a set of management tools (this training built on some workshops conducted in 1978). This set of ten people constituted the "Core Project Team," which subdivided into two subteams—"Core Project Subteam 1," which worked in the Ministry of Agriculture (MOA), and "Core Project Subteam 2," which worked in the Guyanan Electricity Corporation (GEC). The former created two management-improvement teams (MIT)—Hydraulics MIT, which worked in the Hydraulics Department, and Lands and Surveys MIT, which worked in the Lands and Surveys Department. Core Project Subteam 2 created one management-improvement team in the Guyanan Electricity Corporation. The two core project subteams diagnosed the management problems and opportunities in their agencies, suggested strategic responses to these problems, built and trained a management-improvement team from agency staff to implement the solutions by applying the new management techniques, and assisted the agency team as necessary.

Core Project Subteam 2 began its intervention in GEC with a six-day diagnostic study using the organizational diagnosis protocol (developed by the Core Project Team) and intensive interviews with top management. It identified management problems and proposed eight management-improvement projects for addressing these problems to a top management team consisting of the Executive Chair, General Manager, and the Heads of Departments. This top management team selected two projects for implementation: a program for clarifying overall organizational objectives and responsibilities, and an interdepartmental management-improvement project for a specific facility. The latter project was selected for implementation because "it was felt that single-focused projects provided the optimum vehicle for addressing and testing solutions to all of the problems and management-improvement ideas developed for the organization as a whole."[26] This judgment proved to be profoundly correct and a major factor in the success of the intervention.

Core Project Subteam 2 conducted a two-and-a-half day residential training workshop for the thirty most senior managers of GEC. The workshop instructed participants in a series of management tools for use in clarifying organizational goals and planning toward them. "Workshops assisted participants to operate as departmental and interdepartmental management teams to develop a clear mission statement, set of performance indicators, and allocation of organizational responsibilities for the Corporation."[27] The publication of the synthesized mission statements successfully completed the first project.

The second project called for an interdepartmental management-improvement project for a specific facility as a test site for the management-improvement team (MIT) procedures. The eight MW generating station at Versailles, which was in almost total disrepair, was selected. Core Project Subteam 2 selected a MIT for the Versailles Improvement Project and together they prepared a detailed performance-improvement plan for the generating station. This plan was presented to both the top management of GEC and the Versailles plant employees. It was well prepared and well accepted. Then the MIT implemented the plan, which consisted mainly of instituting a problem-solving team approach to problems, developing a management information system for planning and scheduling maintenance, developing a system for identifying and purchasing needed spare parts, and producing more detailed budgets and financial arrangements. After four months the MIT intervention had the engine rehabilitation two months ahead of schedule, had developed the information system which was almost ready for testing, had developed a training program for plant operators, and had prepared and costed plans for engineering changes. Although the report was drafted before the concrete results of the Versailles MIT could be assessed, the project was widely perceived, nevertheless, as very successful.

Working in the Ministry of Agriculture, Core Project Subteam 1 began its intervention with a ten-day diagnostic study of MOA and also, at the suggestion of the Ministry Permanent Secretary, a diagnostic study of the Hydraulics Department. The weaknesses were identified and twelve projects were drafted for consideration. The proposed projects were ranked in importance by Core Project Subteam 1 and separately by the senior managers of MOA. Both rankings agreed on the implementation of two projects: one to create a team to link MOA with the new Planning Department and one to install a MIT in the Hydraulics Department. Core Project Subteam 1 clarified the goals of the Hydraulics Department, drafted an operations manual for the Hydraulics Department MIT, and conducted an intensive two-day workshop for the people selected for the MIT. Then the MIT started work on its first project, to reform the over-centralized procedures for certification of expenditures. Unfortunately, the solution required the placement of auditors in the field, an action which was beyond the MIT's control and was not yet performed after five months. Thus, the MIT lacked a tangible success to give it momentum and promote the MIT approach. The MIT then planned an agenda of projects and began working on some of them, but had not completed any by report time. The MIT was having other difficulties as well: team meetings were too poorly attended for team effectiveness, the teams' mastery of the key tools and skills was inadequate, and enthusiasm had waned.

Despite the problems of the Hydraulic Department MIT, Core Project Subteam 1 accepted the assignment of installing another MIT in the Lands and Surveys Department. The second assignment started with a workshop, selected a pilot project, and established a MIT to conduct the pilot project. This MIT was created too close to the time of the report to be evaluated, but it was having many of the same problems as the Hydraulics Department MIT.

To summarize, the overall project goal was to train a management-improvement team (the Core Project Team) within the Public Service Ministry that could, in turn, train management-improvement teams in government ministries and public corporations. The training involved solving real problems in those organizations. By and large, the project did succeed in training a highly competent core management-improvement team that created and trained management-improvement teams in three organizations. Core Project Subteam 2 in the electric utility was quite successful in selecting a workable project for a MIT to execute, creating an interdisciplinary MIT of GEC personnel, and training the personnel in the new management and problem-solving techniques. The MIT, in turn, was successful in solving some concrete organizational problems. Core Project Subteam 1 in MOA created and trained two interdisciplinary MIT's. The first MIT worked on problems in the Hydraulics Department but encountered severe resource problems and did not accomplish much beyond the diagnosis and planning stages. The Lands and Survey MIT was created too recently to be evaluated. While the report indicates that other agencies are interested in having management-improvement teams, which should diffuse the new technologies, the intervention failed to institutionalize these management procedures within these organizations. A permanent structural change has not yet been achieved.

Performance and Output Gaps

This intervention did not begin with a perceived performance or output gap, which then led to an invitation to intervene. Rather USAID was convinced that new management technologies could improve the performance of Guyanan government agencies and it was willing to pay for an experimental low-cost project to train a Guyanan management-improvement team which would test and diffuse the new technologies. By means of a series of workshops a number of government managers identified some general management areas which needed strengthening (performance gaps) and were introduced to some new management tools. As a result, the Guyanan government saw some potential benefits from the new technologies and was willing to experiment with them if USAID paid the costs. Previously, the government was not unaware of many of its problems, but it had always related them to scarce resources rather than to management practices. The project itself, therefore, had not only to sharpen the government's perceptions of performance or output gaps as it progressed, but needed also to relate these gaps to poor management practices. From beginning to end it had to demonstrate that the new managerial technologies could greatly improve productivity and thereby create a demand for training in the new technologies. In this it succeeded. In fact, after the first MIT had been working in the Hydraulics Department for a while, the Secretary of the Lands and Surveys Department requested a MIT, as have other agencies in the meantime.

It was relatively easy to create perceptions of performance and output gaps in management practices. In the preproject workshops group discussion was used to delineate causes of poor performance. The top management participants agreed that they had four classic organizational difficulties: inadequate delegation, unclear objectives, poor communication, and lack of motivation. These are the types of problems which organizational design management technologies are designed to solve.

Once the Core Project Team subdivided into two subteams, one in the Ministry of Agriculture and one in the Guyanan Electricity Corporation, each subteam had to generate perceptions of gaps which were related to management techniques and thus establish legitimacy. Both agencies had immense problems; however, there appears to have been much more of a sense of crisis in the electrical utility because of the widespread publicity about power failures and reductions (output gaps). Official investigations were being threatened and there was a public outcry, all of which created a much greater pressure for change, and a greater legitimacy for the MIT, in the GEC than in the Ministry of Agriculture.

Environmental Context: Opportunities and Constraints

This is one of the few reports we have read that truly takes culture into account. It notes that the essentially informal and open interaction pattern of the Guyanese allowed for this type of intervention. Although this factor was a constant for this study (it applied to both settings), nonetheless it was important to the intervention itself. The introduction of managerial improvement teams is more likely to flourish in a culture where informal interaction occurs easily.

The report does not indicate differences between the two organizations except that the Ministry of Agriculture had much fewer organizational resources and more financial and management problems than the electrical utility.

> [The Hydraulic Department] was at one-third strength in the management and professional staff grades. Less than 25 percent of its heavy equipment was operating. Pay scales were far below the equivalent in public corporations or outside Guyana. Staff

turnover at all levels was very high. Planning and budgeting procedures had virtually collapsed, and were replaced by monthly improvisations and juggling. Releases of funds for expenditures were running several months behind current operations, and overall flow of resources to the Department was no more than a fraction of that required to meet minimal output commitments of key services. As a consequence, the Department had fallen years behind in sea and river defence maintenance and construction, and in other key areas.[28]

These severe constraints made it extremely difficult for the MIT to function effectively. The team members had extremely heavy duties because most of them had two or three job assignments, with the time they gave to the MIT usually overtime and after hours. It is not surprising that their high initial motivation waned and low attendance at team meetings seriously curtailed its effectiveness. Another reason for failure in MOA was the unfortunate choice of the first intervention by the MIT. It required approval and actions by top administrators who were beyond the range of influence of the team. When a management-improvement team is not strongly supported by a consensus of top management it should start out with safe, workable interventions to build legitimacy. This strategy worked in the power plant because the team focused on changes within the plant and had the authority to make them. In the meantime, the directors of the utility were preoccupied with the energy crisis and the problem of trying to locate oil and let the MIT carry out its plans unimpeded.

The report does not describe many other dimensions on which the two organizations should be compared. We speculate that the Ministry of Agriculture was older and, therefore, probably more centralized and bureaucratic. The report does indicate that the Permanent Secretary of MOA made most of the key decisions on the design and implementation of the intervention, which provides modest support for our speculation. We would also expect that the public utility had been involved in more innovations, at least of a technological sort. This surmise is based on a relatively large literature which indicates that the technology for electrical utilities has improved continually for four decades, so that they are continually adapting new technologies and having to be more innovative. It was also confirmed by personal communication with the author of the report. We conclude, therefore that the utility was somewhat more organic than MOA, although both would be classified as mechanical organizations.

The report notes that organizations with fewer problems are easier to change and are more amenable to a MIT intervention. This is true when many problems demand so much attention that no attention can be given to instituting changes. It must be remembered, however, that under the right circumstances, a crisis will motivate people to change. Furthermore, organizations that have changed in the past and therefore are likely to have fewer current problems are easier to change because of their history of organizational change. Indeed, *from the perspective of a change agent, one simple diagnostic is knowing how many changes have occurred in the past ten years as a predictor of the degree of success of almost any intervention.*

Another important constraint which applies to both the MOA and the GEC interventions is the extremely short time frame of eight months for the project. It is extremely difficult to institutionalize the management-improvement team approach in an agency and develop the capacity to diffuse this approach throughout the government in so short a time.

Structural, Design, and Environmental Changes

The intervention involved a relatively simple change in both organizations, i.e., the creation and training of a management-improvement team. The change was essentially the same in the two organizations but with a few critical differences. One MIT was created in the electrical utility and two MITs in the Ministry of Agriculture. In the electrical utility the MIT decided to focus on one specific power plant to see if its performance could be improved. The Ministry of Agriculture MITs focused on two separate functional departments, but the major problems of these departments could not be solved inside the departments.

The addition of a management-improvement team, in turn, introduces further changes in any organization. The main change which MITs introduce is the use of multispecialty problem-solving teams. These tend to decentralize decision making and make the organization more organic. MITs also introduce a variety of management technologies, some of which would increase delegation, team building, problem solving, or flexibility, making the organization more organic, and some of which would increase rationality, planning, role definitions, routinized procedures, supervision, or monitoring, making the organization more mechanical. These changes in opposite directions may appear contradictory but such changes are often appropriate. Some organizations need to be changed from traditional, patrimonial, or inefficient bureaucracies to more mechanical and, therefore, efficient bureaucracies, at the same time that they have to become more organic to increase their problem-solving capacity.

A critical dimension of the MITs in Guyana was their impermanence. While the project envisaged establishing MITs in many agencies of government, it is not clear how long the current MITs will function after the project ends and foreign consultants are withdrawn. The national members of the Core Project Team have the necessary skills to carry on and establish MITs in other agencies, but will the government sufficiently support the effort? We suggest that a permanent management-improvement department within the government is needed to diffuse the MITs throughout the government and assist struggling MITs. Otherwise, agencies with MITs are likely to regress to less effective, but quicker and less complex, management procedures. This case, therefore, raises a generic design issue: whether to establish temporary task forces or permanent departments. The impacts of task forces can erode but, on the other hand, departments can become rigid and perfunctory. Peters and Waterman argue for task forces, but perhaps departments are a better option for LDCs. Even when one opts for task forces, however, the issue still remains of how long the management consulting team should remain in place, or how many visits it should make so as to obtain maximum impact at reasonable cost.

Another critical dimension of MITs is their breadth. Normally they must be as broad in the organization as the factors they have to influence. In the Guyanan interventions they had to cut across functional departments to be successful. The MIT in the power plant had a multidepartment perspective and multidepartment members. This was both natural and necessary. The MIT in the Ministry of Agriculture was assigned to the Hydraulics Department and later another MIT was created in the Lands and Surveys Department. In the Hydraulics Department the MIT tried to deal with problems which required changes in the activities of other departments and at higher levels, and it failed.

The Nature of the Approach

The intervention level was organizational in the case of the electrical utility and departmental in the case of the Ministry of Agriculture. Since two separate departments were involved in the latter, department MITs were formed in each.

The project's tactics were data collection, training, experimentation, and problem-solving groups, and these overlapped. Data collection was used in the diagnostic phase and it identified performance and output gaps and specified some of their causes. The basic training was in working together as a multispecialty problem-solving group, and it involved practicing on real problems or learning by experimenting with new managerial technologies. After the basic training and using newly developed selection methods, the Core Project Subteam selected a problem to be solved. The Core Project Subteam then added multidisciplinary agency members to the team. These agency members of the subteam became the MIT for solving the selected problem. The problem was the pilot project for the MIT and for employment of the new managerial methods. In both organizations the original Core Project Subteam members trained the added agency members to solve the problems of the pilot project as a MIT. The project assumed that if the pilot projects were successful, the MITs would tackle other problems, the Core Project Subteams would receive requests to train special MITs in other units of their target ministries, and the Core Project Team would receive many requests to establish MITs in other ministries.

This project emphasized training and participatory workshops, using them for two purposes. First, they helped identify performance and output gaps and mobilize commitment to organizational change for solving them. Once the Core Project Subteam established itself in each organization, it identified and prioritized problems (or performance gaps) and selected a set of problems for presentation to top management. Then, top management selected the problems to be addressed first. In this way top management became more aware of problems, selected ones it was most concerned about, and became more committed to the intervention.

The second objective of the training and workshops was the obvious one of developing the capacity of managers to use the new managerial technologies and to work in teams as problem-solving groups. The objective of the whole project was to improve through training and practice the performance of managers in the Guyanan Government and to build within the government the capacity to train managers in the new management technologies. Critical to its success, therefore, would be declining dependence on the consultant.

In both organizations the MITs were used as problem-solving

groups. It must be remembered that this organizational change effort occurred in 1978-1979, before quality work circles and task forces became popular parts of the American management lexicon. Thus, the approach is much more innovative than it may appear today. To our knowledge, the use of MITs (quality work circles at the management level) previously had not been used self-consciously in LDCs, yet they have much to offer. They require time, energy, and high-level support, but they greatly increase problem-solving capacities and make organizations more adaptive (and more organic).

Both interventions trained and employed MITs in a problem-solving effort, but there were some fundamental differences between the two interventions. The top management of the electrical utility participated in an additional training session after the problem-selection process had been completed. The focus of this workshop was to clarify goals, create interdepartmental teams, and decide how to allocate responsibilities more effectively. In effect it helped to build a positive value climate for change and team work, and helped to create a "strong" culture at the top of the organization, where it is usually most needed. This did not occur in the Ministry of Agriculture where decisions were made by the secretary and the intervention was not made at a sufficiently high level to solve the selected problem.

We have already suggested that training people in new techniques, including managerial technologies, tends to meet with little resistance. There was little resistance in this case and the final report noted that the agencies' staff was very interested in the new technologies. The project used terms like "matrix management" which had positive valence for the Guyanans, probably because the introduction of this new technology did not imply past failure on the part of managers. Thus, the opportunities for change are increased by "selling" organizational design as a new managerial technology.

The major resource required by this intervention is time. MIT members have to put in extra work while trying to do their regular jobs. While this makes the project inexpensive, it runs the risk that MIT members will have too little time or energy to work together for the MIT to act truly as a problem-solving group. In fact, this is perhaps the main cause of failure of the MIT in the Hydraulics Department. Work pressures were an enormous constraint in this project.

Results

Not unexpectedly, because of all of the contrasts described, the intervention in the electrical utility was successful while the intervention in the Ministry of Agriculture was much less so. According to the report, the following results were achieved in the electrical utility intervention:

> After four months of project work, the engine rehabilitation was two months ahead of schedule and, by the end of December, the station began to contribute an additional 746 megawatts per month to the grid. A major clean-up campaign had been initiated and completed at the plant. Planned maintenance schedules and an integrated management information system for identifying, ordering, tracking, and allocating spares had been developed and was tested in January. . . . A formal training program for plant operators, including instruction in minor maintenance activities, had been developed. Plans for necessary structural modifications have been prepared and costed, and a schedule and system of performance reporting devised."[29]

The MIT in the Hydraulics Department encountered many difficulties, carried out fewer activities, and was close to failing. It failed to achieve a successful solution to its pilot problem or the other problems addressed later. It met too infrequently and too few members attended for it to work effectively. Its mastery of skills and key tools was inadequate.

The report explains the differential success of the two MITs by the differences in leadership of the MITs and the degree of organization pathology (obstacles). There were substantial differences in these factors and they were important; we would add, however, three other factors favoring the intervention in GEC. There was a much clearer perception of a crisis in the utility, the intervention level was high enough to encompass the actors who were critical to the success of the project, and the climate was more favorable to working in multispecialty teams.

Conclusion

This intervention does not involve a structural change per se; rather, it is an organizational design change, which added temporary problem-solving groups acting as task forces to an organization. The time span of the consulting was short and the large number of unfavorable conditions in the Department of Agriculture made any kind of intervention there difficult. Nevertheless, the project has trained a number of managers in new managerial techniques, which have proven their utility in a number of applications, and a core management training team is ready to diffuse the MIT approach and the managerial technologies throughout the government, if the government makes the team permanent.

Project Development Resource Team
for Organizational Planning (Jamaica)

The second management training intervention was conducted by Merlyn Kettering in Jamaica over a four-year period.[30] An important feature of this intervention was the continuous presence of the consultant over the four years. In contrast, the management consulting team was present for only short periods in the Guyanan and Colombian cases. Also, the management-improvement team which was created in Jamaica eventually became a unit or department in a new organization. This location was not part of the original change strategy; nevertheless, it increased its effectiveness.

The emphasis in this change effort is on what is labeled "action learning" or "action training." Multidisciplinary teams are taught to prepare project profiles and to plan the implementation of projects. They work on their own projects as part of the learning process. Thus, the training is made directly relevant to their ongoing work. Furthermore, the emphasis is much more on training *per se* rather than on problem-solving, although some workshops dealt with this.

Synopsis

In the mid-1970s Jamaica was relatively ineffective in obtaining external funds from donor and lending agencies for development projects. The government believed that this failure was due to its lack of capacity for preparing attractive project proposals and for planning the implementation of projects. The Jamaican Government requested USAID for help and the National Planning Project (NPP) was initiated in late 1976. The three major purposes of the NPP were: "(1) to improve the capacity of the Jamaican Government to plan and carry out development projects, (2) to increase the flow of development capital, and (3) to improve capital utilization through accelerated and successful project implementation."[31]

The reports on NPP do not present an historical narrative of the project, but the major events of the project's history are the following. A training-consultancy team called the Project Development Resource Team (PDRT) was established within the Projects Division of the Ministry of Finance and Planning. At first it lacked permanent positions and consisted of persons on temporary assignments. "This involved frequent staff position vacancies, uncertain career prospects and in one case a reduced salary."[32] Later the Projects Division became a statutory body called The Project Analysis and Monitoring Co. Ltd. (PAMCO). As a department of PAMCO, PDRT could hire people for permanent positions, which reduced turnover and enhanced team coordination.

PDRT was a multidisciplinary four-person team. Originally it was composed of a financial analyst, an economist, an engineer, and an agriculturalist. During its first two years, it was assisted by two expatriates (an agriculturalist and an engineer). The PDRT members were experienced in project planning and management, and were trained by expatriate consultants, mainly Merlyn Kettering, in the action-training methodology to be employed by PDRT. Then PDRT trained teams in various agencies in preinvestment and implementation planning to improve project proposals and project implementation.

The Development Project Management Center (DPMC) of the U.S. Department of Agriculture participated in the National Planning Project by developing training materials for PDRT and providing both short- and long-term consultants. Between DPMC and PDRT, four manuals on project planning and implementation, and forty-six modules on various management tools, have been produced.

NPP featured the action-training approach to management training, which emphasizes ". . . on-the-spot training of persons actually responsible for 'live' projects. . . . Action training makes use of their own project activity experiences and project problems as focal points of the training."[33] The process began when an agency selected a project, assigned a work group to design it, and requested the assistance of PDRT to train the work group for its task. PDRT gave them a brief initial training during which the project team began to plan the project. Afterward PDRT provided consultations and workshops until the project plan was completed. This pattern was repeated for projects which were authorized for implementation. A project implementation team was appointed, PDRT gave it an initial training during which it began to develop the implementation plan, and it completed the implementation plan aided by PDRT consultation and workshops. The project teams worked on their real-life projects but they learned a general methodology, which they could apply to other projects. The PDRT members also continually learned from the trainees about environmental constraints, management problems, and adaptation of procedures to agency realities.

PDRT began its action-training program with project teams in the Ministry of Agriculture and later worked with project teams in the Ministries of Health, Industry and Commerce, and Education. It provided training and consultation in response to requests from various agencies. In less than three years, "PDRT ha[d] given training workshops and consultation to over 492 persons for various aspects of project planning and implementation and ha[d] conducted seminars in which over 510 other persons [were] introduced to key concepts and skills."[34] "There [has] been direct assistance to over 40 projects through project planning workshops, 28 projects through implementation workshops, 50 projects through planning consultations, and 14 projects through implementation consultation."[35]

One of the accomplishments of the NPP was the development, refinement, and institutionalization of a Jamaican Project Planning System. Prior to the intervention there was no coordinated system for project identification, appraisal, planning, and approval. The new system involved standardized formats for project documents, and a rational set of steps from project identification to project authorization, included a project profile, prefeasibility, and feasibility study. The project profile used a standard format and existing data to provide a relatively short but complete description of the project. It was easy to complete and it answered the basic why, what, who, when, how questions on the project. Since it was easy to compile, it became widely used. Even field staff used it to propose projects and it increased the flow of ideas to decision makers.

The project profiles were submitted to an interministerial Preselection Committee (PSC) which judged the project's merits in light of national and sectorial priorities. The PSC could promote the project for a financial feasibility study, recommend implementation, request clarification, or reject it. The PSC decisions were reviewed by the Economic Council before becoming official.

The PDRT action training became organized around the new Project Planning System. Action training was focused mainly on the five areas of project profile preparation, project implementation planning, project management, project administration, and project appraisal (depending upon the tasks of the project team being trained). PDRT established the Project Planning System and trained a substantial number of people for their roles in that system.

The NPP could claim considerable success in building the capacity of the Jamaican Government to draft project proposals, plan project implementation and manage project implementation. It still had an agenda for developing or completing management tools, but USAID did not extend the project beyond the original contract. The loss of USAID support signals the fact that NPP was not integrated into the USAID Jamaica program. There were several USAID projects which never used PDRT as a resource when such a step would have greatly benefited the USAID projects. The reports indicate that there was considerable friction between NPP consultants and USAID.

Performance and Output Gaps

The major performance gap, namely lack of capital flows to Jamaica, appears to have been great enough to be recognized by the government and the USAID mission alike. Also, many projects were being rejected by the Ministry of Finance and Planning because of their poor preparation—it was clear that the various agencies lacked the capability for preparing proposals for funding. The performance measure here was fairly clear and the output gap was quite noticeable. This created considerable pressure for change. Over time, other gaps were also perceived including the inability to use funds or implement projects effectively.

Environmental Context: Opportunities and Constraints

The materials reviewed did not consider what might have been favorable external conditions. We can speculate that the attitudes and values of Jamaica as a former British colony were perhaps more congruent with managerial technologies from the United States than they might have been in former French or Spanish colonies. Another probable favorable condition was the number of Jamaicans trained in the United States. In the previous discussion of the Philippine case, we mentioned how American education can facilitate the use of teams.

The major opportunities for the project were the resources it enjoyed. The NPP was liberally endowed with three resources: time, personnel, and power. Because it was a four-year project, it was able to institutionalize a project planning system and train a large number of personnel in planning and other management tasks. Four years is enough time to effect permanent improvements in management practices. The provision of personnel was also generous. The long-term consultant resided in Jamaica for the four years and other consultants were available as needed. The PDRT personnel were a problem at first, because of high turnover, but the problem was corrected with the establishment of PAMCO. NPP enjoyed the strong support of the Jamaican Government because it had requested the project after recognizing an output gap about which it was very concerned. Later, the support remained strong because the government perceived that the project had closed the gap considerably.

Two major constraints appear to have been the problems of interministerial transfers and USAID mission turnover. The former constraint was overcome by the creation of PAMCO as a separate organization with permanent positions. The latter constraint led to the termination of the National Planning Project by USAID Jamaica at the end of the contract.

Structural, Design, and Environmental Changes

The change had two stages. At first, a training team called the Project Development Resource Team (PDRT) was created in the Ministry of Finance and Planning. Eventually this became a department or group in a separate public organization responsible to the Ministry of Finance and Planning called PAMCO. This kind of institutional base provided PDRT with a legitimacy and stability it would otherwise have lacked. It is also important to note the multidisciplinary character of PDRT. It possessed a range of skills beyond training skills and could function as a flexible task force.

The targets of the change intervention were, first, its own ministry, the Ministry of Finance and Planning, and, second, the Ministries of Agriculture, Health and Social Security, Industry and Commerce, and Education. Its objective was to improve the capability of the Ministries to gain funds and to better implement projects. It worked with a large number of projects within these Ministries. Thus, it sought to improve the performance of a large number of different government activities as compared to the Guyanan case, which worked with few actual projects.

The major design change introduced by the NPP was the Jamaican Project Planning System, which routinized the process of identifying, appraising, planning, and authorizing projects. A project profile was drafted in a standard format for initial determination by the interministry Preselection Committee and the Economic Council. After initial approval it proceeded through a set of feasibility and planning studies in preparation for final PSC authorization, guided by formats for documentation. PAMCO served as secretariat to the Preselection Committee and guided the appraisal of the projects seeking final authorization. In addition, PDRT had contributed greatly to the standardization of the planning of project implementation and the monitoring of projects. An important result of the project, therefore, was that all the relevant agencies shared the same basic planning, authorizing, implementing, and monitoring process. These changes made the participating Ministries more mechanical through standardizing these processes and defining them more clearly. It also greatly increased the competence, efficiency, and productivity of these Ministries.

The NPP also modified the Ministries in the organic direction. It increased communication and participation through training multispecialty teams in working together in project planning or implementation planning. According to the report the mandate of PDRT included ". . . increas[ing] project planning, implementation planning, and management capabilities throughout the government, especially at implementing levels, [and] support[ing] policies of government decentralization. . . ."[36] Also, the project profile ". . . increased the number of project ideas flowing into Ministries [and] the participation of field staff in project preparation. . . ."[37]

The Nature of the Approach

The intervention level of this particular change effort in one sense was the entire government. The Project Development Resource Team was located in the Ministry of Finance and Planning but provided training and management tools for all the agencies of the government. It also developed the Jamaican Project Planning System, which was developed on the basis of interviews with officials throughout the government and which affected the planning process for all agencies. The officials had also recommended that the project focus on planning and that it emphasize the Ministries of Agriculture and Industry and Commerce. In addition, PDRT later emphasized the Ministries of Health and Education, and also focused on implementation and monitoring.

The dominant tactic used in this intervention was training, with the second most important tactic being problem-solving groups. Small interdisciplinary teams were action trained in proposal preparation and implementation planning.

The key feature of the action training involved working with actual projects, first in the planning stage and then the implementation stage. Courses, workshops, and consultations were combined during each of the two stages of a project: design and implementation. This program of learning by doing is an old idea with a new application. It was the essence of Dewey's approach to education and is common to other educational models.[38] This approach is especially desirable for skill learning, which is exactly what was needed here. The motivation for change came from the action learning itself because the training was relevant to the individual's work. Because the trainees were taught to solve the problems which were confronting them, they were highly motivated to learn.

This intervention also did some restructuring. First, it created a new unit in the Projects Division of the Ministry of Finance and Planning, which became a department in PAMCO. Second, the institutionalization of the Jamaican Project Planning System set up an interministry review committee and broadened the participation in proposing projects through the simplified project profile step. The Project Planning System was a design change which made government procedures more mechanical, while the project file was a design change that made them more organic.

This project did not require many resources. PDRT had only four national members and only two expatriate members for two years. One expatriate consultant served for the four years of the project.

Results

PDRT's accomplishments were considerable. It steadily increased its consultations, planning and implementing courses over the three years the project was in full swing, specifically 1977–1980. It gave training workshops and consultation to over 492 persons and gave seminars for another 510 people. Clearly, this approach proved to be very popular. In fact, the intervention had a much wider impact than was originally planned.

The Administrative Staff College incorporated some of PDRT's managerial technologies in its courses for high-level government officials. The National Planning Agency and some other training institutions also adapted the action-training approach and materials to their needs. Some of the specific managerial technologies, most notably the project profile, were widely adopted throughout the government. Four manuals on planning and implementation and forty-six modules on management tools were published. As a result of these means of diffusion, more and better information was being used in the ministries.

The speed of the proposal preparation process was considerably increased. When extensive flooding occurred in 1979, the Emergency Relief Committee was able quickly to develop a number of proposals using the format of the project profile. New processes for the planning and implementation of projects were established which have been more effective than the old. The bottom line is that the flow of capital for projects into Jamaica increased considerably, marking the project as a success.

Within specific Ministries, changes occurred which were similar to the changes at the government level. The Ministries were rationalizing their project planning, appraisal, implementation, and monitoring systems or procedures. The PDRT was assisting with the development of these systems

One negative result was the termination of the project at the end of the contract by the USAID mission in Jamaica. While PDRT maintained good relations with the many Jamaican agencies, it had difficulties with the donor agency. Nevertheless, PDRT was institutionalized within the Jamaican government and no longer was dependent on foreign technical assistance, even though more assistance could have been profitably utilized.

Conclusion

This case involved a design change, the addition of a new unit or department in the Ministry of Finance and Planning. It also involved a strong management training program using the action-training approach. The effort of the consultant was sustained and long term, i.e., for four years. The intervention improved the performance of a variety of government agencies.

Integrated Planning and Implementation of Rural Development (Colombia)

This intervention was a management-improvement project that has many similarities to the Jamaican and Guyanan cases, although it had little direct connection with USAID.[39] Like the Jamaican project, it placed a great deal of emphasis on learning by doing; like the Guyanan project, it involved a lot of problem solving. Although O.D. is involved in various degrees in all of the previous interventions, only this one reports the use of T-groups to heighten sensitivity and improve working relationships. It also emphasized training, data collection, data discussion, problem solving, and other tactics of this approach. Little is reported on the nature of the team that did the intervention, nor is its composition and location clearly described.

This was a complex intervention. It involved a management-improvement team from the Inter-American Institute for Cooperation on Agriculture, which trained personnel in the Integrated Rural Development Program (DRI) to increase their planning and implementation capacity. As in the Jamaican case, the management-improvement team worked with a broad set of agencies and associations, all those involved in integrated rural development. The focus was on combining planning and implementation into one integrated process and on improving the coordination between agencies.

Synopsis

In 1978 the Planning and Project Management Division (PROPLAN) of the Inter-American Institute for Cooperation on Agriculture (IICA) began a project of technical cooperation with the Colombian Agricultural Institute (ICA). The project began with the First National Seminar on Management of Regional Rural Development Projects conducted by the PROPLAN management-improvement team with the participation of several agencies serving the rural sector and the Colombian Agricultural Institute. In this seminar/

workshop the participants identified critical areas of project management at the regional and local levels that needed strengthening
and identified some of the management needs of the participating
institutions.

This seminar led to a project to strengthen the management of
regional rural development projects by providing training and consultations to four of the participating organizations for developing
management models and redesigning administrative procedures.
During implementation this project was revised in two important
ways. First, the PROPLAN management-improvement team
limited its attention to ICA with the idea of later adapting the new
management models, procedures, and tools to the other organizations. This management model was developed by the joint efforts of
PROPLAN and ICA. Second, it substituted learning-by-doing
methods of training for the more standard seminars and workshops
that had been planned.

In itself, this project was not very important, but it provided a
learning experience for drafting a second and much larger project,
the PROPLAN/A Colombian Project. The materials and procedures developed for two districts in the first project were judged to
be appropriate for extension to other districts in the larger project.
The PROPLAN/A project also drew upon the multicountry experience of PROPLAN. It was attached to the Integrated Rural Development Program (DRI) and it sought to improve the planning-
implementation process of the interinstitutional and multisectoral
rural development projects of DRI.

As with the earlier project, PROPLAN/A began in only two districts. It conducted learning-by-doing training courses and developed management models. These were perceived as successful
and were extended to two other districts where the methodologies
and tools were further revised. Later, they were adapted to the regional level and eventually to the national level. A year later, the
project was expanded to all DRI districts in the country.

Since the PROPLAN/A project succeeded in diffusing the project management model and assorted management technologies
throughout the Integrated Rural Development Program (DRI), it
is appropriate to describe this program. It was the major program
in Colombia that was targeted at the small-scale farmer. It was a
large program with a budget of $670 million for the 1977-1985
period. It served more than 800,000 peasants in 3,800 villages in
17 of the 23 Departments of Colombia. It was important to the gov-

ernment's overall social agenda because it sought to increase small farmer productivity. This was seen as the best way to increase the food and nutrition levels of the country. Its activities included programs in research and extension, credit, marketing, conservation and use of natural resources, training and community organization, health, potable water, school buildings, teacher training, school kitchens and gardens, roads, and electrification. Over twenty public agencies provided infrastructure and services for agricultural production and the rural population, and participated with DRI. The DRI programs were implemented through subprograms of fifteen public and private-sector institutions, and the DRI offices coordinated these programs at the local, district, regional, and national levels. DRI was headed by the Council of Directors, which established policies, and chaired by the Minister of Agriculture.

The objective of the PROPLAN/A Project was "to strengthen the planning and management system of the Integrated Rural Development Program (DRI)."[40] The PROPLAN/A Project evaluated and improved DRI's existing instruments and developed additional managerial tools based on IICA's multicountry experience and specific DRI institutional contexts.

The subject areas covered by the project were: preparation of microregional diagnoses, preparation of district development plans, preparation of general guidelines, preparation of operational programs, analysis of existing mechanisms for citizen participation, design coordination mechanisms, and design a follow-up and evaluation system. In most of these activities specialists from PROPLAN Central Group (international office) and PROPLAN Colombia worked together with national specialists. The *microregional diagnosis* was developed mutually by the Central Group of PROPLAN and PROPLAN's Colombia office and tested out in DRI. The *district development plans* were developed by PROPLAN Colombia in conjunction with the Colombian Agricultural Institute (ICA) based on earlier work by the Central Group; they were tested in one district and adjusted for another district. Then the DRI General Office decided to apply the methodology in all twenty-seven DRI districts. The *general guidelines* were based on a general methodology designed by the Central Group of PROPLAN, adapted and applied to one district by PROPLAN Colombia and DRI, and revised for nationwide use at the request of the DRI General Office. In the area of *operational programs,* PROPLAN

Colombia worked cooperatively with the agencies involved. For *mechanisms for citizen participation,* PROPLAN Colombia did a study of their use and planned to recommend improvements. PROPLAN Colombia developed preliminary methodologies for *institutional coordination* and a *progress follow-up system.*

The PROPLAN/A Project emphasized cooperation. The technical assistance to agencies involved joint efforts with agency staff to test and adjust selected management methodologies and instruments. It involved the transfer-by-doing approach. Also, the training activities used the learning-by-doing approach. "This format always began with the presentation of methodologies developed by the [Central Group], followed by examples of its application, specific actions for adapting it to the conditions of the DRI Districts, and followed with experimental testing in situations simulated by national specialists."[41]

We illustrate the dominant pattern for the implementation process of the PROPLAN/A Project by describing the development of the district development plan. First, project management problems were identified and a framework was developed for designing a project management plan. This step was tackled by a team consisting of specialists from local, regional, and national levels of the Colombian Agricultural Institute, representatives of the users of ICA's services, and representatives of organizations interacting with ICA. This group was given team work training and management training to help it produce the problem identification and framework for designing a management plan.

The next step was to create four task forces of ICA specialists to develop management technologies for four areas of project management: (1) reviewing project objectives and developing project strategy in light of the contextual realities, (2) planning specific projects and the use of resources, (3) interinstitutional organization and coordination, and (4) managing information and monitoring the project. Guidance on each of these tasks was available from the methodologies developed by PROPLAN Central Group but these had to be tested and adapted for the conditions of ICA districts.

Performance and Output Gaps

There was widespread recognition among public agencies in the agricultural sector of the need for better project management skills. This perception was sharpened by the First National Seminar on

Management of Regional Rural Development Projects, which identified problem areas of project management. As a result a project was started to address these problems. Since the Colombian agencies requested help, the project operated in a favorable climate. On a smaller scale problem identification seminars were regularly employed at the beginning of specific interventions to identify performance gaps.

Environmental Context: Opportunities and Constraints

The public sector in Colombia was among the most developed and well organized in Latin America. Within the public sector, the integrated rural development approach had become institutionalized and DRI was staffed with many specialists. Thus, the PROPLAN/A Project sought to change a fairly dynamic, professional, and organic set of organizations. DRI and related agencies such as ICA were open to change and interested in a management-improvement intervention. The Council of Directors of DRI strongly desired to improve its performance, and the staff desired new management technologies.

The PROPLAN/A Project, therefore, had strong support from the beginning. What was more surprising was the strength of the support as the project evolved. When management planning and implementation systems were developed and tested in one or two districts, DRI quickly extended them to other districts. Extensive changes occurred rapidly, demonstrating how open DRI was to change.

Another favorable circumstance was the research and development that had preceded the intervention. The PROPLAN department of IICA had been developing and testing planning and implementation systems in many contexts that could serve as a base for the systems used in DRI. The PROPLAN/A Project only required the adaptation of these systems to the specific districts or regions. Furthermore, the work of PROPLAN with ICA in a prior project had prepared the way by developing the framework and establishing working relationships.

There were surprisingly few constraints to this intervention, which testifies again to the popularity of the management-improvement approach. The one constraint we would mention was the difficulty of integrated rural development. It is normal for government agencies to be highly centralized in LDCs, which makes the coordinated activities of several agencies at the local or district levels extremely difficult. Therefore, DRI's task of integrated rural development may have been easy to design on paper at the national level, but was very hard to plan and implement smoothly in the communities. The use of multidisciplinary multiagency teams was essential in order to take the full range of important factors into account. On the other hand routinized procedures facilitated getting things done without reinventing wheels, as long as they were not too rigid. The PROPLAN/A Project emphasized problem-solving teams, routinized planning and implementation systems, and constant adaptation and flexibility. In summary, the DRI mandate was extremely difficult, making the PROPLAN/A Project a complicated task, but the project approach was well-suited to the difficulty of its task.

Structural, Design, and Environmental Changes

Integrated rural development requires integration at national, regional, district, and local levels. To be effective the involved agencies must locate considerable discretion and power at the district level, and probably at the local level for some activities. These agencies therefore must not be too centralized in those components that participate in the integrated rural development program. The report on Colombia indicates that the PROPLAN/A Project was to assist in the decentralization of the DRI program. It aided decentralization by developing effective planning and implementation systems for the district level. These systems enabled multidisciplinary district teams to successfully plan and manage the integrated rural development programs in their districts. This aid made the districts more self-sufficient and autonomous in their managing projects, and made it safer for higher levels in DRI to devolve some power and authority to the district levels.

One of the main reasons for decentralization in an agency such as DRI was to make it adaptive to local conditions and needs, and flexible in providing suitable services. Local "markets" (service areas) for integrated rural development are relatively unique, at least standard formulas can not be followed slavishly. Another feature of integrated rural development is the complexity of the task, as discussed previously. It requires, therefore, relatively high-level skills. These features together, relatively unique markets and relatively high skills, spell out the contingencies that call for an organic organization, and DRI was relatively organic. The intervention made it more organic in emphasizing the use of multidisciplinary teams and facilitating decentralization. On the other hand, the intervention also made it more mechanical by increasing the routinization of planning and implementing procedures. This was necessary because the management skills were not high enough at the district level effectively to coordinate and direct complex multiorganizational programs. The new routinized management tools compensated for this deficiency and aided the planning and other management functions in support of the multiagency programs.

A major design change was the liberal use of task forces. They were used as problem-solving groups at all levels and to address the following four generic problems: reviewing projectives and strategy, planning specific actions and the use of resources, interinstitutional organization and coordination, and managing information and monitoring.[42]

The first task force developed a system of priorities based on the participation of representatives of the key agencies and beneficiary groups. This activity included the identification of performance and output gaps. The task force also analyzed the forces favoring or blocking a program. This activity paralleled the task in our analytical framework of identifying opportunities and constraints. Next the task force set objectives and adopted a strategy for pursuing them.

One of the management tools that a project task force developed was the Operational Management Summary to address the issue of project objectives. It was ". . . used for presenting a comprehensive, clear and quantified vision of the objectives and goals pursued, and the activities and resources available for achieving them."[43] Thus, it addressed the first two problems presented previously.

Two task forces worked on interinstitutional organization and coordination. The first task force worked on the District Development Plan, which was a methodology for planning and implementing integrated rural development at the district level. It dealt with the coordination for district level programs of the organizations participating in DRI and their relationships with beneficiaries. The other task force dealt with the coordination of local, regional, and national levels of the DRI program.

Another task force created a monitoring and management information system, which focused on the district level management information needs but also provided useful information for regional and national offices. It included representatives from the local, regional, and national levels. They analyzed methodologies and instruments currently in use and revised them. The new instruments were synchronized with the other managerial instruments developed by the Project.

The Nature of the Approach

The intervention is of special interest because of its complexity and scope. The intervention level was first interorganizational, secondly at the top of the organization, thirdly at the district level, and finally at all levels of the organization. It tried to build better coordination between various organizations and improve planning and implementation within the relevant agencies. Integrated rural development is an extremely complex task because of the large number of different organizations and community associations involved. The PROPLAN/A Project changes, therefore, affected many interorganizational relationships. The entrance level was at the top of DRI, but the focus of attention was on the district level. Nevertheless, it generated managerial technologies and training for all levels of the organization.

The change tactics reflected almost a pure O.D. approach with the use even of T-groups. Specialists from the Colombian Agricultural Institute working at the local, regional, and national levels were given an introductory seminar on O.D. so that they could learn to work together. They were also taught how to run group meetings and data discussions as a way of identifying problems.

The tactics which were emphasized in the intervention were decree, data collection, group discussion, group problem solving, T-groups, experimentation, and training. Decree was used to implement new managerial technologies widely throughout DRI after they had been tested and revised. T-groups were used to make some of the task forces work effectively together.

A key element in the change strategy was the use of experimentation. The project involved a number of small pilot projects at the district level. When task forces had developed management systems and tools, they were applied and tested in one or two districts and revised before wider application.

Group discussion and group problem solving were employed not only in the training and functioning of the task forces, but also at each step of the process. The complexity of integrating many organizations required considerable use of group discussion and group problem solving to take the many perspectives and factors into account in planning and implementing rural development. Project personnel provided direct technical support activities for these task forces or problem solving groups. The project team helped them use the instruments for collecting and analyzing information and for preparing the managerial systems and management tools. The project team also used T-groups as a way of improving the performance of the team members on the task forces.

Training was a key tactic. Once management systems and materials were developed, tested, and decreed for widespread adoption, training was provided at many levels in their use. Training was also provided on how to work in teams which included techniques such as nominal groups, force-field analysis, and brainstorming.

Data collection was used in the preparation of the management systems and tools. Data collection was especially important in obtaining community inputs for designing DRI programs. Many methods were used for this purpose including surveys, consultation meetings with the general population, district meetings, and research. They used almost the full array of information gathering tactics suggested by O.D. change agents.

The major resources used in this intervention were knowledge and power. Knowledge from many sources was used in the development of the managerial systems and tools. Systems and tools developed by the Central Group of PROPLAN on the basis of international experience were adapted to the DRI context. The adaptation process required the perspectives and knowledge of many organizations and all levels of the staff. Even community and district knowledge of conditions was important. Once these systems and tools were developed and tested, they were implemented widely and quickly by decree. This intervention was second only to that of T and V in the power employed in instituting the changes.

Results

The major results that were reported were the development and institutionalization of a number of managerial systems and tools. We are left to assume that performance improved and gaps were closed. The actual numerical increases in community participation or in interorganizational communication were not reported. The de-

velopment of an environment that stimulated learning and problem solving was reported but not documented. The report also
claimed that the project was developing national self-sufficiency in
continuing the objectives and activities of the project upon its com-
pletion. "Project activities have thus been aimed at forming a
group of DRI Program national level staff, who would be responsible for extending the instruments developed in the various participating institutions, and leading the training activities required
for achieving this goal."[44]

Conclusion

This case was a management intervention that was relatively
unique in the breadth of its scope, both in terms of the number of
functional areas and the complexity of the task of integrated rural
development. The change target was a relatively organic bureaucracy that needed to be made more organic through the widespread
use of problem-solving teams, especially at the district and local
levels, for integrating the activities of several organizations and
community groups. The intervention also made DRI somewhat
more mechanical through the institutionalization throughout it of
standard managerial systems and tools. However, the DRI pattern
was to use teams to adapt standard managerial technologies to specific settings, so that this intervention maintained a balance between organic and mechanical processes. We would also point out
that this intervention was unique among our cases in that it used
the full range of O.D. tactics.

THE SIX CASES SUMMARIZED

Before analyzing the six cases for their implications for change
agents, we present capsule summaries of them to aid the reader in
the following discussion. These cases are also summarized in
Figure 3.1.

NIA in Philippines

The National Irrigation Administration hired community organizers to mobilize farmers through irrigation user associations to better operate and maintain communal irrigation systems. It also

began pilot projects in two communities that integrated community inputs with engineering procedures. At the same time a high-level National Communal Irrigation Committee was created to guide the integration of the community participation capacity into NIA. Then, one pilot project of the same type was started in each of the twelve regions covered by NIA to help diffuse the new program throughout NIA. As a result NIA became more responsive to community needs and more successful in providing effective and sustainable irrigation systems.

T and V in India

A successful pilot extension system was institutionalized widely throughout India. The new system had a new organizational structure and a new strategy. It was hierarchical, highly structured and routinized, and single purposed, i.e., to transfer effective technologies to farmers. (The previous extension had sought also to provide farmers with inputs and credit.) The new extension agents activities were scheduled on a two-week basis. From Monday through Thursday for two weeks the agent visited different groups of farmers on a fixed schedule. Friday was for training in the technologies to be taught in the next round of visits; Saturday was a make-up day; and Sunday was the agent's holiday. Then, the two-week schedule was repeated. This system was more highly organized and more mechanical than the previous extension service, and was spreading rapidly because evaluations reported that it was much more effective than previous systems.

AUPHA in Jordan

As recommended by a study of the management problems of the Ministry of Health, the Health Management Appraisal Methods Project was initiated to develop a methodology for self-assessment of the management of health services. Foreign consultants held seminars on using existing data (mainly health, medical, and financial data) for management purposes. The project also provided training in new management practices. The Ministry was in the process of decentralizing to a regional structure at the time of the project and the training was given to the regional directors and their staffs. As a result, the role of managers was dramatically reoriented from ineffective supervision and monitoring to more teaching and motivating of subordinates based on good information. A badly needed financial control system was also implemented through retraining.

Management Improvement Teams in Guyana

American management consultants trained Guyanese management consultants in the Public Service Ministry in a set of management tools. Then the group of American and Guyanan consultants subdivided into two groups to work in two agencies. Each subteam added agency members whom they trained to be a problem-solving management-improvement team. The two agencies were the Ministry of Agriculture and the Guyanan Electricity Corporation. The management-improvement team in each agency selected, with official approval, an agency problem to work on as a pilot project for using the new management technologies. In the Ministry of Agriculture, this special MIT worked in the Hydraulics Department and had difficulty implementing its solution to its pilot project problem. Later, a MIT was created and trained to work in the Lands and Survey Department. The MIT in the Guyanan Electricity Corporation did succeed in dealing with its pilot project problem. The long-term purpose of the intervention was to train agency staff in new problem solving and management techniques to build new capacities into the agencies. Real progress toward this purpose was made during the brief time of the intervention, but the intervention failed to institutionalize the new management procedures in these organizations.

PDRT in Jamaica

A multidisciplinary training team was established in the Ministry of Finance to train personnel throughout the government to propose, plan, and implement projects more effectively. It used an action-training approach in courses, workshops, and consultations, which gave project officers on-the-spot training using their own live projects as learning materials. The team introduced new management practices and developed a planning process for the Finance Ministry. The services of the team were in great demand, and some of the new management practices diffused widely.

Integrated Rural Development in Colombia

A management training and development program was instituted between the Inter-American Institute for Cooperation in Agriculture and the Integrated Rural Development Program in Colombia to improve management skills and practices in DRI, as well as in a number of institutions that participated in the Integrated Rural Development Program. Training was provided at the national, regional, and district levels. In addition task forces were created to do problem solving around four critical management problem areas. Two objectives of the management-improvement program were to improve the integration of rural development activities and to increase the participation of farmers and rural associations in the development programs. The program employed a rich variety of O.D. tactics.

IMPLICATIONS FOR CHANGE AGENTS

These cases have several implications for change agents, most of which are derived inductively rather than deductively. We discuss these implications under three major themes: performance and output gaps, the nature of the approach, and structural and design changes.

Performance and Output Gaps

All of the successful interventions involved a gap in performance or output. This has proved to be one of the insights of the organizational theory literature that appears to be transferable to the LDC context and spans a wide variety of cultures. The absence of examples in former French colonies, however, limits the generalizability of this finding. Nevertheless, the implication is that most people are motivated to do well and to make their organizations more effective.

The gap or failure is sometimes obvious and the desire to do something about it fairly strong. One example would be a failure to produce electricity.[45] Other outputs, however, require measurement, and thus data collection, to demonstrate a lack of effectiveness in goal achievement. The more successful change efforts focused on demonstrating output gaps to ensure that there was no

Figure 3.1 Characteristics of Six Cases of Organizational Change in Third World Countries

Cases	Performance and Output Gap	Opportunities	Constraints	Changes	Tactics
NIA (Philippines)	poor maintenance, improper use of system	visible failure, communal tax on construction, relative equality, top support, high education level, open to change, absence of problems	some engineers resisted, centralized ministries	community organizers, problem-solving groups (high and low levels)	pilot project, data collection and discussion, group decision-making, group problem-solving, restructure
T & V (India)	general recognition of extension failure, cost-benefit failure	reputation for success	resistance by some field agents and bureaucrats	reduced agents' tasks, centralized power, monitoring system	decree, restructure, training, pilot project, data collection
AUPHA (Jordan)	statistics on health problems, recognition of poor management	support of Minister of Health and physicians	none mentioned	new management practices, decentralization, new information system, reoriented supervision, new financial control system	group problem-solving, training, data collection and discussion, group decision-making, decree, experimentation, restructure
MIT (Guyana)	low productivity, management defects, low motivation	support of top (utility), crisis in utility-supported change, conducive culture	other responsibilities of team members, MOA more centralized and bureaucratic, short time frame	created three task forces	group problem-solving, data collection, training, experimentation
PDRT (Jamaica)	few projects funded	Jamaican culture conducive to teams, many U.S.-trained	no permanent staff, high turnover, trouble with donor	implementation team, new management practices, new department	action training, group problem-solving, new department
DRI (Colombia)	recognition of inadequate planning skills	developed public sector, requests for assistance	not discussed, the complexity of integrated rural development	new management practices, broadened participation in decision making, interagency task forces	action training, group problem-solving, data collection and discussion, group decision making, T-groups, pilot project, decree

Figure 3.1 (continued)

Case	Intervention Level	Motivation	Resources	Results	Form Before → After
NIA (Philippines)	top, bottom, strengthening village association	rewarding interaction, top level support	funds from Ford	better canal placement, better maintenance, innovations, institutionalization, strengthened associations	mechanical → became more organic, decentralization
T & V (India)	top to bottom	contact with supervisor continual training	funds from World Bank, agricultural research centers helped	increased contact with farmers, increased learning	mechanical → mechanical, more mechanical, centralization, more rational, more standardized
AUPHA (Jordan)	top and regional levels, a few aspects at the bottom	learning, top level support, desire of physicians to solve problems	USAID funds, low cost	results beyond the changes were not discussed	became both more mechanical and more organic, decentralization, more rational, more supervision
MIT (Guyana)	organizational level in utility and department level in MOA	not discussed	commitment of top in utility, USAID funds	improved performances in utility and not in MOA	little change in form, both more organic and more mechanical
PDRT (Jamaica)	entire government, all levels	solving problems, learning	two expatriate advisors, USAID funds	high demand for training, more projects accepted, new management practices	not much change in form but more organic
DRI (Colombia)	all levels, started at district level	not discussed	IICA funds and experience	better planning and management, increased participation, new management practices adapted but effects not described	mechanical/organic became more organic

159

doubt about the need for the change. On the bases of these and other cases we studied, we observe that *the less successful change efforts did not demonstrate and emphasize output gaps as much as the more successful interventions.*

Five of the six interventions focused on the *performance* of efficiency. The exception is the Philippines where the focus was on sustainability of irrigation systems. We find this common interest in efficiency somewhat surprising because we originally assumed that variation in cultural values would lead to more variation.

Are there *outputs* that are valued in many cultural contexts? We are impressed with how widespread the support for meeting basic needs is in the public agencies.[46] We suspect that there are other outputs that are highly valued in many cultures and can motivate public agencies. Possible candidates are technological development and reducing dependencies. Both of these contribute to national pride and status and should be appealing to many LDC organizations and to political elites. Finally, as was the case with Jamaica, many countries would want to obtain more development capital.

The Nature of the Approach

In Chapter 1 we delineated three change strategies, although in the real world these are mixed together in a variety of ways. Two general observations can be made about the role of these strategies in our cases. First, all except T and V in India, *employed one or more of the change tactics associated with O.D.* Of the interventions, only two, the interventions in Jamaica and Colombia, used T-groups as a way of teaching people to work in teams, but most used group discussion and all but T and V used group problem solving.[47] Second, all of these interventions employed a combination of tactics. This leads to a simple observation that a more complex strategy with multiple tactics is more likely to be successful than a simple, one-dimensional strategy.

The interventions in the Philippines, Colombia, and Jordan are almost textbook cases of how to alter an organization. Almost all of the tactics of change were employed in each of these cases. *The combination of the best features of these three interventions provides a very effective change process for most situations.* The best features are:

1. A very clear perception at the top of the organization of performance or output gaps that need addressing
2. The use of multidisciplinary problem-solving groups for designing and implementing changes
3. The involvement of top decision makers in problem solving
4. The use of data collection and discussion to document the performance and output gaps and to inform the design and implementation of the changes
5. Restructuring the organization, if necessary, to be more organic if more innovation, adaptation, and flexibility are needed, and to be more mechanical if more efficiency is needed
6. The use of experimentation and pilot studies to test and revise the changes before widespread implementation
7. Training people for their new roles or in the new skills required

The *intervention level* varies enormously in the six projects. The three most successful interventions—NIA in the Philippines, T and V in India, and MOH in Jordan—are distinguished from the others in that they were begun with strong support from the top person. The DRI intervention in Colombia appears also to have been successful and it had fairly strong support from the Council of Directors. It would be wrong to conclude, however, that top-level support is simply the result of unusual leadership. *The projects in one way or another kept top leadership informed and involved in solving problems.* This involvement seems to be a key factor in the success of these projects.

All of the tactics identified in Chapter 1 were employed in at least one of our six cases, but the reader may have noticed that our discussion of tactics throughout this chapter has been dominated by the discussion of teams. Almost all the projects used *teams,* although in a variety of ways. As pointed out in Chapter 1, teams can be used for group discussions, group decision making, group problem solving and group training. They can be temporary, semipermanent, or permanent. They can be interdisciplinary or not. By and large they are effective, but sometimes they fail, as was the case in the Ministry of Agriculture in Guyana. In fact, a general rule found in the literature on small groups is that equality is essential for effectiveness. Hierarchically structured groups are not as effective as those with less hierarchy. We thus generalize that teams must be open to the suggestions of all of their members to be effective.

We believe that teams acting as problem-solving groups have a special role to play in adapting Western organizational change strategies to Third World organizations. Many organizational theory and organizational design ideas have to be adapted to the specific organization, culture, and political climate. Teams are helpful in this process because they include multiple perspectives. They are especially effective when they work with the top of the organization, because top executives can guide the change effort away from the politically impossible and toward adaptations that will be supported. The farther down the chain of command teams operate, the less this is the case.

Teams appear generally to be more successful when they are part of a permanent department, as in the cases of the Philippines and Jamaica. They should be institutionalized as part of an existing organization or as part of a new organization. If they are not made permanent, they should function for an extended period, as was done in Jamaica.

It appears that mixed teams—part U.S. or international and part host country—are useful for transferring and adapting technologies to the local context. This pattern was employed in Jamaica, Guyana, Colombia, and Jordan. The extent of the interaction, however, appears to make a difference as well. External change agents are wise to team with organizational members for successful interventions in order to gain insider knowledge and thereby improve adaptation. In this sense organizational change efforts are like the planning of projects; they require a lot of difficult problem solving with input from a variety of key personnel.

We have been discussing equality and participation in teams but the development administration literature discusses participation in other contexts as well. Often participation in an organization is equated with the bottom-up approach. The commonly used terms "top-down" or "bottom-up" are misleading, however, because they oversimplify. It is clear that in all of these change efforts there was support from the top, and thus in this sense they were top-down. We also find in all cases that there was some form of participation, and in this sense they were bottom-up.

What does *participation* mean in the context of development organizations?[48] For many writers participation refers to the contribution of community members to the decisions and actions of development organizations that affect them. This meaning is explored in the next chapter. In this chapter, however, we are concerned with the breadth of participation by members of the organization in the decisions and procedures of organizations. In our definition, participatory organizations are characterized by decentralization of power and especially the power to make strategic decisions. By our definition organizations that allow lower members to voice their preferences may not be participatory. The organization must also give lower members real influence. By this definition, NIA in the Philippines and MOH in Jordan were clearly participatory (possibly also DRI in Colombia). While this type of participation often contributes to project success, it is not always necessary to success, as demonstrated by the T and V case. The mode of participation is also important to its contribution to success. Problem-solving groups, quality work circles, task forces, performance-improvement teams, or simply teams are especially effective models of participation when the task is complex. When the task is simple, teams are less necessary unless they serve important political purposes.

Many of the cases demonstrate the importance of experimentation and pilot studies. This tactic helps adapt borrowed managerial technologies, allows for more participation, and probably facilitates the development of more complex solutions. Experimentation surfaces problems with the proposed organizational change and leads to revisions and better changes before widespread implementation. Admittedly, experimentation is easier in large systems such as NIA.

Training is another commonly used tactic in almost all the interventions. In part this reflects the emphasis on managerial technologies in the cases. It may also reflect a recognition of a need for skills. But again, how the training is done and the content of the training are critical. Training in teams appears to be the most effective; the reason, we suspect, is that it tends to involve group discussion and even group problem solving.

An uncommon tactic in these cases was *decree.* Nevertheless, decree often is very important after the solution has been designed, tested, and revised using problem-solving teams and high levels of participation. Often the debugged solution is decreed for widespread use. This was the pattern in T and V in India, MOH in Jordan, and DRI in Colombia. In contrast, NIA in the Philippines diffused the community organizer approach more gradually and in smaller steps. After the pilot project was assessed in one district, the innovation was not immediately diffused throughout NIA but a pilot project was conducted in each of the other districts before diffusing the community organizer program throughout NIA.

In general, most of these interventions did not require much in the way of *financial resources*. The intervention in the National Irrigation Administration was the most expensive because it added a new occupational specialty to the organization. Most interventions required little more than the costs of the external consultants, which costs were born by donor agencies. The other resources of power, personnel (skills), knowledge, and time were needed in larger measure in several of the cases. Power was the main resource required for T and V in India and a significant resource in MOH in Jordan and DRI in Colombia. Personnel skills were important in the four management-improvement interventions, so that they emphasized training. Knowledge in the form of previously developed managerial technologies was important in DRI in Colombia, and time was important in NIA in the Philippines, in Jamaica, and to some degree in DRI in Colombia. The lack of funds and personnel was responsible for the failure of the management-improvement team in the MOA of Jamaica.

Finally, the role of data collection appears to be a critical part of a change strategy. Data collection helps demonstrate output gaps, problems, and, most critically, the complexity of the situation. It also provides a knowledge base for problem solving. Most of our cases involved informant interviewing and the use of available organizational data. Data collection was also a major part of the solution in two cases. Major changes in the Jordan case were the creation of a management information system and a new accounting system. In the Guyanan Electricity Corporation, a management information system dealing with maintenance schedules and parts inventories was part of the solution to improving plant performance.

Structural and Design Changes

The six change interventions vary in how much they emphasized structural or design changes versus process changes. Although our sample of six interventions is small and nonrandom, they suggest that structural or design changes are longer lasting. Both NIA and T and V made major structural changes in the whole organization, which appear to be fairly permanent. MOH in Jordan was in the process of making a long-term change to a regional structure. In the three interventions that were primarily management-improvement changes and not part of a major restructuring effort, the management-improvement teams were more successful when institutionalized as a department. Processual changes, therefore, seemed to be strengthened when they operated from a strong structural base; some structural changes may be necessary to more effectively achieve processual changes.

At the same time structures can not be effectively changed without training and process changes. Indeed, we conclude that the structure versus process dichotomy is misleading because successful change efforts usually involve both. Mixing change strategies appears to increase the chances of success. In other words, *major organizational change usually requires changing structures, job descriptions, and the people who fill the jobs.*

One lesson these cases provide is that change agents tend to think in processual terms and to emphasize the processual aspects of organizational change. Several reports describe NIA as an example of learning by doing, but this intervention involved important structural changes. Similarly, the relocation of PDRT in Jamaica to the public corporation PAMCO appears to have greatly facilitated its work even though the importance of this structural change was not emphasized in the report. Only the T and V case emphasized structural changes rather than the process of instituting the change. Considering that the extension service was entirely restructured, this emphasis on structure is not surprising. We conclude that change agents usually ignore the structural side of change more than they should. They may be more effective if they pay more attention to the structural and design implications of their interventions.

The most important finding in these cases about structural change is that improving organizations (including public bureaucracies) requires changes in different directions in different circumstances. Some bureaucracies need to be changed in the mechanical direction of greater efficiency; others in the organic direction of greater innovation or adaptiveness to local conditions. T and V is perhaps the clearest example of change in the direction of becoming more efficient, but many of the other cases involved the addition of more efficient bureaucratic practices under the guise of managerial technologies.

The organizations in Guyana, Jamaica, Colombia, and Jordan were being changed or altered to become more effective bureaucracies. Although they had been called bureaucracies before the interventions, they had deviated greatly from bureaucratic principles—some of them had aspects of patrimonial bureaucracies, lacking clear lines of authority and responsibility, emphasizing personal loyalties, and being governed by political factors. Thus, they actually became more *effective* by becoming more *bureaucratic. The direction of change in these organizations was toward rational legal bureaucracy in the classical sense of the term.*[49]

Another lesson from these interventions is the benefits of adding a new occupation or department. Examples include the training team in Jamaica and the addition of community organizers in NIA. Permanent additions may be expensive changes, but they involve structural changes with long-term results.

Unfortunately, we are not able to determine how much the specific opportunities or constraints contributed to the success or failure of each of the cases. Many of the organizations were ready for change interventions and many appeared to be less bureaucratic than the LDC norm. *The lesson for change agents is that they should intervene first in those organizations that have the most opportunities and fewest constraints.* Although it is not widely recognized in the organizational change literature, most radical, new education innovations in the United States required either new organizations or else innovators had to leave their organizations and find universities that were open to their ideas.

Another factor that contributes to the success or failure of the intervention is the nature of the personnel who are involved in change efforts. NIA, the electrical plant, and MOH were probably easier to change than most public bureaucracies because they did not involve civil servants. They involved engineers, physicians, researchers, or people in other occupations who were more experienced in solving practical problems and more open to change. Civil servants are more prone to be rule followers, lack initiative, and be less flexible, as we saw in the Ministry of Agriculture in Guyana where more difficulties were encountered than in the electric utility.

It is interesting to observe that, with the exception of the Guyanan intervention, there was little discussion of the strategy for the diffusion of the change. The basic strategy that we have recommended was demonstrated in this case. The management-improvement team in the GEC intervened where it was easiest, demonstrated success, then diffused the change more broadly.

Finally, we observe that these six cases illustrate a wide variety of institution-building strategies. The first is to make an organization more organic, as in the Philippines, in order to make it more responsive to local needs and more innovative. The second is the more common strategy of reforming a bureaucracy to make it more efficient, as in T and V (India) and Guyana. The third strategy is to decentralize to the regional level, as in Jordan. The fourth is the creation of a department or team that offers management services to other organizations, the thrust of the intervention in Jamaica. The fifth is the development, testing, and diffusion of new managerial technologies, as in Colombia and Jordan. These do not represent an exhaustive list of institution-building strategies, but they represent quite distinct ways of thinking about the problem of making institutions stronger. The question remains as to when one should use one strategy or another, a question to which we will return in Chapters 5 and the Epilogue.

Despite gaps in reports, the six cases illustrate a wide variety of lessons about successful change strategies, most of which were derived inductively. Only a few fit neatly or exclusively into one of the literatures on organizational change, whether O.D., O.T., or organizational design. Two overarching themes emerge. First, the greater the number of approaches used and the more that the system is altered, the more likely the change is to be successful. Second, change should not always be in the same direction; a contingency approach should be used to determine the direction of change that is appropriate for the problem at hand.

Notes

1. Alfred D. Chandler, Jr., 1963, *Strategy and Structure* (Cambridge: M.I.T. Press); and his 1977 *The Visible Hand* (Cambridge: Harvard Graduate School).

2. Note that Francophone countries are not well represented.

3. A large number of documents is available, the most useful of which is Benjamin Bagadion and Frances Korten, 1984, "Developing Irrigation Organizations: A Learning Process Approach to a Participatory Irrigation Program," in Michael Cernea, *Putting People First: Sociological Variables in Development Projects* (Balti-

more: Johns Hopkins Press), which provides an extensive bibliography. In addition we recommend Benjamin Bagadion and Frances Korten, 1980, "Developing Viable Irrigators Associations: Lessons from Small Scale Irrigation in the Philippines," *Agricultural Administration*, vol. 7, pp. 273-287; and Romana de los Reyes, 1983, "Process Documentation: Social Science Research in a Learning Process Approach to Program Development," paper read at the Social Development Management Network Meeting, April 14-16. David C. Korten has written a large number of papers providing insights into the general framework, the most important of which is his 1980 "Community Organization and Rural Development: A Learning Process Approach," *Public Administration Review*, vol. 40, no. 5, pp. 480-511.

4. Korten, 1980, *op. cit.*

5. The reports make clear that three successive administrators supported the project but they do not analyze why.

6. John Cohen *et al.*, 1981, "Development from Below: Local Development Associations in the Yemen Arab Republic," *World Development*, vol. 9, no. 11, p. 1053.

7. Cohen, *et al.*, 1981, *op. cit.*

8. *See* N. S. Carey Jones, 1983, "Decentralization and Delegation in Agricultural Development," *Agricultural Administration*, vol. 13, pp. 187-199; and Dennis Rondinelli, 1983, "Implementing Decentralization Programmes in Asia: A Comparative Analysis," *Public Administration and Development*, vol. 3, pp. 181-207.

9. Thomas Peters and Robert Waterman, Jr., 1982, *In Search of Excellence: Lessons from America's Best-Run Companies* (New York: Warner).

10. Romana de los Reyes, 1983, *op. cit.*

11. Korten, 1980, *op. cit.*

12. *See* among other publications: Michael Cernea, 1981, "Sociological Dimensions of Extension Organizations: The Introduction of the T and V System in India" in Bruce Crouch and Shankarich Chamala, *Extension Education and Rural Development*, vol. 2 (Chichester: John Wiley and Sons), pp. 221-235; Gershon Feder and Roger Slade, 1984, "A Comparative Analysis of Some Aspects of the Training and Visit System of Agricultural Extension in India," (Washington, D.C.: Research Unit, Agricultural and Rural Development Operational Policy Staff, World Bank), unpublished paper; John Howell, 1982, "Managing Agricultural Extension: The T and V System in Practice," *Agricultural Administration*, vol. 11, pp. 273-284.

13. Feder and Slade, 1984, *op. cit.*

14. Daniel Benor and James Harrison, 1977, *Agricultural Extension: The Training and Visit System* (Washington, D.C.: World Bank).

15. Herbert Kaufman, 1960, *The Forest Ranger* (Baltimore: Johns Hopkins).

16. Benor and Harrison, 1977, *op. cit.*

17. *See* Howell, 1982, *op. cit.*; Feder and Slade, 1984, *op. cit.*; Cernea, 1981, *op. cit.*

18. Cernea, 1981, *op. cit.*, p. 230.

19. Michael H. Bernhart, 1981, *Health Management Appraisal Methods Program: Jordan Case Study* (Washington, D.C.: Association of University Programs on Health Administration), mimeo.

20. Dennis A. Rondinelli, 1981, "Government Decentralization in Comparative Perspective: Theory and Practice in Developing Countries," *International Review of Administrative Sciences,* vol. 47, no. 2, pp. 133-145; Rondinelli, 1983, *op. cit.*

21. Bernhart, 1981, *op. cit.*, p. 6.

22. Bernhart, 1981, *op. cit.*

23. Bernhart, 1981, *op. cit.*

24. *See* Practical Concepts Inc., 1979, *Improving Organizational Effectiveness,* vol. 1, Final Report for the Government of Guyana and USAID/Guyana (unpublished report). Information was also obtained from Larry Cooley, project manager.

25. *See* Stanley Davis and Paul Lawrence, 1977, *Matrix* (Reading, Mass: Addison-Wesley). For a simple introduction, *see* Richard L. Daft, 1983, *Organizational Theory and Design* (St. Paul, Minn.: West), pp. 237-246.

26. Practical Concepts, Inc., 1979, *op. cit.*, p. 22.

27. Practical Concepts, Inc., 1979, *op. cit.*

28. Practical Concepts, Inc., 1979, *op. cit.*

29. Practical Concepts, Inc., 1979, *op. cit.*

30. *See* Merlyn Kettering, 1980, *Final Report of the National Planning Project,* USAID/GOJ 532-0039 (Kingston, Jamaica), mimeo; Merlyn Kettering, no date, *Trip Report for September 1– October 10, 1980* (mimeo from the files of DPMC, USDA, plus 14 attachments); Project Analysis and Monitoring Co. (PAMCO), *Project Planning and Management Series,* modules 12 and 31 (Kingston, Jamaica), mimeo; Merlyn Kettering, 1980, *Action Training in Project Planning and Management* (Washington, D.C.: DPMC, U.S. Department of Agriculture), mimeo; and interviews with Merlyn Kettering.

31. Kettering, 1980, *Action Training, op. cit.,* p. 1.

32. Kettering, 1980, *Action Training, op. cit.,* p. 16.

33. Kettering, 1980, *Action Training, op. cit.,* p. 2.

34. Kettering, 1980, *Final Report, op. cit.,* p. 2.

35. Kettering, 1980, *Final Report, op. cit.*

36. Kettering, 1980, *Action Training, op. cit.,* p. 5.

37. Kettering, 1980, *Action Training, op. cit.,* p. 10.

38. Laurence Arthur Cremin, 1961, *The Transformation of the School: Progressivism in American Education* (New York: Knopf).

39. Inter-American Institute for Cooperation on Agriculture, 1983, *A Guidance System Improvement Effort: PROPLAN/A Cooperation with the Colombian DRI Program* (PROPLAN Internal Document 85, April); and Inter-American Institute for Cooperation on Agriculture, 1981, *Improving Rural Development Planning and Management: Proceedings of IICA-PROPLAN/USDA-DPMC Seminar* (PROPLAN Document 18, San José, Costa Rica, December).

40. Inter-American Institute, 1981, *op. cit.,* p. 51.

41. Inter-American Institute, 1981, *op. cit.,* p. 54.

42. Inter-American Institute, 1981, *op. cit.,* p. 56.

43. Inter-American Institute, 1981, *op. cit.,* p. 57.

44. IICA, *op. cit.,* p. 12.

45. Visibility of performance has not been stressed much in the literature. For an exception, see Selwyn W. Becher and Gerald Gordon, 1966, "An Entrepreneurial Theory of Formal Organizations—Part I: Patterns of Formal Organizations," *Administrative Science Quarterly,* vol. 11 (December), pp. 315-344; and Selwyn Becher and Duncan Neuhauser, 1975, *The Efficient Organization* (New York: Elsevier); Jerald Hage, 1980, *Theories of Organizations: Form, Process and Transformation* (New York: Wiley-Interscience), Chapter 7.

46. Rondinelli, 1983, *op. cit.* mentions this as some of the motivation to decentralize governments.

47. The reports do not in all cases state that the groups were problem solving; thus, in some instances we are inferring this.

48. See Norman T. Uphoff, John Cohen, and Arthur Goldsmith, 1979. *Feasibility and Application of Rural Development Participation: A State-of-the-Art Paper* (Cornell University, Rural Development Committee).

49. See Max Weber, 1964, *The Theory of Social and Economic Organization,* translated by A. M. Henderson and Talcott Parsons

(New York: Free Press), pp. 341-358.

    50. Weber, 1964, *op. cit.*

4

Delivering Services to Communities Through Organizational Change

The previous chapter focused on institution-building strategies for organizations. The vast bulk of the development administration literature, however, deals with improving service delivery to communities and strengthening community organizations and associations. The rural development capacity-building approach discussed in Chapter 2 is a good example of this concern. Although our primary focus in this book is on organizational change, we look at community development in this chapter because communities are where many development organizations deliver their services. Also, making community associations more effective is a very important development strategy.

The study assumes that part of the problem of performance and output gaps resides in the local community where services are delivered. Outside organizations, including government agencies, can provide services but the local people must "make things happen." Development must take place in communities for these service organizations to be considered successful. They must link in some way to the local community and generate local assistance in providing the service. The way in which outside organizations link to local communities can greatly affect the extent to which services are created or utilized; thus, this chapter focuses on the organization-community linkage. This chapter is not a study of community development per se. It examines how outside organizations can change to improve their services to communities or to mobilize the communities to participate in the provision of services, thus making the outside organization more effective.

Several examples are in order. Chapter 3 noted the success of the National Irrigation Administration in the Philippines. The organizational changes which were discussed, however, are only part of the story. Equally important are the changes in the community associations themselves and the linkages between them and NIA. Another example of the importance of the community activity for organizational success is the case of the Training and Visit (T and V) Agricultural Extension System in India. The main measure of its effectiveness is the extent of the adoption of new food production technologies. Yet, this is something farmers do, not the organization. How T and V relates to farmer associations or work groups, therefore, influences the effectiveness of T and V, since ultimately its effectiveness depends upon what the communities or individuals do in response to it. Finally, DRI in Colombia sought to provide integrated rural development, which always depends upon community participation to be effective.

The outside organizations that deliver services to the community range from national ministries, such as the postal service or the department of roads, to extension services, school systems, or national community development organizations. Commonly, these establish a station or agency in the community or have agents who visit the communities. Some of these organizations, such as the postal service, do not require significant community participation and do not concern us in this chapter. Here, we look at organizations that depend on community inputs and we focus on their articulation with the host community and the receivers of their services.

Community organizations and instrumental voluntary associations that we consider from an organizational change perspective include: farmers' cooperatives, other cooperatives, irrigation user associations, farm settlement organizations, local development associations, local political organizations, village health committees, urban community centers, community schools, marketing associations, worker self-management businesses, self-help housing associations, and other instrumental voluntary associations. These organizations or associations tend to articulate goals and then implement plans to achieve them. They are purposeful collectives which are designed, rather than "natural" collectives. In most cases these are associations in which members volunteer their services for some collective benefit or public good. In a few instances, they are very small embryonic organizations where one or several individuals work part-time and are paid for their services.

We present six case studies of organizational changes which helped develop communities. The first four involve outside organizations, and the other two involve community organizations and instrumental voluntary associations. The six cases were selected to cover a range of examples across the following dimensions:

1. Urban-rural
2. Sufficient-scarce funds
3. Public-private
4. Multi-single objectives
5. Local-supra-local control
6. Untargeted-targeted to the poor

The first four cases—Brazil, Sri Lanka, Senegal, and Burma—involve instances where organizations attempted to deliver services, but found that in order to do so, they had either to change the nature of their linkage to the community or construct a linkage from scratch. The cases provide an interesting variety of ways in which linkages can be made. They all stress some community control and some community provision of resources. The fifth case describes a national government which tried to encourage local development associations to conduct development activities because it could not provide any itself. The sixth case describes the linkage between the national office of an association of milk cooperatives and the local cooperatives.

LINKAGE OF OUTSIDE ORGANIZATIONS
TO COMMUNITY DEVELOPMENTS

Municipal Services in the
Favelas of Rio de Janeiro (Brazil)

The municipal government of Rio de Janeiro wanted to extend a number of municipal services to the favelas or shanty sections of the city but lacked the resources to do so.[1] This situation of an acute imbalance between a large public demand or need for a service and the agency's miniscule resources for meeting that need is a common problem in LDCs. The solution is obvious but seemingly impossible. The agency must obtain additional resources from new sources, but what new sources can they mobilize? Foreign lending and aid agencies might be able to help in a few cases, but their resources are only enough to meet a small percentage of the needs. The only answer is that the extra resources must come from the community or people served. The key question, therefore, is how can communities be mobilized to provide labor, capital, knowledge, and/or organization to help meet the communities' needs? The Urban Community Development Project in the Municipal Secretariat for Social Development in Rio is a fairly successful example of a program that enlisted substantial community inputs in municipal service provision, and provides a model for the development community.

This case, as well as the Colombo, Sri Lanka case which follows, is an example of a government agency using community mobilization to provide a *wide* range of services in the community. In the subsequent Senegal and Burma cases, a government program mobilizes community inputs in providing a *narrow* range of services in the community. The latter two cases involve the development of program formulas which standardize a service and thereby make it widely available at low costs through minimally trained local or volunteer providers. In the former two cases the communities select the services which they need so that the agency program must be uniquely adapted to each community and can not be standardized. Thus, programs like those in Colombo and Rio de Janeiro, must be relatively organically organized and linked to many community activities. The Senegal and Burma service organizations, however, could be more mechanically organized and linked to few community activities. Nevertheless, all four cases depended heavily on community participation.

Synopsis

Rio de Janeiro, like most Latin American cities, has poor areas with minimal housing, little infrastructure, and almost no municipal services. In Brazil, these areas are called favelas and their existence demonstrated the failure of the municipal government to provide for the basic needs of burgeoning urban populations. They are acute output gaps for urban governments, which appear to be helpless before the needs of the urban poor.

Over the years a number of community groups had sprung up

in Rocinha, the largest favela in Rio, to meet some of the critical community needs. They were supported by local churches and outside institutions. Their activities included day-care centers, health posts, community schools, youth clubs, and task groups for attacking problems such as sanitation and health. These community associations also provided an ideal opportunity for a new municipal program.

In 1979 UNICEF and the Municipal Secretariat for Social Development (SMD) established an Urban Community Development Programme (UCDP) for launching services in the favelas. The strategy of UCDP was to rely on as much community participation as possible. In the first stage, an interdisciplinary team of four consultants from Rio was hired to recommend a plan of action for the UCDP, a participatory methodology for community development in favelas, and a set of specific municipal actions for Rocinha. It drew upon UNICEF's basic services strategy but had to adapt it to the urban setting. For example, UNICEF's strategy strives to increase the degree of self-sufficiency of the community, but a favela needs to obtain municipal services, not learn to do without them.

The team decided to develop the participatory methodology for community development first, then propose some specific projects to test and revise the methodology, and finally propose an appropriate structure of institutional support. The main axiom of the methodology was the strengthening of the community's capacity to plan and implement development activities. The second axiom was the maximization of direct returns to the community. Based on these two axioms the team proposed a methodology which emphasized four features. First, it would involve widespread participation of the community in the decisions of the program and give the community real decision-making power, not just the right to ratify or reject agency decisions. Second, training would be provided to community members who volunteered their labor to the programs. Third, as many community members as possible would be hired by SMD to provide the services. Fourth, the program should maximize the use of existing local resources and should strengthen existing local structures.

The team worked with the community groups in Rocinha and on the basis of community priorities recommended three pilot projects for the next stage: basic sanitation, community schools, and community health. UCDP provided funds, and an Implementation Commission, dominated by community representatives, reformulated the proposals and devised implementation plans. Most of the work was to be carried out by paid community auxiliaries. All forty seven community auxiliaries and five of the six technical assistants were recruited from the local population. Only two community technicians (a social scientist and a sanitation engineer) and one technical assistant were outsiders. In addition, the implementation of the projects involved constant voluntary participation by the community itself including the donation of services and labor.

The education team renovated a run-down school in a poor area, constructed another school in another poor area, and started teaching classes for children in the morning and for teenagers and adults at night. The construction utilized the volunteer labor and materials of residents and the assistance of experts provided by SMD. The education team also provided a two-month training program for forty-five interested potential teachers, thirty-three of whom were later selected for employment in the SMD/UNICEF project. Over time the community schools transformed their curriculum to better enable their students to enter into the public schools more successfully.

The sanitation team began with an assessment of the sanitation needs of the area. Then they developed several proposals for actions through group discussions and a workshop on sanitation problems with representatives of municipal agencies. These projects were carried out with considerable community inputs in terms of ". . . labor, organization, and administration of the work journeys, equipment, and construction materials. It is calculated that the residents absorbed 25 percent of the costs for the purchase of materials. . . . The Rua 3 project would have cost 217 percent more if it had been carried out by conventional methods."[2]

The health team worked closely with the Rocinha Health Group (RHG), a local health organization which had existed for two years, and their memberships overlapped considerably. RHG had surveyed the health needs and services of Rocinha and had developed a set of projects for their improvement. The health team, therefore, provided support for RHG's activities and took action on the remaining projects. It assisted in four municipal and three national vaccination campaigns, taught health classes to groups of pregnant women, and improved drinking water by distributing calcium hypochlorite. To conduct these activities, the team was trained in research procedures and in water purification.

During the progress of the project through four phases, several changes were made in SMD. In the first phase, the team of four consultants was established in SMD as an autonomous unit for planning the project. It answered directly to the Secretary who allowed it almost complete discretion; the major influence on this team being the community. In the second phase, the UNICEF funds were passed through SMD to an autonomous body, Fundo Rio, to implement the project. The consultancy team acted as managers of the project and established appropriate administrative mechanisms. In the third phase, four highly qualified experts in SMD were added to the consultancy team and the enlarged working group directed the SMD role in the Rocinha projects, articulated the Rocinha project with other relevant institutions, and expanded the methodology to other favelas. In the fourth phase, the UNICEF project and funds were to be ended and the Urban Community Development Programme (UCDP) was to become supported solely by SMD. The working group, minus the consultants, would continue to integrate the UCDP into SMD by advising the Secretary and the SMD project managers. The working group was also to become part of the SMD Executive Committee.

The report was written before the fourth phase but considerable results of the project were documented. The projects under the three teams were implemented and the methodology extended to other favelas. A community school was established in another favela with SMD money and the help of several Rocinha residents. The media reported on the project and news traveled through the favelas' grapevines. As a result there were many demands for SMD assistance in similar types of community development. In the area of basic sanitation SMD responded to these ". . . demands in terms of basic materials for small sanitation projects to be conducted by the communities themselves. The SMD will also help with technical assistance and general supervision of the process. There are now over 60 requests for this course of action from the favelas; mutual aid sanitation projects will be implemented in 30 favelas in 1982."[3] Finally, in the area of health, the project provided experience for the development of a community involvement program for public health clinics in low-income areas. Community auxiliaries trained by SMD and attached to clinics served as outreach agents with an education function and the Municipal Secretariat of Health provided the health care in the clinics.

Performance and Output Gaps

The output gap in this case was obvious to everyone. The municipal government provided almost no services to Rocinha and other favelas. Widespread recognition of this gap, however, did not create pressure for change until the authorities came to believe that services should be provided and could be provided. The report claims that serving low-income areas was ". . . being defined as a priority concern of the municipality. . . ."[4] so that the government thought that services should be provided. This concern probably resulted from the increased pressure from the favelas as they were becoming more organized and vocal. The government, however, did not think that more services could be provided because it lacked the resources. UNICEF, believing that more services could be provided without increasing costs if a new methodology involving community participation were used, was willing to pay for the chance to demonstrate its idea. The entire project, therefore, was an experiment in how to generate more services in low-income areas with very little increase in costs.

Environmental Context: Opportunities and Constraints

This project followed one of the cardinal principles of our strategy of organizational change. It selected a target group for the intervention which was most congenial to the change. It selected Rocinha, a fairly well-organized and active community. Prior to the project, various community associations in Rocinha were conducting a variety of community development activities. As we have said before, social collectives which have experienced considerable change are more open to change.

There were several other favorable conditions for a participatory project in Rocinha. First, the project had support from the Secretary, who gave the consulting team a free hand. Second, Rocinha was not homogeneously and desperately poor. It was heterogeneous in income and skill levels, so that, considering how poor the area was generally, it had a fair number of fairly skilled residents. Since it was not at the bottom of the barrel, a participatory program had a better chance. Third, the project had the prestige of UNICEF behind it. The community was much more receptive to the intervention because it respected UNICEF. Fourth, there is no mention in the report of racial, ethnic, or cultural conflict which can hinder community participation programs. Fifth, Rocinha was favorably located geographically because it bordered fairly wealthy areas, which provided employment opportunities for Rocinha residents and greater visibility for Rocinha's lack of municipal services.

Several constraints were mentioned in the report. First, Rocinha had hilly portions which created special problems for obtaining city water. In fact, the water system in Rio is limited to serving the areas of the city which are less than thirty meters above sea level. Second, the class separation between the consultancy team and the residents created some distrust in the residents which required special measures to dispel. Part of the social distance was professional style. The report mentions that a document produced by the consultancy team ". . . was not easily absorbed by the local community, due to its size and academic language."[5] Third, the autonomy of the consultancy team at first led to some disassociation of the staff of SMD from the project, which was viewed as a UNICEF project, until the four experts from SMD were added to the consultancy team.

Structural, Design, and Environmental Changes

This program was based on two important organizational changes: the creation of the relatively autonomous, highly placed, policy-making and planning work group in SMD and the community-dominated implementation teams. The former reported directly to the Secretary of SMD. In the first phase, it consisted of the four consultants and was viewed in SMD as a UNICEF group. Later, four SMD staff members were absorbed into the work group, which helped institutionalize it into SMD. This group orchestrated the expansion of the program from Rocinha to other favelas. Its autonomy gave it the flexibility to experiment with methods for articulating with the favelas. The second innovation was the staffing of implementation teams with as many people as possible from the favelas. This enabled the team to work closely with and to have the support of the community. These policies helped maintain the motivation of members of the favelas to participate and to provide resources, mainly consisting of their labor.

The structural changes definitely made SMD somewhat more organic. Project decisions were made by a multidisciplinary team with approval by the Secretary, on the one hand, and by the community representatives, on the other. At a lower level, the implementation teams combined community representatives who knew the community with SMD experts and project directors. Both problem-solving teams dealt with complex problems involving diverse viewpoints and specialties. They produced programs which were adapted to the special circumstances existing in Rocinha at that time. Even the planning methodology which the consultancy team developed was not a standard formula, but was a dynamic process for communities and agencies to create mutually programs adapted to the specific needs of the community.

Nature of the Approach

The intervention affected several levels of SMD. The entry was at the top, with the consultancy team that designed the project reporting directly to the Secretary. It was given a relatively free hand to experiment and develop a new participatory approach. Later, it was institutionalized as part of the Executive Committee of SMD. The greatest change, however, occurred at the middle level, where project directors had to work with implementation teams which were dominated by community representatives. This was a substantial break from previous operating procedures which were much more hierarchical and mechanical. At the lower level SMD generally supplied materials and the community supplied the labor.

This intervention used a wide range of tactics including:

1. Data collection and discussion
2. Experimentation
3. Restructuring
4. Problem-solving groups
5. Training

The tactics which were emphasized were restructuring and problem-solving groups. We have described the structural changes of the high-level consultancy team and the community-dominated implementation teams. We have not yet explained, however, the strategic importance of the community involvement in the implementation teams. Community participation in decision making generated community inputs of labor and knowledge. The project depended upon community labor and other inputs for success, and as a general rule community inputs will not be forthcoming in good measure for projects unless power is shared with the community. Also, community members have a valuable understanding of community needs and attitudes, and therefore can help fit projects to local conditions. For these reasons, decision-making power must be shared with the community to effectively provide appropriate nonstandardized services to the community.

Related to the tactic of restructuring is the tactic of problem-solving groups, which the restructuring involved. The top-level consultancy team designed and provided high-level management for the project and guided its institutionalization into the agency. Such tasks are best accomplished generally by a multidisciplinary problem-solving group, such as the consultancy team. The implementation teams had the task of guiding the implementation of specific team projects. This required some technical skill and linkages with SMD and other involved agencies. These functions were supplied by SMD team members. The task also required knowledge of the community and the ability to mobilize the participation of residents. These functions were provided by the community team members. This fruitful combination of experts and residents is noted in the report: "Although technical expertise was of considerable import in the proposals produced, the community auxiliaries' knowledge of local conditions (both physical and social) was also fundamental."[6]

Data collection was important to this intervention because the implementation teams needed to know the needs of the community and their priorities. The project had scarce resources and had to direct them to priority matters. This was particularly true of the health program which had to assess the health needs of the community residents and their rates of utilization of services. Before the project, a group of concerned community members had surveyed the four local clinics and found that together they only offered fifty six hours per week of medical services to sixty thousand to eighty thousand residents. The project itself conducted health surveys of families to guide its health program and devised careful descriptions of environmental and social conditions to guide its sanitation program. These data-collection efforts accomplished two purposes: they documented the magnitude of the output gaps and they contributed to the design of effective projects when used in conjunction with group discussions.

Most of what the Urban Community Development Programme did were pilot projects. Each implementation team selected projects to implement which not only sought to accomplish specific needed tasks, but also would demonstrate the usefulness of the participatory methodology of the project. Furthermore, the project it-self was a pilot project.

Another common tactic in this project was training. Residents were trained in sanitation and health, auxiliaries were trained for their employment service, implementation teams were trained in research methods, and teacher candidates were trained to teach in the project schools. The project depended upon community actions but these actions are more fruitful if the actors are given more skills first.

The main resource used in this intervention was community inputs of labor and knowledge. The project helped the community provide services to itself. It was not an expensive project because it was designed to increase government services without increasing government expenditures. Outside funds were required, however, to pay for the experimentation required to develop the new, more productive methodology. The project also needed strong support from the top.

Results

The report does not document carefully the results but it describes the rapidly growing demand for similar services from other favelas. The project was perceived as successful, became institutionalized in SMD, and was beginning to diffuse to other ministries. In fact, the report gives a glowing report of the project, but we should note that the authors of the report are the four original consultants.

Conclusion

This is an important case because it describes an apparently successful effort to generate more services in low-income urban communities without increasing costs significantly. The methodology is designed to generate substantial increases in community inputs, mostly labor and knowledge of the community. Structurally it requires implementation teams dominated by community representatives; a high-level multidisciplinary task force to design, manage, and link the program; and sufficient program autonomy to experiment. (The last feature may diminish when new methodology is more widely institutionalized.) This project's guiding principle is that power must be shared with the community in order to obtain high levels of community participation. This case demonstrates that a participatory methodology can greatly increase the production of services in low-income areas where almost no services were being provided before. We shall see that this principle is the dominant lesson of this chapter because it recurs in most of the other cases.

Environmental Health and Community Development Project (Sri Lanka)

Colombo, Sri Lanka had 585,776 people living in fourteen square miles in 1981, with about half of the population living in slums and shanty settlements.[7] The conditions in these slums were horrid. Infant and childhood deaths were significantly higher there than in the rest of the country. Gastroenteritis was common and caused about one-sixth of the deaths suffered by small children. These slum areas also had high rates of cholera, typhoid fever, and infectious hepatitis. Very few households had piped water and most used roadside taps, which were not widely available. The report describes the miserable conditions of the few sanitation facilities as follows:

> Almost none of the slum and shanty areas was sewered. The sewer pipeline serving the city today was laid in 1906, with no comprehensive overhauling since then. The available latrines were constructed years ago, and were found to be dilapidated due to inadequate or no maintenance. The city had over 5000 bucket privies, which posed a great challenge to the municipal conservancy services. Many of the gardens [neighborhoods] had no toilets at all, and while the adults were forced to use a public lavatory on the road, the children simply used the open drains running through the compound.[8]

It seemed impossible for the Colombo government even to begin to deal with these conditions. What could be done? Additional resources had to be obtained somehow, so the Common Amenities Board (CAB), a statutory body under the Ministry of Local Government, Housing, and Construction, requested assistance from UNICEF for improving the amenities of these slums. UNICEF provided small funds and some amenities were built. These facilities, however, were not maintained. When the Board requested more funds for a five-year program, it recognized that a new approach was necessary. The community had to be mobilized to maintain the facilities. In the early stages of planning, the community mobilization feature was tacked on to a basically traditional top-down mechanical approach. In the later stages of the implementation of the project, however, community mobilization was the main feature of the project. In the end this project demonstrated the lesson of UCDP in Rio that additional services and facilities can be provided with little extra expense if community inputs are mobilized.

There were two major differences between the Colombo and Rio UNICEF projects. First, Rocinha had a number of active community associations and the slums of Colombo had almost none; in other words, Rocinha was partially mobilized, while the Colombo slums were not. Second, the critical component of the Colombo project was the "Health Wardens," recruited and trained specifically for this project, whose task was to mobilize the Colombo slums; but the critical component of the Rio project was the three project-implementation teams, which were dominated by community representatives. The implementation teams capitalized on the existing community associations while the Health Wardens had to create community associations.

Synopsis

In 1979 UNICEF funded the Environmental Health and Community Development Project (EHCOP) to upgrade sanitation facilities and improve health in the slums and shanties of Colombo. The project established a three-tier community development council system, with a council for each "garden" (neighborhood). Representatives from garden councils formed a district council, while representatives from district councils formed a citywide council. The major implementing agencies were the Municipal Public Health Department of Colombo, which recruited and trained a cadre of young Health Wardens, and the Common Amenities Board, which provided facilities throughout the city. The Health Wardens helped the communities (gardens) organize community development councils to identify their health and sanitation needs. Community leaders were also identified and given some training in workshops. Community Development Councils selected and implemented health and sanitation projects on a self-help basis and petitioned the government for badly needed amenities.

EHCOP was designed by government officials and UNICEF staff, without any inputs from beneficiaries. It was designed, however, to receive considerable feedback from the communities when they had become organized and were represented by the three levels of councils. The first step, therefore, was for the Health Warden field workers to mobilize the communities. They were given two months of preservice training in a wide variety of health and sanitation subjects including ". . . primary health care, health education, nutrition, physiology, garbage disposal, environmental sanitation, parasitic diseases, common infections in the city, pest control, social diseases, and family planning. . . ."[9] Later, they were given a seven-day inservice training in community leadership and organization. They frequently visited the slums of their wards to gain rapport with the residents. They began discussions of community health and sanitation needs, and helped the residents organize a council to be a part of the new Community Development Council scheme of the Municipal Public Health Department. "At the outset, it was difficult to sell the idea to the communities, but once the idea gathered momentum, requests came in regularly from gardens for assistance in organizing a council."[10] In the first year the project established more than one hundred Community Development Councils (CDCs).

The second step was to identify and train community leaders. More than one thousand leaders were identified and given leadership training in one-to-three-day workshops or orientation courses.

> Under their leadership, the Community Development Councils are responsible for implementing the project activities on a self-help basis. This includes the maintenance of common amenities such as water taps and toilet facilities, the collection and use of pooled resources for environmental sanitation, immunization, and nutrition and health education. . . . The meetings are open to any residents who wish to attend, and serve as a forum to discuss problems of common interest, to review their involvement in community welfare work, and to plan future community social development activities.[11]

The third step was to create District Development Councils (DDCs) under the District Health Officers in each of the six health districts of Colombo. Each DDC included the Assistant Health Education Officer, the District Municipal Engineer, elected representatives from each CDC, and representatives from interested voluntary organizations. The DDCs coordinated the activities of various departments with the CDCs' projects, and removed bottlenecks and delays in the delivery of services to the communities. They also ". . . have assured more frequent visits by different officials to the slums and shanties than was the pattern previously. In addition, these councils organize inter-ward programs aimed at improving the health and sanitation conditions, and the cultural and social lives of the people."[12]

The fourth step was to create a City Development Council, which would include elected representatives from the DDCs and be a policy-making body. Top government officials objected to this much decentralization of power and vetoed the idea. The community leaders, however, gave an ultimatum—unless they were allowed to participate at the city level, they would *not* participate at the community level—with the result that the City Development Council was established.

With the three-tier council system in place, the municipal agencies formulated an Annual Work Plan at the beginning of each year. This was reviewed by the City Development Council, which noted any suggested changes. Progress reports were reviewed monthly by the agency officials on the City Development Council and the full Council with DDC representatives reviewed the semiannual progress reports. Information on this meeting was passed back to the CDCs for the coordination of community activities with the government's activities.

Performance and Output Gaps

The output gap was obvious. Almost no services were provided to the slums, and the facilities that had been installed were in disrepair. The Common Amenities Board, which supplied facilities throughout the city, recognized its failure to provide adequate amenities in these areas and wanted to close this output gap but lacked the resources to do so. It sought external funds from UNICEF and with these funds provided some amenities. These amenities were not maintained, however, and another output gap was recognized. It was concluded that the communities must help maintain facilities for amenity projects to be successful and that a new type of program was needed. (In other words, there was a common recognition for the need for organizational change in the direction of greater community participation.) The project ended up with more participation than it bargained for but only because the communities became mobilized, and the results were quite positive.

There was another widely recognized output gap that created considerable pressure for change. This gap was the high death rate and especially the infant mortality rate in the slums. A survey in 1978 documented the deplorable health and sanitation conditions and the high dropout rate from school in these areas. It is hard for a government to continue to do nothing in the light of such reports. Furthermore, the central government had shifted its own development goals to emphasize social development, which made a participatory project more acceptable and output gaps in the area of sanitation and health for the poor more visible.

Environmental Context: Opportunities and Constraints

The main feature of the environmental context in the Colombo case was the lack of adequate resources in the municipal government to provide much service to the slums. This situation also existed in Rio and in many cities of the Third World. A major difference in the environmental context of Rio, however, was the much greater degree of organization of Rocinha, which presented a grand opportunity for a participatory program there. The lack of organization in the Colombo slums was a severe constraint, which had to be overcome by the Health Wardens before the project could move on to concrete actions.

Three other conditions provided opportunities for a participatory program. First, there was considerable equality in the slums of Colombo, even if it was an equality of poverty. Equality of poverty tends to breed mutual self-help in thousands of little ways among people who know each other, which made organizing and mobilizing the slums easier. Second, the development literature had been promoting participatory programs for some time and the designers of this project were influenced by these views. Third, there is no mention in the report of political interference. The project was somehow insulated from much of the political influence that afflicts many urban projects. The funds were earmarked for urban slums and, since UNICEF remained continuously involved, there was less opportunity for diversion of funds than normally occurs in LDCs.

Three conditions provided constraints to a participatory project. First, the slums had major ethnic and religious divisions among Tamils, Sinhalese, Muslims, Hindus, Buddhists, and Christians. At the same time these groups were relatively well integrated for an Asian country, but such divisions were bound to hinder interethnic organizations. Second, the slum residents were very ignorant of health principles and sanitation practices. "Total ignorance of and/or indifference to health care and sanitation practices was considered to constitute an obstacle to any effort to improve the living conditions and health status of these communities."[13] Third, the top-level officials resisted community representation on the City Development Council, but the district and community councils had enough power to overcome this resistance.

Structural, Design, and Environmental Changes

The major environmental change was the creation of the three-tier system of development councils. In two-and-a-half years, the project helped create 291 Community Development Councils covering about 15 percent of Colombo's slum and shanty population. Above the CDCs, the project created six District Development Councils, and above these the City Development Council. The development council system institutionalized community participation in the selection and design of the projects of participating agencies for the slums. This represented significant decentralization and was resisted by top officials who were losing some relative power. At the City Development Council-level this system allowed representatives of the communities to monitor projects and feed back their opinions to the directors of projects. In summary, several highly hierarchical and top-down municipal agencies were changed to include some bottom-up mechanisms with more feedback, becoming more flexible; and, furthermore, some power was devolved to the mobilized communities. These changes made the agencies slightly more organic.

Another structural change for the Municipal Public Health Department was the addition of a new occupation, the community organizers called Health Wardens. Not only did the ninety-eight Health Wardens mobilize the communities, they also linked the Public Health Department to the community and facilitated the implementation of self-help, agency, and mixed self-help/agency projects. The addition and integration of an occupational specialty into an agency makes it more organic and able to deal with more complex tasks.

Nature of the Approach

The intervention level was environmental and organizationwide. A three-tier council system for community participation was created in the environment of the municipal agencies and the agencies were changed to be responsive to community inputs. The changes were made at both the top and bottom of the organization. Some of the power of the top officials was shared with the City Development Council and top officials had to become more responsive to the demands of communities. At the bottom level community organizers were hired and integrated into the organization.

The major tactic used in this intervention was restructuring, involving the system of councils and the community organizers described above. The Municipal Public Health Department became more organic and all of the participating agencies became more decentralized and responsive to local communities.

Three other tactics were heavily utilized: data collection, training, and group decision making. The report mentions numerous surveys of the needs and conditions of the slum residents, which were used to guide the design of specific projects. The Health Wardens conducted health surveys and devised immunization and education programs on the basis of the data collected. Other agencies also conducted community needs studies. One survey by the Women's Bureau deserves special mention because it was conducted by low-income women who had been trained by the Women's Bureau.

Training was an important tactic at lower levels and in the community, although not at higher levels. The Health Wardens had two months of preservice training in practical health and sanitation matters, and had a seven-day inservice training in community leadership and organization. The one thousand community leaders were trained in one-to-three-day workshops on community leadership. Such training is very important because a major problem for many community organizations and associations is the lack of leadership and managerial skills. If anything, the community leaders in Colombo probably should have had more training. Training was also provided to community residents on specific subjects relating to the areas of service of specific agencies. For example, a nutrition program taught mothers recipes for inexpensive and nutritious foods, as well as the hygenic preparation of these foods.

Group decision making was another important tactic. The CDCs decided what local actions should be taken and what requests to make for new amenities. We doubt whether these CDCs acted as true problem-solving groups because they were not trained for that task; rather, they seemed to have chosen among well-known options. The City Development Council may have acted as a problem-solving group, but the report is not clear on its mode of operation. In any case, this intervention did not feature problem-solving groups, but did feature decision-making groups.

Results

As a result of the program, sanitation and health needs greatly improved (from a very low level), and the communities were taking better care of their own needs. Furthermore, through the three levels of councils, the poor participated in government decisions affecting their lives: The councils had been given real power and their recommendations were accepted.

The specific results, after only two years, were impressive and covered a wide variety of areas. They included widespread immunization, health and nutrition education, and the addition of many cement garbage bins, 543 new stand pipes for drinking water, 723 latrines, and 340 bathrooms, with 2200 bucket latrines converted to sanitary latrines. The motivational consequences of these visible signs of progress were naturally profound. The extra resources also helped provide a great deal of motivation in the community, with the financial support of UNICEF helping enormously. It then became the job of the Community Development Councils to help keep all the new facilities properly maintained and to provide individual and community cleanup efforts.

If the participatory approach had not been used the results would have been less and they would have been different. The influence of the council system redirected the project activities and made them more relevant. Furthermore, participation itself should be viewed as a positive result. These results are summed up in the report as follows:

> An immunization coverage of 80 percent in 23 council areas, the mass legalization of unregistered marriages in the slums, and the efforts to obtain national identity cards for those who had none were direct results of the people's participation in decision making at these three-tier council meetings. In addition, perhaps for the first time in the history of local government in Sri Lanka, the citizens have been able to participate in the planning of programme activities to enable the municipal authorities to deliver the basic services that they really want.[14]

Conclusion

This project illustrates the importance of independent community associations for providing services to poor areas. In this instance they were created by the project itself. To accomplish this objective, community organizers had to be hired and trained. The project also illustrates that the linkage between agencies and community associations may require negotiation for the agencies to share sufficient power with the communities. Agencies want the benefits of community help and even advice but they usually want professionals to make the final decisions. In Colombo, the communities would not accept this pattern and demanded real power. Independent voluntary associations representing the communities helped overcome the resistance of top officials. When power was shared, the project produced considerable results with incredible speed: productivity increased substantially and the new model for servicing slums was diffused to other cities.

Rural Health Huts (Senegal)

The Sine Saloum Rural Health Project (SSRHP) was a more radical community mobilization project than the UCDP in Rio or the EHCOP in Colombo.[15] UCDP built upon community associations in Rocinha and hired community residents in the provision of services to the community. EHCOP mobilized communities into voluntary associations to help select, plan, implement, and maintain services and facilities provided by the municipal government. The contribution of the communities was large in both of these projects, but the role of the government was also large. In the health hut project in the Sine Saloum region of Senegal, however, the community did practically everything after the health hut staff was trained. The Senegal government only provided some supervision.

SSRHP was designed to enable the communities to serve themselves without continuous government assistance. To accomplish this, the Ministry of Health in the Sine Saloum region was restructured by adding a new level of health service at the bottom. Before SSRHP, the Ministry of Health (MOH) had roughly three levels: hospitals at the regional level (eight regions), health centers at the departmental level (nine health centers in Sine Saloum), and health posts at the Communaute Rurale level (seventy-nine health posts in Sine Saloum). SSRHP was to add six hundred village health huts to form a level beneath that of the health posts. The top three levels were staffed by permanent government employees and provided free health services. SSRHP was to mobilize the villages, providing three villagers from each village for brief training by MOH as part-time health workers and creating the health hut. Each village also was to provide a health hut management committee which received brief training from the Promotion Humaine, an agency which was responsible for community development. Thereafter the health hut was essentially on its own. As a result, health huts greatly expanded health services in Sine Saloum with very little expansion of government expense—these services were partly provided by voluntary labor and partly paid for by users.

Synopsis

The Sine Saloum region of Senegal had very poor health conditions and the government provided very little health care there. "Most rural people do not receive even the most rudimentary modern health care because there are not enough Health Posts, the lowest level of government facilities, and these do not receive adequate financial support."[16] In fact, there was only one physician for every 77,000 persons and only one nurse for every 4,800 persons. The $5 million Sine Saloum Rural Health Project (SSRHP), funded largely by a $3.4 million grant from USAID, was initiated in 1977 to provide badly needed health care with very little increase in government staff.

> [SSRHP] . . . was to create a network of *self-supporting* rural "health huts"—i.e., village-based health facilities. Active participation of villagers was sought for constructing the huts, encouraging use of the new services, and for payment of salary to part-time village health workers (a health assistant, trained midwife, and sanitarian) and payment for drugs received. The huts would provide the basic, primary health care services that would address the major causes of poor health in the region and become part of a comprehensive primary health care system. Cases requiring greater medical knowledge or skill could be referred to "health posts" at the next higher level of the hierarchy.[17]

Originally, the project was to be overseen by a Project Executive Committee, chaired by the Governor of Sine Saloum, and run by the Project Director under the direct supervision of the Médicin

Chef du Région. However, the Executive Committee and Project Director were never appointed; instead, "the Regional Governor has apparently taken direct personal charge of project administration."[18] As a result the project was poorly managed and government support and supervision of the health huts was very inadequate.

At the bottom level, SSRHP worked as follows. Project staff visited villages and sold them on the health hut program. The village built the hut, organized the management committee, and selected the three part-time health workers. MOH trained the health workers and Promotion Humaine trained the management committee. The health hut functioned under the medical supervision of the nearest Communaute Rurale health post which was headed by a nurse.

USAID evaluated the project in 1980. More than four hundred villages had constructed health huts and organized health committees, and hundreds of villagers had been trained as health workers. The project, however, was a failure and nearing collapse. Patients were not being charged enough to cover salaries nor the cost of medicine. Many health huts ran out of medicines and closed. It was also plagued by other severe problems. Supervision was inadequate, some huts were located too close to health posts, which distributed free medicine, and attrition among health workers was high.

As a consequence of the output gap documented in the 1980 evaluation, the program was redesigned. A Project Director was assigned; fees were set more realistically, and the Ministry of Health charged fees for medicine at the health posts; and much greater control over the health hut was conferred on the village health committees. As a result of these changes, "Today [1983] villages in Sine Saloum are covering 100 percent of the direct costs of primary health care services at the community level: villagers are paying for medicines, compensating the community health workers, and maintaining the village health huts."[19] The program was a success and served as a model for similar programs in other countries. According to Bloom, the key to its success was community management, which was facilitated by the training of all members of the village health committees in health hut operation. Thus, the villages provided all of the components of the program that they could, and the Promotion Humaine and the Ministry of Health provided the training that the management committee and health workers needed.

Performance and Output Gaps

There were two widely perceived gaps that motivated the creation of SSRHP and its reorganization. The first was the critical shortage of health care in Sine Saloum described previously. The second was the failure of SSRHP to resolve this shortage due to decapitalization of the health huts' inventories, lack of supervision, health worker turnover, and other problems. A thorough evaluation of the project by USAID in 1980 documented the performance and output gaps. Sometimes such reports are suppressed, but not this time.

> The 1980 Sine-Saloum evaluation had far-reaching effects. Rather than ignoring its conclusions and recommendations, the AID mission in Senegal and the Government of Senegal immediately undertook a series of additional reviews and rapidly instituted corrective measures. Among the steps taken were a review of the project by Senegal's National Assembly, and the appointment of new project staff—including project managers from both countries. The project was then redesigned to incorporate the evaluation's recommendations.[20]

Environmental Context: Opportunities and Constraints

There were many more constraints operating in this case than opportunities. First, Senegal was in severe financial difficulty with a large national debt, few natural resources, foreign exchange problems, and budget deficits. Second, the proportion of the national budget devoted to health had declined from a high of 9.2 percent in 1969/70 to 6.0 percent in 1978/79; thus, health programs in Senegal were already under stress. (This constraint, however, also provided an opportunity for a project which would expand health services without expanding costs.) Third, free medicine was available at the health posts which were normally only five to fifteen kilometers away from the health huts. Since the health huts had to charge for medicine to survive, they had trouble competing with the health posts. Fourth, cultural attitudes toward women were a constraint. There were few women on the village management committees even though they were the primary clients of the health huts. Later, in a way which was consistent with traditional values, the project reform corrected this problem by creating women's committees parallel to those of the men. Fifth, the centralization of government agencies in Senegal constrained this village-based program. The personal direction of the program by the Governor was not an asset but a liability because it resulted in ineffective management. Sixth, the limited adult literacy in French in rural villages hindered the project. "The project designers decided that health workers should be literate in French to facilitate training, bookkeeping and transmission of information."[21] (These health workers, however, were upwardly mobile, younger, and relatively unattached to the village, so that many of them left relatively quickly.) When many of these problems were corrected by the reorganization and reform of the project, SSRHP began to succeed.

One other constraint, which would have doomed SSRHP after USAID funding ceased, was the lack of transferability between line items in the MOH budget. As a result, the MOH budget for personnel for the health hut program would barely increase and could be absorbed by MOH, but other budget items would increase greatly and would not be absorbed by MOH. The 1980 USAID evaluation reported the following:

> At the Sine Saloum regional level the Common Expenditures budget item would have to increase by 310 percent when A.I.D. funding ceases. Similar large percentage increases will occur throughout the detailed budget line items on which the project depends for the supervision and support function. Resources to cover such large increases appear unlikely to be available. [An evaluator,] Over's conclusion is: "The result will be that the Project will be starved of supervision from above and thus will function poorly or cease to function at all."[22]

One opportunity was the glaring, documented imbalance between health care services in different parts of Senegal. The Cap Vert Region, which included Dakar, received 45 percent of the 1973-1977 health budgets but contained only 19 percent of the population. In contrast, the Sine Saloum region received only 9 percent of the budgets but contained 20 percent of the population. In fact, Cap Vert had twenty times as many doctors per hundred thousand population as did Sine Saloum. An inequity of this magnitude cried out for redress and mobilized considerable support for the health huts project. When it was evident that SSRHP was failing, the national government was quite concerned and acted quickly and decisively to correct the problems.

Structural, Design, and Environmental Changes

SSRHP restructured Senegal's MOH by adding relatively autonomous village health huts at the bottom of the organization.

Since these health huts were under the direction of the village management committees, and only given mild supervision by the nearby health post nurse, this was a radically decentralized service. However, for such a radically decentralized service to succeed, there has to be adequate training. Training was provided but more was needed, especially in health hut management. The reorganization and reform of SSRHP provided this much needed additional training. Even though SSRHP was radically decentralized at the lower levels, the MOH management of SSRHP was highly centralized in the beginning under the control of the Governor. The reform decentralized the MOH top management of the project, thereby making it more effective. The reform also decentralized management at the local level. In the original project, the health post ". . . over[saw] the activities of the Village Management Committees, receive[d] money from them for medicine resupply, and decide[d] how the village health workers [would] be paid."[23] The reform allowed the village health committees to keep all their income and to manage their own affairs without outside control. The health workers, however, were assisted by periodic medical supervisory visits.

The major structural change in MOH caused by SSRHP was neither organic nor mechanical; rather, it was a craft change. SSRHP added a bottom level to MOH of craft organizations (technically they were not full organizations by our definition). At first, significant control was maintained by MOH, which incorporated the craft units into the mechanical structure of MOH. Later, when the village health huts were more autonomous, they fit more truly the craft form. The craft involved was nursing, but, since only a small range of the nursing profession was involved, we call this the truncated-craft form. We point out that this form is not found in Western contingency theory. We "discovered" it in our study of Third World cases. In fact, we claim that it is an important finding because it is an organizational form which has great promise for Third World settings, involving as they do the contingency of a severe lack of resources. This theme will be discussed in Chapter 5.

The other major change occurred in the environment of the health huts. MOH took the politically unpopular step of charging uniform user fees at all levels of the health care system. This put MOH on a better financial footing and financially saved SSRHP.

Nature of the Approach

The intervention level was mainly at the bottom and in the environment. A bottom level of village health huts was added below the health post level and the communities were mobilized to build, run, and manage the health huts. The intervention levels for the reorganization were top, bottom, and environmental. The top management of the project was removed from the Governor's hands and given to a full time project Director. The village health huts were made more autonomous and the authority of the village management committees was greatly strengthened. A common fee structure was instituted for the provision of health services at all levels of the health care system, enabling the health huts to compete.

The tactic of change was primarily restructuring, as described above, and, secondarily, training. To institute the new structure of health care the project staff served as community mobilizers, MOH provided modest training for the health workers, and Promotion Humaine provided modest training for the village management committees. The reorganization involved further restructuring to a more decentralized system of health care, with greater amounts of training. Also, in the reorganized system the village management committees had to serve as simple problem-solving groups.

Data collection was a crucial tactic for bringing about the reorganization. The very negative evaluation report documented a very wide performance and output gap and stimulated other evaluations which concurred. As a result, bold major changes were made in the project. It should be pointed out also that the evaluation was more than mere data collection; it contained analyses of the problems and recommended solutions. The evaluation team, therefore, worked as a problem-solving group.

It is worth noting the absence of two tactics: decree and experimentation. The health hut system could not be decreed because it depended upon voluntary participation; instead, it depended upon persuasion by the community mobilizers. On the other hand, experimentation was both possible and desirable but not used. The evaluation report severely criticized the project for this failure.

> Although the amount of the grant is relatively small, the scale of the project, with 600 individual units, is very large and administratively difficult. To jump into such an undertaking without a thorough pilot project is folly.[24]

Many of the problems which afflicted the project would have arisen in a pilot project and revisions could have occurred without the widespread disappointment the original project produced when so many health huts closed. The villagers supplied materials and labor to build the huts and their pride was hurt when those huts were abandoned.

The resources used most heavily in this intervention were the voluntary labor from the communities and the financing of the services by users' fees. These substituted for MOH's scarce financial resources. At first, the voluntary labor was too unskilled to manage successfully the health huts and the fees were set too low to pay for the service. As a result, the health huts failed. Later, the fees were set higher and the volunteer village management committee members were better trained, and the project succeeded. In one sense, power was another resource which was used because power was shared with the village to obtain village inputs.

Results

The results of the original project were a flash in the pan. After a slow start it had rapidly picked up momentum—huts were opened in more than four hundred villages and thousands of people received health services. Nevertheless, half of the huts early to open were closed by 1980, and most huts would have closed shortly thereafter if drastic changes had not been made. In contrast, the reorganized project was quite successful. By 1983, health huts that were 100 percent self-supporting in terms of the direct costs of medicine, health workers, and health hut maintenance were operating in over 370 villages. MOH had only had to pay for training and supervision. In fact, SSRHP became so successful it has been diffused to other countries.

Conclusion

SSRHP demonstrates that services of resource-scarce agencies to poor communities can be greatly multiplied by mobilizing and training the community to provide the simplest of these services for themselves. A great deal of power must be shared with the community and adequate managerial and technical training must be provided to make such a community self-service program work. The early project had insufficient power sharing and training, and failed. The revised project had sufficient power sharing and training, and succeeded. Therefore, the type of linkage between service agency and community associations is critical.

National Literacy Campaign (Burma)

The National Literacy Campaign (NLC) is an extreme example of a government accomplishing a great deal on a shoestring budget.[25]

The government of Burma wanted its entire population to be literate. This meant teaching over a million illiterates to read—a very large task, requiring large sums of money if done by paid teachers. Instead, Burma mobilized over two hundred thousand volunteer teachers who were given room and board by host villages. The production of learning materials was the major expense of NLC for the government, but all authors whose works were used waived their remuneration, and the sale of postcards, publications, flags, and other items was used to finance the printing of materials.

The NLC's organizational form was a mixed mechanical-organic national organization which trained and dispatched extension workers with truncated-craft-type skills. It also linked with national-, district-, township-, and village-coordinating committees. The design of the program, the creation of materials, and the development of a system for teaching reading were created by organic organizations, working groups, or individual experts. This was the organic portion of NLC. The recruiting, training, assigning, and managing of the volunteers and the administration of the other activities were done by a mechanical bureaucracy. At the bottom of the organization the volunteer teachers carried out the routinized teaching program under the supervision of the village rather than the NLC organization. The teachers performed the craft of elementary teaching, but not the full range of the craft—they only taught reading and the recognition of numbers. We call this a truncated-craft activity.

Both this and the Senegal case demonstrate that tremendous increases in productivity at very small costs can be gained by using truncated-craft workers on a volunteer or low pay basis. The workers have to be trained in a simple skill that provides a widely needed and desired service, while some form of radically decentralized management and support must be provided. The latter was provided by the villagers in both these cases.

Synopsis

Education has always been emphasized in Burma since independence in 1948. When the Revolutionary Council came to power in 1962, it made even a stronger commitment to educating everyone to increase their dignity and enhance their livelihood. This commitment eventually was translated into the National Literacy Campaign (NLC), after several pilot programs developed an effective methodology based on volunteer literacy teachers. The first initiative was taken by a college professor and his students in 1964. He trained them to teach reading to adults and they went to rural villages during their summer vacation to work with illiterates. In 1966 this program grew into a national movement which was centrally directed.

> Up to 1968, experiments were conducted throughout the country regarding the mode of organization, the mode of study— preparation of teaching materials, method of teaching, production of learning aids, determination of optimum period required to become literate, and the follow-up measures to avoid the relapse into illiteracy, etc.[26]

NLC finally selected a seven-week program involving no more than two hours a day and a primer that utilized words and events common to village life.

In 1969 the Central Literacy Supervision and Coordination Committee (CLSCC) of NLC selected the Meiktila district as a pilot area for the total eradication of illiteracy in one year. The next year two more districts were selected for saturated coverage, four more in 1971, and four more in 1972. In this way the country was eventually covered. The program was strongly promoted and given much publicity in the target areas; national and target district leaders were involved. The campaign was made a high-profile event in order to motivate village participation and to pressure illiterates to enter the program as their national duty.

CLSCC, which guided the NLC projects, contained members from the involved ministries and from universities, peasants' and workers' councils, the media, and other organizations. Similar committees were formed at the district township and village level to provide coordination, support, and supervision.

The volunteer teachers were university students who would work with volunteer village teachers and literates. The latter two groups gradually took over when the college students returned to school. The students paid their own transportation costs and depended on the village for their support. They were very dedicated and enthusiastic, and made the program work.

Performance and Output Gaps

In this case, the output gap was not due to the failure of the educational system, but due to a new definition of national goals. The educational system was doing as well as was expected of it, and was even doing better than other educational systems of countries at

similar income levels. The new government, however, set the elimination of illiteracy as a national goal and thereby created a wide
output gap. On the other hand, the new government was not going
to give the Ministry of Education large funds to achieve the goal of
full literacy. A different, relatively cost-free educational system
had to be created to close the new gap, and the volunteer students
did the job.

Environmental Context: Opportunities and Constraints

There were several cultural factors which were particularly conducive to a voluntary educational campaign. We have mentioned the
historical emphasis on education (e.g., 56 percent male literacy
rate as early as 1930) and the extraordinary emphasis upon education for all the people by the Revolutionary Council. Strong educational values are not just the ideology of political leaders, but are
based also on widespread religious and philosophical ideals.
Burma had a tradition of its people participating in education so
that parents, students, and communities commonly contributed
labor and some money to build or repair schools and other community facilities. In fact, most Burmese believed that they had a duty
to contribute in some way (usually via volunteer labor) to the bet-
terment or maintenance of the community and its facilities. NLC
channeled these motivations into the elimination of illiteracy. The
students volunteered to teach and paid their own travel expenses;
the community offered to provide for the volunteers; and even the
illiterates felt a duty to participate in the program and try to become literate. Another opportunity was the Burmese language itself, which is relatively easy to learn to read.

There were two main constraints: the lack of resources to provide paid teachers to teach literacy, and motivation, since this was
a voluntary program based on volunteer teachers and volunteer
students. The tradition of volunteerism mentioned previously and
the high purpose of the movement motivated the teachers. The
greater difficulty was convincing the last ten percent of illiterates
to make the substantial effort required to become literate. This
problem was dealt with by the movement fanfare, which included
media hype and public preaching on literacy as a civic duty: Becoming literate was portrayed as helping to build the nation. The
teachers made special appeals describing the advantages of reading religious literature and instructions for practical affairs. Thus,
national and traditional values and self-interest were used to moti-

vate participation. The fact that the teachers were volunteers who were sacrificing to help others also helped them persuade many illiterates to participate.

There was one other, apparently major problem—the difficulty of educating the practically uneducatable—but this constraint was largely defined away.

> Since it was not possible to teach everyone to read and write it was ultimately decided that in assessing total literacy, people who were extremely weak and feeble, those who migrated to other villages or towns, and those unable to learn due to mental retardation, should be excluded from the list of potential learners. A village was considered to have attained total literacy if 96 percent of the remainder became literate.[27]

Structural, Design, and Environmental Changes

The report on NLC does not clearly describe its organizational structure, but it does identify four basic components. First, the national administration was centralized and mechanical. Second, the creative work of developing materials and curriculum was performed by teams of university professors who donated their services, making this component of NLC organic. Third, policy/coordinating committees were established at all levels. It is not clear how much they worked as problem-solving groups, but it is clear that they mobilized political support and secured the involvement of relevant groups and organizations. Fourth, the program was implemented at the village level by volunteer teachers under the control of the village, which made the program highly decentralized. (We have identified this latter component as truncated craft in form.) NLC, therefore, was a mechanical organization with organic and craft components.

NLC's organizational structure was relatively unique in two ways. First, it involved an extraordinary degree of participation in terms of both volunteered labor and in decision making and control. Second, it was both centralized and decentralized. The administrative structure, training of volunteer teachers, and uniform materials and curriculum—developed at the central level and used throughout the nation in conjunction with a standardized teaching program—were centralized. Implementation, on the other hand, was decentralized to the village level where the literacy teachers were almost entirely responsible to the township and village leaders.

This case also involved substantial change in the environment. It mobilized inputs from professors, volunteer teachers, villagers, the media, political leaders, and numerous organizations. It promoted the literacy campaign as a noble cause and the response was extraordinary. The program was completely dependent upon the contributions of the villages, since they absorbed the total costs of the volunteer teachers. They did this by rotating the visiting teachers in ones and twos among families for housing and having them eat different meals in different homes. The burden was thereby widely shared.

Nature of the Approach

NLC involved new organizational structures at all levels and in the environment. It developed from small-scale nongovernmental literacy projects to become a national campaign. Materials, curriculum, and teaching methods were developed experimentally for small projects and then one set was selected and decreed for uniform use throughout the country. Temporary volunteer teachers were sent to villages, which supported and directed them. NLC thus involved many organizational innovations and changes at all levels.

The five predominant tactics used were: (1) Restructure, (2) Research, (3) Experiment, (4) Training, (5) Group decision making. NLC's structure has been described previously. It was unique among the programs in the Ministry of Education in the system of multiple-tiered policy committees, volunteer curriculum development groups, volunteer teachers, and community support and control at the local level.

The main role of research was the development of materials, curriculum, and the teaching method. Research was crucial in one other decision. The Central Literacy Supervision and Coordination Committee chose the Meiktila district for the first total saturation effort to eradicate illiteracy, but it had first researched which district would provide the best opportunity of success. CLSCC wanted an early success to create enthusiasm for the program because it judged that a poor start would lead to demoralization and the failure of the campaign.

Experiment, training, group decision making were standard features of NLC. The period from 1964 through 1969 was largely experimental and involved many pilot projects. Even the saturated

coverage of one district in 1969 was a pilot project to see if saturation was more effective than dispersing the teachers. Training was
critical for making the volunteer college students effective reading
instructors. Group decision making was employed by the countless
committees involved in NLC. These committees also may have
done group problem solving but the report is not clear on this point.
Most aspects of the program were routinized, which would have left
relatively small room for group problem solving.

The main resource used by NLC was the two hundred thousand
volunteer teachers. Another resource was moral influence, a type
of symbolic power. Most of the work on the campaign was done for
symbolic rather than monetary rewards.

Results

Between 1965 and 1974, NLC helped over a million illiterates become literate. It was widely acclaimed as a success and won international recognition. NLC had provided a large amount of additional educational service for very little cost to the government.

Conclusions

NLC devolved more control of its program to communities than was
true in the Brazil, Sri Lanka, and Senegal cases. Additionally, NLC
relinquished control over its lowest-level workers, the volunteer
teachers. These power concessions were necessary, however, to obtain the inputs from the community and the participation of
teachers on which the project was totally dependent. Power sharing
proved to be a very profitable exchange; it allowed much to be accomplished with very little resources and provided an example
worth emulating by others.

One feature of this case was somewhat unique for highly participatory programs. The NLC volunteers who provided the services to the communities came from outside of the communities.
Most participatory projects train locals for simple service and construction tasks, as was the case in the Sine Saloum Health Hut
Project. NLC tapped an underutilized source of skills and enthusiasm, college students during summer vacations. The lesson
we derive from this innovative policy is that Third World countries
should be creative in designing new ways to generate additional
resources.

IMPROVING OR CREATING COMMUNITY
ORGANIZATIONS AND ASSOCIATIONS

The remaining two cases deal with the formation and/or strengthening of community organizations and instrumental voluntary associations. In these cases the community associations attempted to provide most of the personnel, and technical and financial resources for the program with only a little assistance from the outside.

Local Development Associations (Yemen)

The failure of the national government of Yemen to provide local services in rural areas was the output gap that the Local Development Associations (LDAs) were created to address.[28] LDAs were independent community development associations that had government recognition and moral support. While the government could contribute few resources to their projects, it encouraged districts and villages without LDAs to form them to begin meeting the very great local needs through cooperative action. In this way, LDAs were to fill the void left by a very weak central government that could not provide infrastructure and services to the most rural areas. The people wanted better infrastructure and social services, but had to produce them through their own cooperative actions—very much in accord with Islam's values of self-help, community involvement, and care for the poor.

This case is similar to the previous four cases in that the government sought to use community inputs to provide services in poor areas when it lacked the resources to provide the services itself. It differs significantly, however, in that the government provided so little assistance to the communities that the Local Development Associations were largely on their own. The national government was limited to encouraging the formation of LDAs and very occasionally assisting them with materials, advice, or minimal services. In the four previous cases the communities participated in the government program. In this case, there was no concrete government program in which to participate. Nevertheless, this case makes an important point: *When the national government can not provide badly needed services, the communities must provide them for themselves.*

Synopsis

Yemen is one of the poorest and least developed countries of the world. Its government lacks the resources to provide services in rural villages where most of the people live. From its beginning its policy has been to encourage local actions and in 1963 it issued an ordinance that provided the legal basis for local associations concerned with development. In 1968 the government created the Department of Social Affairs, Labor and Youth within the Ministry of Local Administration to promote LDAs for economic and social development. Then in 1973 the Confederation of Yemeni Development Associations (CYDA) was formed and put in the new Ministry of Social Affairs, Labour and Youth (MSALY). CYDA conducted some donor-funded development projects and provided occasional technical and financial support to LDAs. Almost all rural development activities, however, were still conducted by LDAs, i.e., independent community associations not officially attached to the state.

There were four levels of administration in the LDA system that paralleled the government levels: village Development Cooperative Committees (DCCs), governorate/district LDAs, governorate Coordinating Councils (CCs), and a national Confederation of Yemen Development Associations (CYDA). CYDA encouraged the formation of village committees that provided an organization for carrying out village projects, usually financed by local taxes. The villages elected representatives to the district LDA general assembly, which in turn elected an administrative board that selected the officers of the LDA. Commonly, these hierarchical positions were filled by sheikhs of appropriate eminence. Ironically, this elitism had an egalitarian component. The sheikhs' authority rested on social trust, and, as LDA officers, they had to influence members to support their initiatives. Generally they did this by knowing and advocating the popular will. Cohen *et al.* make the astute observation that the idyllic harmony experienced by the newly formed system might not last beyond the honeymoon period. "It will be the second generation projects and the maintenance costs of the initial ones that test the harmony between LDA officers and local people."[29] Holding office in an LDA may have been an honor but it was not much of a privilege. It was not financially rewarding and was frustrating and time consuming. Many served one term and resigned. Furthermore, impressionistic observations

"suggest that a fairly large number of LDA officers have been removed or voted out of office over the past five years [i.e., by 1981]."[30]

The two levels of the system which carry out projects are the
village DCCs and the district LDAs. Some projects are carried out
by the villages without outside help. Other projects are proposed to
the LDA by the villages. The LDA then selects a set of locally requested projects (usually infrastructure projects) and seeks funds
for the projects largely from local contributions, but also from tax-
and fee-generated funds, CYDA, and the central government.
Much of the labor usually is provided by the villages. By these arrangements many more development projects have been completed
than was the case where the system was not in effect.

Performance and Output Gaps

The almost total failure of the government to provide services to
rural villages was a glaring output gap, but since it lacked the resources to provide more services, it stood helpless before the gap.
All the government could do was encourage districts and villages
to take care of their own needs and provide institutional (but not
financial) support for LDAs. LDAs themselves had quite a variable
record of success. They did quite well on very simple projects, but
failed when they got too ambitious. Their performance and output
gaps were generally due to the lack of appropriate skills. LDAs
could have been greatly strengthened, therefore, if training or
technical assistance could have been provided to them.

Environmental Context: Opportunities and Constraints

The environmental context is very prominent in this case, which
means that generalizing from it to another case is risky. There
were numerous opportunities and constraints, which greatly influenced the functioning of the LDA system for local development. We
begin with the opportunities, which included relative equality,
favorable traditions, and increasing resources. First, participatory
or cooperative activities are severely impeded by gross inequalities, but in rural Yeman inequalities were relatively mild
for a Third World country. Cohen *et al.* estimate ". . . that the ratio
of economic distance between the upper and lower 20 percent
groups [was] less than six to one [in 1981]."[31] A narrow range of

inequality tends to increase the agreement between elites and the poor on development priorities.

Several traditions of rural Yemen were favorable to the LDA development approach. First, Yemen has a tradition of local rule which is based on fiercely independent tribal divisions. Second, Islamic traditions emphasize active participation in the affairs of the community and the mosque. Third, religious welfare associations commonly take care of the poor and maintain the mosques. They served as worthy precursors of the village development cooperative committees. Fourth, traditionally, leaders identify community needs and mobilize the community to address these needs.

> Most communities have a long history of local notables organizing people and resources for local projects, sheikhs identifying local needs and taking responsibility to see that the community acts to resolve them, or groups of local people forming a transitory organization to carry out a specific project in the community's interest.[32]

As resources gradually increased, more opportunities were created for LDAs. Taxes from the local area were in large measure returned to LDAs to support development projects in the area, and these taxes increased over time. Furthermore, the formation of CYDA helped obtain funding from foreign donors, which was then channeled through line ministries to local projects or directly to LDAs for projects. Another source of additional resources were migrants to the oil-rich countries, who sent home their earnings, and later returned home with new ideas for community development.

Numerous constraints affected local development activities, including kinship divisions, the lack of institutional development, and the lack of needed skills. Rural communities in Yeman are sharply divided into kinship groups, tribal units, Islamic sects, and occupations. These divisions made cooperative development activities more difficult.

Another difficulty was the newness of the four levels of development associations. The lack of experience of all levels with each other produced numerous misunderstandings, frustrations, and disappointments. Typically, LDAs were frustrated by the inadequacy of and delays in the financial and technical assistance from the Coordinating Councils and CYDA. At the same time, CYDA and the CCs perceived the Local Development Associations as being too impatient and demanding. Other tensions between levels could be cited, but some of them can be expected to smooth out considerably over time as some of the bugs are worked out in the institutionalizing process.

Another serious constraint on a locally based development program is the lack of necessary managerial and technical skills in the communities. Many LDAs lacked minimally satisfactory accounting systems because of an acute shortage of accounting skills, as well as numerous other essential skills, as this 1981 indictment demonstrates.

> Many LDA projects are poorly planned and managed. LDAs have trouble obtaining technical advice on design work and their officers lack the administrative and budgetary skills to effectively supervise project implementation or to manage financial resources. Hence, little attention is given to technical aspects of design, cost-benefit considerations, budget calculations, ecological impacts, maintenance programmes or future recurrent costs. For example, roads are carved on hillsides with little concern for grades or drainage culverts. Agricultural terraces below roads are destroyed by debris from construction and erosion from uncontrolled runoff. Budget overruns are common and generate suspicion of the fiscal integrity of [LDA] officers as local people are asked to donate additional funds and communities are faced with unanticipated maintenance expenses. Unless the causes of such problems can be corrected, the presently positive attitudes of rural people may sour.[33]

Structural, Design, and Environmental Changes

The structural change involved in this case is the creation and gradual institutionalization of a four-level system of development associations. The village Development Cooperative Committees (DCCs) were ". . . intended to provide an organization for village level activities and to deal with demands that locally collected taxes be used to finance local projects."[34] This level was the least developed organizationally. Villages were often mobilized to conduct projects, but few organized into official DCCs to do so.

The major actors in the four-level system of development associations were the LDAs. They were governed by a general assembly of representatives elected by villages. The general assembly elected a Local Development Board (LDB) of five to seven members to run the LDA. The LDB met once a month to identify local project needs, submit project plans up the line to the CC for approval for assistance, raise local contributions, and supervise the implementation of projects. The day-to-day affairs of each LDA were administered by the LDB president. The CCs and CYDA were supposed to provide technical assistance and partial financial support for selected projects, which they had approved. In rank order, they emphasized construction of rural roads, construction and staffing of village schools, construction or repair of village water systems, and preventive health care services.

Nature of the Approach

This case involves organizing development associations at four levels from the nation to the village. The key level in this system was the district level, the level at which LDAs functioned. This level was sufficiently large to support a development association with the capacity to manage the implementation of a range of projects, and sufficiently small to be in close touch with local groups. Nevertheless, there were important functions which had to be handled at higher or lower levels.

The major tactic employed in creating the system of development associations was restructuring (actually, structuring). The LDA program built on a variety of precursor local development projects and attempted to diffuse throughout Yemen a strongly participatory model of a local development association. The LDA system did not regularly involve data collection, experimentation, or pilot projects. It also provided little training, which is perhaps the main reason why the results were not much greater. It did involve group discussion in the various general assemblies and group decision making in the LDB and executive boards of the other levels. It is a notable case, however, for the narrow range of tactics used.

The major resource employed in the LDA system was volunteer labor. All other resources were scarce. The most harmful resource deficiency, in our judgment, was the lack of skills. The LDA system could have been improved considerably if simple managerial and technical skills were taught to those who needed them.

Results

In general, Yemen's LDAs have a proud record of accomplishments. They built roads, schools, water systems, and clinics, and provided some welfare services. They also developed community capacity.

On the negative side, many LDA projects were poorly planned and managed. They lacked the technical expertise to carry out many of their projects effectively. They needed to receive technical assistance through extension services of CYDA or the central government, but neither one was prepared to provide those services. Even though the LDA system had many faults one program evaluator stated that it was ". . . the only institution in Yemen operating at a level of the mass of peasants in the countryside which holds the promise of assisting the poorest of the poor [to] meet their basic needs."[35]

Conclusion

The LDA system in Yemen was not very successful by the standards of much more developed societies because many projects were poorly planned and executed. It was quite successful by Yemen standards, however, and produced a range of development activities when little would have occurred without it. This case again demonstrates the great value of mobilizing local inputs in producing facilities and services in poor areas when government resources are scarce. It also demonstrates the need for technical assistance to local associations in managerial and technical skills to make them effective.

National Dairy Development Board (India)

The previous five cases addressed the problem of how governments with little financial resources could provide services in poor areas. These cases demonstrated that some form of community participation was the solution. The case of the National Dairy Development Board (NDDB) differs from the previous cases because scarce resources were not a problem for it—the NDDB and its thousands of milk cooperatives were self-financing through the sale of milk.[36] Nevertheless, NDDB shares with the previous cases its dependence on effective local participation for success. The National Dairy Development Board was mandated by the government of India to develop the dairy industry in India by creating village dairy cooperatives and supporting them with marketing, processing, and technical services. The NDDB and the system of milk producers' cooperatives which supported it were very successful because they were appropriately structured and employed appropriate tactics.

Synopsis

The National Dairy Development Board (NDDB) was the top administrative layer of a vast system of village-level dairy cooperatives and district-level cooperative unions. It traces back to a group of dairy farmers who boycotted the unsatisfactory, government-sponsored milk-marketing program and formed the Kaira District Cooperative Milk Producers' Union (AMUL) in 1946. By 1947 eight village cooperatives were operating under the cooperative union. A few years later, Verghese Kurian became manager of the union and built it into the NDDB, which, in 1976, was comprised of 4,530 village cooperatives and two million farmers. These numbers continued to grow as NDDB continued to promote dairy cooperatives throughout India.

AMUL began with a few village cooperatives in 1946 and grew to include 850 village cooperatives by 1978. Similar milk producers' cooperatives were established in other districts of Gujaret with AMUL's assistance. The AMUL pattern was based on village-level cooperatives whose member farmers paid a $1.50 membership fee and agreed to sell a specified amount or more of milk a year. The members elected a managing committee and the committee elected its chair. The cooperative employed three to six part-time workers to measure and test the milk collected at the collection station and to make cash payments to sellers on the same or the following day. A cooperative union, which served some eighty village cooperatives, would collect the milk twice a day from each village, process it, and sell it in the cities through the Federation of Dairy Unions. The District Union provided a number of services to village cooperatives including help in getting started, guidance and monitoring, veterinary services, feed supplies, and other services to farmers. In return, the cooperative agreed to a set of by-laws established by the union. This is a fairly simple and effective system. Cash benefits were immediate and reliable. Village cooperatives were continuously audited and they had a good record of being honestly run. They prospered, built up reserves, paid bonuses, and donated funds to build schools, roads, and other village facilities.

The AMUL pattern was one of several milk producing and marketing patterns in India, but it was perceived as the most successful. In 1965 the government of India established the National Dairy Development Board (NDDB) in the town of Anand where AMUL was headquartered and made Verghese Kurian, the manager of

AMUL, its Director. NDDB was to diffuse the AMUL pattern throughout India, but it only had the power of persuasion to overcome the entrenched interests supporting other milk producing and marketing schemes. Some of the competing schemes were organized and run by state governments and most of them were performing badly. For example, some were operating at only 30 to 40 percent of capacity. Nevertheless, no states willingly changed to the AMUL pattern, and NDDB accomplished little expansion at first. Therefore, NDDB drafted a proposal for a national program of dairy development known as "Operation Flood" and the government of India approved it and funded it with $130 million. This was a multifaceted program that focused on increasing the capacities of publically owned city dairies and reorganizing the urban milk market. These developments, however, were coordinated with the development of eighteen rural milksheds in different regions of the country in the AMUL pattern of district unions and village cooperatives.

Performance and Output Gaps

AMUL was created because of farmer discontent with a government milk procurement program, and it expanded throughout the district and the state of Gujaret because it offered farmers a better program than those of competing options. Beyond Gujaret, however, glaring performance and output gaps did not lead to the adoption of the AMUL system because of entrenched dairy interests. NDDB finally succeeded in spreading the AMUL system by working with, instead of against, key interest groups. It instituted a program in many states involving investments in plants, which resulted in a tripling of the processing and marketing capacities of the publically owned dairies of Bombay, Delhi, Calcutta, and Madras. This forced the urban "cattle colonies" to the rural areas. As the demand for rural milk production increased, the AMUL program was instituted in eighteen rural milksheds. In this case, therefore, the demonstration of gaps did not lead to change; rather, the old system had to be shaken up first with a program that offered substantial benefits to powerful interests. Then, the highly regarded AMUL system was established to meet the increased demand for rural milk and to replace the weakened parts of the old system.

Environmental Context: Opportunities and Constraints

As was pointed out, the vested interests behind alternative milk schemes greatly constrained the expansion of the AMUL pattern initially. Another constraint was NDDB's lack of power. It was established in 1965 to develop the dairy industry in India, but was invested with only advisory power, which the vested interests had no trouble resisting. Opportunities were scarce and NDDB had to make its own, which it did. It obtained over one million tons of skim milk powder free from the United Nations World Food Program, which it sold to urban dairies to obtain money for capital investments in city milk processing plants. The expanded processing capacity created a greatly expanded need for rural milk production and, therefore, for the AMUL system.

At the cooperative level, both opportunities and constraints operated. Indian farmers had considerable experience with cooperatives and were motivated to join them if they produced tangible benefits. Another opportunity was the prominence of cattle in the Indian society. A major constraint against cooperatives in India, however, was the remaining influence of the caste system and other social divisions. The AMUL system managed to overcome these traditional divisions by insisting on democratic practices. As a result members of all castes and groups waited their turn together in the common collection line.

Structural, Design, and Environmental Changes

In this section we do not describe the change of an organization but the institution of a new organizational pattern in AMUL and, later, in NDDB. The NDDB system had to compete against other organizational patterns in the Indian dairy sector and it proved to be superior. The NDDB system had three levels, which provided vital functions for each other. The village cooperative was democratically organized. It was managed by an elected management committee, which hired several part-time workers to conduct the daily tasks of collecting, testing, weighing, and paying for the milk. The district union collected, transported, processed, and marketed the milk and was a full scale economic organization. It provided a battery of services to the village cooperatives and the farmers: It supported, guided, and advised the cooperatives on their organization and operations and helped build them into strong and effective associations. It provided veterinary services, taught farmers inexpensive but nutritional cattle feeding formulas, and sold feed concentrate mixtures for supplementing available farm residues and herbage at good prices through the cooperatives. AMUL and some other district unions also had some research capacity for studying the feed, breeding, and disease problems of cattle in the district. According to Paul, "Extension, training, and supervision were strong features of AMUL from the beginning. Simple accounting and information systems were developed for managing the affairs of the village [cooperative] and systematic training was given to the officials at the village level. AMUL also provided a supervisory service to cooperative societies to examine their operations periodically and tune up their management."[37]

The AMUL system had two levels: the district cooperative union, i.e., AMUL, and the village cooperatives. The government of India created NDDB as a national level above the district level. Its responsibilities were to set up AMUL-type systems throughout the nation and then develop programs that would strengthen the district and village organizations and improve the farmers' milk production. It also had broader responsibilities to develop the dairy sector of India, but we limit our attention to its relations to the district unions and village cooperatives. NDDB created a Division for Organizations and Animal Husbandry to assist farmers in setting up milk cooperatives in the AMUL pattern. For this purpose it used a

> "spearhead team," consisting of veterinary doctors, dairy technologists, and extension workers who worked alongside a "shadow team" deputed by the state dairy development corporation in each district. They set up cooperatives, organized technical input services, trained cooperative workers, and assisted in milk procurement. The teams would also stay in a district for several years, if necessary, to ensure that the cooperative and milk procurement systems ran smoothly. The shadow team which worked with the spearhead team was to be the core group for the state implementation agency to continue this work in other parts of the state once NDDB's spearhead team was withdrawn.[38]

For the first two years NDDB was supported by grants from the national government. The grants were accompanied by stifling financial controls so that NDDB requested and was granted the right to support itself by charging its clients (state governments, cooperatives, and other agencies) for its services. This arrangement gave NDDB autonomy and forced it to produce quality service for its clients. Thus, in the NDDB system, NDDB was the servant of the village cooperatives and district unions, not vice versa.

Nature of the Approach

The NDDB system involved new organizational structures and linkages at village, district, and national levels. In addition it had profound impacts on the entire dairy sector of India.

A variety of tactics were used in creating the AMUL and NDDB systems. The most prominent tactics were

1. Experimentation
2. Restructure (structuring)
3. Decree
4. Training
5. Problem-solving groups

The system was built in stages, which allowed time for trial-and-error learning. According to Korten:

> Once a successful prototype program had been worked out, largely by the farmers, it was not passed to some established organization for broader replication. Rather, a new organization grew around the prototype—from the bottom up—gradually building and testing its own capacity to provide effective support to federations of primary cooperatives and adding additional layers at its top as the program expanded. Appropriate management systems were worked out through experience to meet the demands of the program.[39]

Since this case involves the creation of new organizations the tactic of structuring was central. Usually the organizations were created through a negotiation process involving the members; nevertheless, the tactic of decree often played a role. For example, AMUL required new cooperatives to adopt its by-laws for cooperatives.

Our earlier discussion pointed out the importance of training the cooperatives' officers and employees, and of extension education to farmers in the AMUL pattern. We also pointed out the role of the problem-solving group called the "spearhead team" in establishing new village cooperatives and district unions. Problem-solving groups also developed some of the new programs or technical packages that were tested and then offered throughout the system.

The main resource used in the construction of the AMUL and NDDB systems was the money generated from the sale of milk. Effectiveness and success earned income and provided more resources for expansion and improvement.

Results

AMUL and NDDB were highly successful and so recognized both nationally and internationally. NDDB surpassed its national target by serving twelve thousand villages by 1980. Farmer incomes had increased substantially by then, too. "Field studies have shown an increase in income ranging from 50-100 percent among members of cooperatives. The rate of return for an average farmer is estimated at 31 per cent."[40]

Conclusion

NDDB was a highly successful cooperative movement built on voluntary associations. The voluntary association had to manage a good deal of daily activity for which it needed a simple but smooth running organization. Some managerial or technical expertise was required for certain positions so that training had to be provided. The cooperatives maintained farmer participation through economic benefits. Either NDDB or the district union provided training and technical advice to the local associations and in turn depended upon them for financial support.

NDDB demonstrated the potency of community associations when they have sufficient training in managerial and technical skills. Local associations by themselves are limited in what they can handle effectively. Local associations linked with a higher-level organization, which can provide training and timely resources, have a large potential. It is important that the link does not breed dependency, but allows considerable local initiative and self organization.

IMPLICATIONS FOR CHANGE AGENTS

This section attempts to cull from the above examples some lessons on organizational change and building community capacity. The characteristics of the above six case studies are outlined in Figure

4.1. These cases exemplify all three organizational change strategies and many specific tactics. All of the cases involved high levels of community participation and the establishment and strengthening of community associations. All cases involved an output gap. In all but the Indian case, the gap was the lack of or inadequacy of services to poor communities. The major constraint on the delivery of those services was the lack of funds. To generate the necessary resources, the communities had to be mobilized to provide inputs. But community inputs were not provided for free; they cost the service organization some power—control over the program had to be shared. Sometimes this required a restructuring of the service organization, and sometimes this required the building of more effective community associations. The most common way in which the community associations were strengthened was by involving local groups and associations in the design, implementation, and maintenance of the projects.

The major community input in most cases was voluntary labor. In several cases, however, the beneficiaries also contributed financially to the project. Projects were paid for by local taxes in Yemen, users paid fees in the Senegal health huts, and the dairy associations in India were financed out of the milk proceeds.

In addition to the above observations, there are a number of important lessons to be drawn from these case studies. First, participation strengthens linkages with communities. Second, the most successful formula for providing better delivery of services to poor communities is generally for community associations to work with outside organizations rather than going it alone. Third, decentralization of the service organization is often necessary to improve linkages with communities. Fourth, the importance of training needs to be emphasized. Finally, leadership is crucial to the success of voluntary associations. These lessons are elaborated in the following paragraphs.

Participation Contributes to
Stronger Linkages with Communities

Participation is such a value-laden word that development administration might be better advised not to use it. The Cornell reviews indicate that it is used to cover a variety of meanings and that it overlaps with other concepts.[41] For our purposes the most common

Figure 4.1 Six Case Studies of Improving Services to Communities

Case Before/After	Service Area	Before Organizational Form	Before Community Participation	After Organizational Form	After Community Participation	Contribution to Community Association
1. SMD/Reoriented by UCDP (Brazil)	municipal services	mechanical	low	more organic, truncated organic	high; helped design and implement	training, inputs, hired members
2. CAB & MOH/added Development Councils and Health Workers (Sri Lanka)	health and sanitation	mechanical	low	more organic, truncated organic, added new specialty	high; helped design and implement	mobilizing, training inputs
3. MOH/added Health Huts (Senegal)	health and sanitation	mechanical	low	mechanical with craft field activities, added craft health huts, truncated craft	high; implemented and managed	training, redesigned signed program, changed environment
4. MOE/added Literacy Campaign (Burma)	literacy education	mechanical/organic	moderate; volunteer labor	mechanical with organic development department and craft field activities, truncated craft	moderate; managed and supported teachers	provided teachers and trained some village teachers
5. —/LDA Movement (Yemen)	rural development	—	little activity	voluntary association	moderate; very high relative to outside help	occasional inputs, limited help
6. government programs/NDDB (India)	marketing milk	mechanical	low	mechanical with organic development department and craft field activities	high; ran village milk cooperatives	training, inputs, veterinary services

221

confusion is with decentralization; sometimes participation and decentralization are seen as identical. We will distinguish them in the following manner: centralization/decentralization refers to the autonomy and power of lower-level participants in an organization, and participation refers to the inputs of beneficiaries or the public into the design, implementation, or maintenance of the output of an organization. Schools in which teachers teach a prescribed course content are centralized and schools in which teachers determine their own course content are decentralized. In either case, students might participate much or little in the classroom. While these distinctions are useful, it is still the case that decentralization and participation tend to go together.

Participation tends to improve links with the community and increase the effectiveness of organizations that provide services to communities. In the four case studies previously presented that involve organizations providing services to communities, community participation was critical to their effectiveness. Community participation was essential for UCDP's program in Rio de Janeiro and for the environmental health and community development project in Sri Lanka. In both cases the members were involved in making decisions about the programs. Effective management by community representatives was the key to successful health huts in Senegal. The Burmese literacy campaign involved the control of the villages over the teachers, although not over the curriculum.

The positive effects of participation at the local level of an organization are further demonstrated in the Philippine National Irrigation Administration reported in Chapter 3. In fact, much of the development administration literature demonstrates the benefits of increasing participation for organizations serving communities.[42]

Why is participation so important? *The main reason is that participation can increase resources without significantly increasing costs.* It is impossible to provide needed services to large numbers of poor people at low cost without their participation. In effect, the resources of the poor (primarily voluntary labor) are mobilized to implement programs and construct and maintain facilities. In this process there is an important exchange between the service organization and the community associations. The organization exchanges power for community resources, especially for labor and sometimes even for money. If the organization needs the resources, then it can not dictate. It must involve the membership of the community.

The second way that participation contributes to project success is by providing information on local circumstances and needs that improve the design and implementation of programs and projects. It is not that the villagers know more than the professionals; it's that they know other things than the technical experts do. Most of the services described previously required both local and professional knowledge, and participation brings them together.

The third contribution of participation is to give participants some ownership in the program. Sharing power provides greater motivation, and motivation is the key to generating labor and making voluntary labor work. As we showed in Chapter 2, it is one of two essential factors for effective voluntary associations.

Finally, *participation builds the capabilities of the participants.* This often is a slow painstaking process but is absolutely essential for generating future resources. Success on one project leads to the willingness to move on to new projects, which create both more individual growth and more community development.

It would be wrong, however, to believe that participation is a panacea. First, as we have seen, participation without appropriate training leads to mobilization but not always to effectiveness. This is quite clear in the LDAs in Yemen. Second, participation can not be turned on so easily as a faucet. It requires effective associations or leadership in the community. Third, participation works much better if *local* people are trained to do the simple, paid jobs. This seems especially true for the cases in India, Senegal, and Brazil. Employing local people also provides a sense of community ownership which is needed to make community associations really effective. Fourth, participation is an effective method for generating resources only when the conditions are propitious, such as when there is relative equality in the community or when there is capable local leadership.

Chapter 3 noted that the relative degree of equality found in the rice culture of the Phillipines provided a positive opportunity for developing a participatory organization. The cases described in this chapter confirm that successful participation requires relative equality. Cohen, in his very thoughtful review of the Yemen Rural Development Associations, makes this argument and marshalls considerable evidence to support it.[43]

Successful participation usually depends upon local leadership, and these leaders in turn usually need some training. The Sri Lanka, Brazil, and Senegal cases all provide examples of this. Although the evidence is not conclusive, it does suggest that *partici-pation is a more effective tactic when organizations not only train locals in skills needed for the service but also train leaders in the skills they require.* In other words, participation requires skills in knowing how to negotiate and when to say no to the advice of any particular experts.

Organizational Changes are Frequently Needed to Produce Stronger Linkages

Decentralization was a major theme of the previous two chapters, and the cases described in this section confirm that decentralization can contribute to effectiveness. Strong linkages via participation are only possible when the organization involved decentralizes its own power structure. This pattern was found in the NIA of the Philippines, and we see the same pattern replicated in both Brazil and Sri Lanka. However, participation is not always necessary nor must all organizations be decentralized. The T and V in India is a clear example of an effective, centralized extension service, and even in the Burma Literacy Campaign, some aspects of the program were centrally designed and controlled.

Mechanisms for Creating Communication Linkages

One of the benefits of participation is improved communication, and communication is critical for the effective delivery of services. There are a number of factors other than participation that contrib-ute to communication as well. Hiring local people as workers, as was done in Senegal and in the two slum projects, definitely facili-tates communication. Another communication mechanism is hav-ing workers live in the community if they are not from the same locality; this was the pattern in Burma. Still a third communica-tion mechanism is training leaders in communication skills, as was seen in the cases of Sri Lanka, Senegal, and Brazil. A fourth is the hiring of community organizers as a way of stimulating com-munication, as was done in Sri Lanka and Brazil.

An Organization-Community Linkage Is More Effective than Self-Help Projects

The real issue is which institution-building strategy leads to the better provision of services to communities—community associations working on their own or community associations working in combination with outside organizations that provide some resources? Although these six cases can not provide definitive evidence, they suggest that community associations are more effective if they are assisted by outside organizations. In Chapters 2 and 5, we analyze why this is so.

One key role for the outside organization is often the provision of training. In Senegal, an outside organization trained the health hut paraprofessionals in their specialties and the health committee members in health hut management. In Burma, the National Literacy Campaign trained the volunteer teachers, and in India, NDDB or AMUL trained the officials and employees of the village cooperatives. This training was essential to the success of the program.

Another major role for the outside organization in community development, of course, is to provide the initial infrastructure or basic resources for projects, e.g., roads, irrigation systems, agricultural research, or a water system. The Sri Lanka and Brazil cases exemplify this pattern. The beneficiaries often can pay user fees or maintain the facilities, but they generally can not pay for the initial cost of the facility.

When outside organizations do not provide assistance, the community projects appear to be less successful. The LDAs in Yemen designed and implemented their own development projects and the government ministers only provided some critical services or resources in a few cases. As a result, many of these projects were technically weak.

To sum up, outside agencies are needed to provide some essential services to communities, but they also must seek help from the community. Outside agencies are needed especially to provide resources and training. The best strategy appears to be an agency-community partnership, which can be called participatory.

The Role of Leadership in Community Associations

The exchange that occurs between the outside organization and the local community is more effective precisely when the local association is well developed. In those situations, leaders play a key linkage role.

So far we have said little about the structure of the community associations. Who is going to provide initiative and leadership in organizing the community for participation? We find in these cases that projects are most effective when they utilize "natural" leaders, i.e., people who are accepted by the group being mobilized as appropriate leaders. Our finding does not determine whether elites or non-elites make better natural leaders for community development activities. The few cases at hand do demonstrate that traditional elites can be good leaders for some community development activities. For example, traditional sheikhs provided leadership in the Local Development Associations in Yemen, at some sacrifice to themselves, because they were motivated by a tradition of service to the community. But in most cases exceptional members of lower groups provide the most effective leadership.

The urban development programs in Rio and Colombo involved natural leaders from the poor neighborhoods. They were not people from the middle class, but they were of a higher status than the average shantytown resident. Again, natural leaders seemed to have been selected for the committees that supervised the village health huts in Senegal, and perhaps also for the management committees of the village milk cooperatives in India. Thus, we tentatively conclude that the people who lead the poor in organized efforts in their own behalf generally are themselves gifted members of the poor. They are natural leaders, in the manner of Lech Walesa of Poland.

Notes

1. *See* Ana Maria F. Braseleiro *et al.*, 1982, "Extending Municipal Services by Building on Local Initiatives," *Assignment Children*, vol. 57/58, pp. 67-100.

2. *Ibid.*, p. 86.

3. *Ibid.*, p. 96.

4. *Ibid.*, p. 75.

5. *Ibid.*, p. 80.

6. *Ibid.*, p. 85.

7. *See* Jehan K. Cassim *et al.*, 1982, "Development Councils for Participatory Urban Planning," *Assignment Children*, vol. 57/58, pp. 157-187.

8. *Ibid.*, pp. 158-159.

9. *Ibid.*, p. 163.

10. *Ibid.*, p. 164.

11. *Ibid.*, pp. 164-165.

12. *Ibid.*, p. 165.

13. *Ibid.*, p. 159.

14. *Ibid.*, p. 166.

15. *See* Richard F. Weber *et al.*, 1980, *Senegal: The Sine Saloum Rural Health Care Project,* Project Impact Evaluation No. 9, Agency for International Development (Washington, D. C., October); and Abby Bloom, 1983, "The Sine Saloum Rural Health Project Revisited," *Development Digest,* vol. 21, no. 2, pp. 36-46.

16. Weber, 1980, *op. cit.*, p. 2.

17. Bloom, 1983, *op. cit.*, p. 37.

18. Weber, *op. cit.*, p. 5.

19. Bloom, *op. cit.*, p. 40.

20. *Ibid.*, p. 39.

21. Weber, *op. cit.*, p. 8.

22. *Ibid.*, pp. 7-8. The quote from Over is from A. Mead Over, n.d., 1980, *Five Primary Health Care Projects in the Sahel and the Issue of Recurrent Costs* (draft working paper for Club du Sahel).

23. Weber, *op cit.*, p. 4.

24. *Ibid.*, p. iii.

25. *See* Nyi Nyi, 1983, "Planning, Implementation and Monitoring of Literacy Programmes," *Assignment Children,* vol. 63/64, pp. 87-99.

26. *Ibid.*, p. 90.

27. *Ibid.*, p. 98.

28. *See* John M. Cohen *et al.*, 1981, "Development from Below: Local Development Associations in the Yemen Arab Republic," *World Development,* vol. 9, no. 11/12, pp. 1039-1061.

29. *Ibid.*, p. 1045.

30. *Ibid.*

31. *Ibid.*, p. 1053.

32. *Ibid.*, p. 1043.

33. *Ibid.*, p. 1049.

34. *Ibid.*, p. 1044.

35. *Ibid.*, p. 1043.

36. *See* Samuel Paul, 1982, *Managing Development Programs: The Lessons of Success* (Boulder, Colo.: Westview); and David C. Korten, 1980, "Community Organization and Rural Development: A Learning Process Approach," *Public Administration Review,* vol. 40, no. 5, pp. 480-511.

37. Paul, 1982, *op. cit.*, p. 22.

38. *Ibid.*, p. 30.

39. Korten, 1980, *op. cit.,* p. 486.

40. Paul, *op. cit.,* p. 16.

41. *See* T. Abeyrama and K. Saeed, 1984, "The Gramodaya Mandalaya Scheme in Sri Lanka: Participatory Development or Power Play?" *Community Development Journal,* vol. 19, no. 1, pp. 20-31; Samuel T. Agere, 1982, "The Promotion of Self-Reliance and Self-Help Organizations in Community Development in Zimbabwe: A Conceptual Framework," *Community Development Journal,* vol. 17, no. 3, pp. 208-215; Paris Andreou and Ahmed Ghaui, 1979, "The 'Comilla Model' and Rural Development in Bangladesh," *Journal of Administration Overseas,* vol. 18, pp. 269-275; Luis M. A. Atucha and Catherine D. Crone, 1980, "A Participatory Methodology for Literacy and Health Education," *Assignment Children,* vol. 51/52, pp. 141-161; Derick W. Brinkerhoff, 1979, "Inside Public Bureaucracy: Empowering Managers to Empower Clients," *Rural Development Participation Review,* vol. 1, pp. 7-9; Jacques Bugnicourt, 1982, "Popular Participation in Development in Africa," *Assignment Children,* vol. 59/60, pp. 57-77; Coralie Bryant, 1980, "Organizational Impediments to Making Participation A Reality: Swimming Upstream in AID," *Rural Development Participation Review,* vol. 1, no. 3, pp. 8-10; Diana Conyers, 1981, "Decentralization for Regional Development: A Comparative Study of Tanzania, Zambia, and Papau New Guinea," *Public Administration and Development,* vol. 1, no. 2, pp. 107-21; William J. Cousins and Catherine Goyder, 1979, *Changing Slum Communities—Urban Community Development in Hyderabad* (New Delhi: Manohar); Stahrl W. Edmund, 1984, "The Implementation of International Development Projects: Four Illustrative Case Studies," *International Review of Administrative Sciences,* vol. 50, no. 1, pp. 2-9; Guy Gran, 1983, *Learning From Development Success: Some Lessons From Contemporary Case Histories* (Washington, D.C.: NASPAA, Working Paper No. 9); Mary R. Hollnsteiner, 1979, "Mobilizing the Rural Poor Through Community Organization," *Philippine Studies,* vol. 27, no. 3, pp. 387-411; Mary R. Hollnsteiner, 1982, "Government Strategies for Urban Areas and Community Participation," *Assignment Children,* vol. 57/58, pp. 43-64; Mary R. Hollnsteiner, 1982, "The Participatory Imperative in Primary Health Care," *Assignment Children,* vol. 59/60, pp. 35-56; Are Kolawole, 1982, "The Role of Grassroots Participation in National Development: Lessons from the Kwara State of Nigeria," *Community Development Journal,* vol. 17, no. 2, pp. 121-133;

Cheryl Lassen, 1979, *Reaching the Assetless Poor: An Assessment of Projects and Strategies for Their Self-Reliant Development* (Ithaca: Cornell, Rural Development Committee); Nici Nelson, 1981, "Mobilizing Village Women: Some Organizational and Management Considerations," *Journal of Development Studies,* vol. 17, no. 13, pp. 47-58; Donatus C. I. Okpala, 1980, "Towards a Better Conceptualization of Rural Community Development: Empirical Findings in Nigeria," *Human Organization,* vol. 39, no. 2, pp. 161-169; Theodore H. Thomas, 1973, "People Strategies for International Development: Administrative Alternatives to National, Political, and Economic Ideologies," *Journal of Comparative Administration,* vol. 5, no. 1, pp. 87-107; UNICEF: Community Participation and Family Life Section, 1982, "Popular Participation in Basic Services: Lessons Learned Through UNICEF's Experience," *Assignment Children,* vol. 59/60, pp. 121-135; Alastair White, 1982, "Why Community Participation? A Discussion of the Arguments," *Assignment Children,* vol. 59/60, pp. 17-34; Marshall Wolfe, 1982, "Participation in Economic Development: A Conceptual Framework," *Assignment Children,* vol. 59/60, pp. 79-109; and James Wunsch, 1978, "Voluntary Associations and Structural Development in West African Urbanization," *Journal of African Studies,* vol. 5, no. 1, pp. 79-102.

42. Cohen, *op. cit.*

5

Lessons for Development
Change Agents

We have used both an inductive and a deductive approach in developing effective strategies of organizational change in LDCs. In Chapters 1 and 2 we explicated theories and ideas about organizational change that have been created largely in the developed world. In Chapters 3 and 4 we described and analyzed actual cases of organizational change in LDCs. In this chapter we join these two streams of thought and derive lessons for development change agents. Our major objective is to explain why some organizational interventions are more successful than others.

This chapter has four sections. The first critically evaluates whether the performance-gap strategy is relevant for development change agents in LDCs. It finds that the performance-gap strategy does work in a variety of cultures. The next section examines what to do about a performance gap. It uses organizational theory and organizational design to explain the causes of poor performances. The third section discusses how to change the organization to eliminate the performance or output gap. The fourth section identifies two organizational models that are relevant to Third World contexts but have been ignored in the developed world. These two models illustrate the versatility of contingency theory. When new contingencies are found one can expect to find new models and can understand why the other models have problems in the new contingencies.

Performance and Output Gaps as Pressures for Change

A central theme of the organizational change literature is that there must be some performance or output gap in an organization before change agents can intervene. The elites or other influential groups must perceive that the organization is failing. This performance or output gap motivates members to accept the proposed change, thereby reducing resistance and justifying the presence of the change agent.

According to our case studies, the performance-gap strategy is effective in many different cultures and countries. In each of the interventions described in Chapters 3 and 4 we find that significant actors believed that the organization was not as effective as it could be and therefore were willing to enact reforms. It is also clear from many unsuccessful cases, which we have reviewed but not reported, that the pressure for change is generally slight when the perceptions of performance or output gaps are slight. One role of interveners, therefore, is to raise the influentials' consciousness of performance or output gaps. In some of the interventions, especially the performance-improvement approach used in Jamaica, part of the strategy was to persuade agency leaders of performance gaps.

We did not expect to find the performance-gap strategy to be widely applicable. We assumed that it would work well in some cultures and not so well in others. We expected different cultures to respond to performance gaps differently. Instead, we found performance gaps to be a powerful motivation for reform in all societies studied.

Our study leads us to generalize that most organizational members want their organization to be effective. Effectiveness is one value that appears to transcend all cultures, or at least the ones in which our cases are located. Frequently, "ineffectiveness" is defined as having too low a volume of production, a frequent situation in developing countries where there is a very high demand for services but not enough supply. This gap can create a powerful motivation for change upon which interveners can build.

The performance of efficiency or productivity is another value that appears to transcend cultures. Organizations in many societies are limited in the degree to which they can become efficient, but they generally want to become more efficient within these limits. For example, some organizations can not dismiss ineffective employees, and employees must be selected on the basis of political connections. This pattern was described in Presthus' study of Turkish bureaucracy.[1] Nevertheless, even these organizations wanted to use their employees more effectively. A concomitant motivation is for managerial and technical employees to improve their competence. We found a widespread desire for new managerial tools and procedures in both cited and uncited cases. Some of this interest may simply be an interest in being modern, but we interpret much of it as an interest in being effective.

Our fundamental conclusion from the cases we examined is that cultural values play a surprisingly small role. In retrospect, there appear to be several reasons for this. First, the argument that values decisively affect development refers to the societal level or concerns individual choices such as investing in capital formation.[2] These spheres differ greatly from the actions of employers in instrumental organizations, as in our cases. Managers and technical staff who have to get jobs done seem to be interested in better ways to do it in many cultures.

Another reason for the relative lack of influence of cultural values in our cases is that most of these organizations served fairly basic needs which are valued in all cultures. Inefficiency or failure, therefore, means that people are being deprived of basic needs and most workers would be concerned about the adversity that results. The organizations in our cases served widespread collective needs such as sanitation, irrigation, electricity, health care, literacy, technologies for farmers, and so forth.

There are other kinds of outputs, such as birth control, which are impacted much more by cultural values. Again, a contingency model is applicable. Many needs may be universal, but not all organizational outputs are basic needs. Those that are not basic needs might vary enormously in various cultures. The literature has perhaps focused too much attention on the outputs which are influenced by values and not enough on those that appear to be common across many cultures. At minimum, development change agents should notice the ones that appear to be widely accepted. Failure to meet these needs can generate pressures for change.

Although the performance-gap strategy worked in all cultures observed, it did not work well under all conditions. Certain features of the situation affect the success of this strategy. Success is more likely in organizations with a history of change, leaders who have lived in other societies, and professional personnel rather than civil servants. Furthermore, clear measures of performances and outputs greatly facilitate the perception of gaps.

At various points we have suggested—on the basis of the literature—that organizations that have already experienced some change are more likely to admit the need for further change. Interventions in the Philippines and Jordan succeeded in part because they took place in organizations that were fairly open to change. Some organizations, however, are much more resistant to recognizing output or performance gaps. Typically, these appear to be organizations dominated by civil servants, at least in the cases available to us. In contrast, engineers and physicians were quicker to identify performance and output gaps in the cases we have reviewed. *The lesson we deduce is that it is easier to intervene in organizations with occupations which have included training in cause-and-effect reasoning.* Performance-gap interventions implicitly use this mode of thinking. Many gaps have causes such as inappropriate structures or processes that can be changed.

Clear measures of performance and output help make gaps more visible. The Jordan intervention demonstrated how records can be employed to document output gaps. Similarly, the change tactics of group data collection and discussion and group problem solving call attention to gaps. One advantage of some of the O.D. tactics is that they focus attention on the need for change and build pressure for it.

The role of key leaders in recognizing gaps was important in Jordan and in the electrical plant intervention in Guyana. We were curious as to why some leaders were much more concerned about gaps than were others, and our studies suggest that one answer is exposure to multiple cultures. In fact, exposure to American culture may be particularly eventful for top managers in LDCs. Persons trained in the United States or at an American-sponsored institution, such as the Asian Management Institute located in the Philippines, played important roles in a number of cases that we reviewed but did not present in this work. U.S. training tends to increase the willingness of personnel to recognize gaps. *One implication for development change agents is to seek out those individuals high in the hierarchy who have been exposed to other cultures, especially that of the United States.* They can more easily perceive gaps and be more willing to act as spokespersons for change.

Another lesson which several cases suggest is that output gaps need to be reaffirmed frequently. Recognition of an output gap at the start of an intervention is a necessary condition for success but not a sufficient condition. *Unless the gap is periodically reaffirmed, the motivation or pressure for change can decay across time.* This reaffirmation can be made either with performance data, as in a monitoring system, or simply with operational statistics. Problem-solving groups provide another method for reaffirmation of performance gaps through their diagnostic function, as was the case in Jordan, the Philippines, and Colombia.

We have argued that the performance-and-output-gaps strategy is effective in LDCs and have identified some situational factors that make it more so. Change agents should notice, however, that the gap strategy should be employed diplomatically. The more successful changes appear to have been "sold" to the governments or agencies in question frequently not so much to "overcome failure," as to acquire *new* management tools and practices. We call justifications for change "gaps" for analytical purposes only. *Development change agents generally should accentuate the positive and portray those changes to close performance and output gaps as learning the latest managerial technologies or instituting modern designs. They can also point out that the same problems are also common in the developed world.* We suspect that part of the attractiveness of "new" managerial technologies, administrative policies, and organizational structures is that they do *not* imply failure but suggest that improvement is a continual process. This is the secret of Japanese success and their use of quality work circles. The emphasis is on constant improvement.

One interesting and unexpected finding is that most interventions have focused on output rather than performance gaps, as we have defined them. The organizational theory literature has been built around measures of the performances of innovation, efficiency, and integration. In contrast, the interventions in LDCs have usually focused on output gaps, failures to achieve the goals of the organization or some stipulated criterion, such as the power failures in Guyana, or the lack of sanitation in Sri Lanka and Brazil. One can easily understand this. The problems of LDCs are more fundamental. When organizations are doing reasonably well but want to do better, they become concerned about performances. When they are doing badly, they are concerned about outputs. We believe that this lack of focus on performances such as efficiency or innovation tends to lead to a more microapproach to the changing of an organization and to a greater emphasis on specific tools and techniques rather than on basic restructuring.

Nevertheless, implicit in many interventions in LDCs is the theme of efficiency or productivity, which are performances. Perhaps the best proof of the importance of efficiency is how quickly in some interventions the definition of gaps or problems shifted to the causes of inefficiency such as lack of clear work roles or lines of responsibility. We saw this in Guyana, Jordan, and elsewhere. This desire to find and correct the causes of operational problems is a sign that efficiency is a widespread concern.

In summary, performance and output gaps appear to be generic ways of building pressures for change. Cultural values appear to have less influence on the perception of performance gaps than we had anticipated. Several factors facilitate the performance-gap strategy. A history of change, exposure to other cultures, professional personnel, and good measures of performances and outputs contribute to the perception of gaps and the desire for change. Even when measures do not exist, O.D. tactics are useful ways of creating recognition of these gaps and of reaffirming them.

The Direction of Changes of the System

Although change agents in LDCs have not been guided previously by the contingency theory of organizations, nevertheless, effective interventions conform to the prescriptions of contingency theory. Our review of the twelve case studies of organizational change in Chapters 3 and 4 indicates three major patterns of change. Voluntary associations are strengthened through training and some critical inputs; bureaucracies are made more efficient by making them more mechanical; and bureaucracies are made more adaptive and innovative by making them more organic. We find few cases using the craft or mechanical-organic models, but these models have some characteristics that are well-suited to LDC contexts. Finally, we identify some new organizational patterns that are not identified in the contingency theory literature in the developed world, the latter having been presented in Chapter 2. We have had our theories enriched by our review of successful interventions in LDCs.

Strengthening Voluntary Associations

The most common institution-building strategy in the Third World is the strengthening of voluntary associations. Chapter 4 on voluntary associations is more representative of the development literature than is Chapter 3. While we had difficulties finding cases for the latter, for the former over one hundred references could have been employed.

As we observed in Chapter 4, *the key to strengthening voluntary associations is to select and train leaders and to provide technical skills.* The success of the Senegal health huts and the UNICEF projects in Colombo and Rio de Janeiro depended on the infusion of both leadership and technical skills. The absence of these factors caused the relative failure of the Yemen projects.

The function of community organizers is to provide or develop both leadership and technical skills for creating or strengthening voluntary associations. Another function of the community organizer is to link the national or regional service organizations with the voluntary associations of the communities. This function is important because voluntary associations usually need assistance from outside service delivery organizations.

Generally, the most effective structural arrangement appears to be service delivery organizations working with voluntary associations by providing technical services. The service organization hires and trains the community organizers who then build the voluntary associations. There are a variety of reasons why this combination of a service organization and voluntary associations is effective. The two social collectives represent two different perspectives and interests. The service organization represents the nation, state, and technical interests. The voluntary associations represent the community, native knowledge, and local interests. Both sides are needed for a more appropriate solution. A dialectic also creates a more complex solution. This was amply demonstrated in the Philippine project. Such a dialectic reduces the probability that one group's narrow economic or political interests will dominate, which is a problem with both national and local elites. We also suspect that this combination reduces the probability of corruption.

Another reason the combination of voluntary associations and a service organization has good potential is that each can provide inputs that the other can not provide as easily. The service organization has the economic and technical resources to build infrastructure, such as schools, clinics, and irrigation channels. The voluntary association can more easily handle the limited but crucial task of maintenance, and to a certain extent provide labor for implementation. Thus, the combination is a happy one.

Gran reviews eighteen "successful" projects and identifies several characteristics that were common to them including continuous internal learning and learning from their environments. On the latter he observes, "In many cases service organizations had field workers who were involved in regular learning and participatory research wherein local people designed and implemented some or all of the program."[3] We conclude that the combination of voluntary associations with service organizations produces these two characteristics. The organization is forced to learn and gain increased respect for the environment, to use Gran's terms.

The easiest way to accomplish Gran's objectives is to use community organizers, especially if the service organization is national rather than local. Community organizers are trained to monitor their environments, to pick out natural leaders, and to respect the needs and wishes of the local populace. These tasks can fulfill important needs of national service organizations.

The second key mechanism for strengthening voluntary associations is for service organizations to accept their recommendations. Participation is not genuine unless some recommendations are accepted. Furthermore, accepted recommendations are a reward that maintains motivation and makes the voluntary association important in the eyes of its membership. But to make participation work, the service organization must frequently decentralize its power structure. We saw this most dramatically in Colombo, Sri Lanka, but also in other cases.

Participation, as we have defined it, also has a beneficial effect on the service organization beyond changes in the power structure. Horizontal linkages and increased communication mean better access to local knowledge, which improves the performance of the service organization. Although some of these points are stressed in Korten's work, they are not emphasized enough in the development literature.[4] On this point Galbraith's *Designing Complex Organizations* provides a number of models.[5]

One voluntary association that succeeded without the assistance of a national service organization was the National Dairy Development Board of India. It is not an exception to the rule about the need for outside assistance, however, because the regional and national levels of the NDDB acted like a service organization, providing training and expert consultation to the local cooperatives as well as inputs, such as veterinary service to farmers. We also suggest that the NDDB was successful because of the relatively high equality of dairy farmers and the common rewards of the cooperative enterprise. These conditions make voluntary associations stronger.

Making Bureaucracies More Mechanical

The second common intervention was reorienting bureaucracies to make them more efficient. Many public bureaucracies in LDCs may appear to be mechanical organizations, but they lack many procedures and tools for functioning in true mechanical fashion. Chapter 3 provides several examples of ways to make bureaucracies more efficient by adding new managerial procedures and tools. Many LDC bureaucracies lack a clear-cut system of records, supervision, job descriptions, and other managerial tools. The Guyanan and Jordanian cases are examples of how the performance improvement approach was used to attempt to correct these deficiencies and make organizations more efficient. In the Guyanan intervention the managers agreed that they lacked clear lines of authority, job descriptions, and supervision—the elements associated with Weber's original model of bureaucracy. Their organization therefore had to become more mechanical to become more effective. We have reviewed many other cases not reported in Chapter 3 that also demonstrate the need for more bureaucracy.

In some cases a bureaucracy is insufficiently mechanical because it is based on personal loyalties and patronage. These should be called patrimonial bureaucracies because they differ greatly from a Weberian bureaucracy. Their productivity would increase greatly if they could be made mechanical organizations. Extraordinary political power is required for such a transformation which is unlikely. Nevertheless, they can be made more mechanical by improving their managerial technologies.

The irony is that much of the current development literature pleads for reducing bureaucratic structures and procedures in order to facilitate the delivery of services. We side with those who extol the virtues of bureaucracy—at least for some tasks.[6] *Organizations doing simple tasks and meeting a large relatively uniform demand, especially where capital intensity is great, should be made more mechanical.*

For those who define development as economic growth, bureaucracy or mechanical organizations are the answer. They provide efficiency and productivity, producing standardized services at low cost. The bureaucratic form, therefore, should be promoted widely in LDCs. In Chapter 2 we explicated some of bureaucracy's strong points, some of which are aptly illustrated in Chapters 3 and 4.

Unfortunately, many people have forgotten that the United States, Great Britain, and Germany, in particular, developed with the aid of mechanical organizations that provided many products in large volume at low cost. Chandler describes these organizations in his book *The Visible Hand,* examples of which include the Pennsylvania Railroad, Singer Sewing Machines, American Tobacco, and the A & P Tea Co.[7]

The T and V model of agricultural extension in India is a classic example of a well-designed mechanical-bureaucratic organization. There was one goal and tasks were simplified and formalized. The schedule of the field agent was carefully worked out on a two-week repeating routine and the reliability of the schedule made it easy for farmers to meet with the agents. It also made it easier for the agent to interact effectively with researchers and then supervisors.

Another debate in the development administration literature is over the issue of centralization and decentralization. In our discussion of national organizations working with voluntary associations, we have argued that frequently the service organization had to decentralize. We have also suggested that participation is an effective link between a service organization and voluntary associations. One might deduce that decentralization is a panacea, and some writings seem to suggest this. This position, however, is inconsistent with contingency theory. *Centralization is very desirable in mechanical organizations when they have simple and standardized tasks that must be performed in large volume at low cost.* Many of the most successful organizations in the United States during the nineteenth century were centralized, and many still are.[8] Nor is centralization efficient only in the private sector, as the centralized postal service demonstrates. In fact, McDonalds and the T and V use a similar organizational form.

Paul analyzes why some programs, such as education, health, and population, are more decentralized than others, such as dairy, rice, and tea:

> The explanation lies in (1) the nature of the service, its underlying technology and the need to adapt it to varying beneficiary needs in order to elicit their responses, (2) the need to involve

beneficiaries in planning and implementing the program as a means of creating self-sustained social changes in the absence of the pull effect of any other motivating factor, and (3) the complexity of the environment in terms of uncertainty, diversity, and scope, which renders central information processing for decision making in important areas ineffective.[9]

Thus, Paul's analysis begins to specify when decentralization is helpful and when it is not. As we have discussed in Chapter 2, it depends upon the nature of the task, and beyond this upon the strategic choices made. To work, centralization must be combined with formalization. Formalization is the process of specifying official procedures and responsibilities for the activities and positions of an organization. It tends to limit worker discretion and regularizes behavior of categories of workers.

Making Bureaucracies More Organic

In a fair number of cases, organizations or parts of organizations were changed towards the organic model. The organic model excels in the performance of innovation, but this performance does not have a high priority in Third World countries that are focused on more basic problems. On the other hand, the organic model also increases flexibility and adaptiveness so the organization can be more responsive to client needs. This responsiveness became a goal of NIA in the Philippines, and it became more organic to achieve it. To a lesser degree the organizations in the Jordan, Guyana, Jamaica, Colombia, Brazil, and Sri Lanka cases also became more organic for the same reason.

It is worth reiterating that mechanical and organic are poles on the ends of a continuum. We do not expect the organizations in LDCs to become highly organic but they can become *more organic*. The principal ways organizations became more organic in our cases was by increasing their complexity in the division of labor, decentralizing, increasing use of multispecialty problem-solving groups, and increased communication and feedback.

Many of the successful interventions added new specialties, thereby increasing the complexity of the division of labor, changing the way in which problems were perceived, and leading to more innovative solutions. In the cases reviewed in Chapters 3 and 4 the new specialty was community organizers who were added to public bureaucracies to make them more responsive to human needs. Not all occupational specialties cause an equal amount of differentiation when added to a structure. The greater the difference between the new occupation and existing occupations, the greater the positive impact on innovation in programs and services if the integration problems can be solved. For example, community organizers diverged greatly from the engineers in the National Irrigation Administration and contributed greatly to innovation and adaptiveness.

Decentralization of power is an element in several interventions. The National Irrigation Administration decentralized its strategic planning function by creating a task group at its top level that planned the implementation of the change. The institution of major changes in an organization, such as improving linkages with communities, usually requires special top-level task forces because of the complexity of the task. The creation of problem-solving teams will decentralize the organization, clearly shown in the electrical power plant intervention in Guyana. The organizational theory literature suggests, however, that decentralization without a change in the division of labor is likely to be unstable and revert. On the other hand, decentralization with an increase in the division of labor is likely to remain because the new occupational group(s) will resist reversion.

Organizations are made more organic by increasing their rate of communication, especially in a horizontal direction. Horizontal communications provide valuable horizontal linkages, facilitate coordination and teamwork, and stimulate new ideas. They also make organizations more capable of learning by doing when the horizontal communication stresses feedback of information about problems.

When inadequate communication and/or feedback are responsible for low performance, new channels must be created or old channels restructured. Many of the tactics of the O.D. approach (i.e., teams, problem-solving groups, surveys, and evaluation) improve communications, which contribute to their success. Teams and problem-solving groups increase horizontal communication, while surveys and evaluations provide feedback. Each makes the organization more adaptive to its environment. The importance of communications is illustrated in all six cases in Chapter 3.

Two Underutilized Institution-Building Strategies

The advantage of having an analytical framework is that one can code not only what has been done but also what has not been considered. Most of the literature on organizations in LDCs describes the movement towards the mechanical model. A few describe the movement towards the organic model. None mentions either the mixed mechanical-organic model or the traditional-craft model. The virtues of these two models, however, need to be considered.

Using the mechanical-organic model.   We have already noted that both centralization and decentralization have advantages. The organizational model that tries to realize both sets of advantages is the mixed mechanical—organic form as described in Chapter 2. *The mechanical-organic model is useful when research tasks must be combined with large-scale production of products or delivery of services. It is also appropriate when production can be standardized or mechanized, but delivery requires flexibility, adaptation, and innovation.*

Two cases in Chapter 4, Burma and India, partially exemplify the mechanical-organic model. Both the Burmese Literacy Campaign and the National Dairy Development Board in India had centralized, mechanical, national organizations with organic research and development components. The literacy teaching modules were developed and tested by university and college professors but then became standardized programs. The NDDB had a unit for developing and testing technical packages for standardized implementation in local dairy cooperatives. These arrangements seemed to have been successful.

To be effective, the mixed mechanical-organic model requires that at least one part of the organization use a complex division of labor. For example, in DuPont an organic research center is combined with a mechanical production system. An analogy for LDCs would be organic agricultural research centers combined with a centralized programmed extension service. *This combination of research on appropriate technologies with a mechanical delivery system has much to recommend it and not only in agriculture.* For example, in the Veterans Administration's Hospitals in the United States, research is done in a more organic way, and patient care is performed in a more mechanical way, especially for long-term chronic patients.

Using the traditional-craft model.   Another model of organizations, which is not explored in the development administration literature, is the traditional-craft model. Most organizations in the

LDCs, however, including small businesses, farms, and cottage industry, best fit this model. The motivation of family-owned businesses is exceptionally high both in the developed and developing worlds.[10] Motivation, however, is not the only factor in success. Most small businesses lack the necessary managerial and technical skills, and therefore are not very effective. Development can be induced by upgrading the skills in these organizations.

We recommend that the Training and Visit system of agricultural extension be adapted to small businesses and cottage industry. The T and V model should be applicable to small businesses as well as to small farms. The need for credit and management procedures are common to both. They differ mainly in their technologies, but the training of the extension agents would take this factor into account. This model should be used as the basis for an institution-building strategy because small business and small farm organizations predominate in LDCs, and they can be improved relatively easily and cost effectively. Furthermore, small businesses mobilize a lot of human energy and often can be easily combined with other activities, such as farming, when markets are periodic or take time to build up.

An effective craft organization requires workers trained in the craft. The craft may be teaching primary school, providing simple health care, pottery making, printing, home constructing, or fire fighting. In all cases a set of skills is necessary. Typically, many of these are learned through apprenticeships or internships. The skills do not have to be very advanced, but they do require some training, usually informal.

The craft organization is most effective when the craft workers have considerable autonomy, but strategic discussions are centralized in the administrator. The major deficiency in craft organizations is usually not technical skills, but managerial skills. Most small businesses in the United States fail for this reason—a good idea poorly executed—and we would assume the problem is a universal one.

Many of the local services provided by governments—primary education, public health, fire fighting, and the like—are more effectively organized on the basis of the traditional-craft organization than as part of a national bureaucracy. Craft organization results in local autonomy and village control and therefore fits local needs. Nevertheless, craft organizations can be made more effective through training in skills and we recommend the use of extension agents for this training.

Lessons on the Change Strategies

Once a particular kind of performance gap has been recognized and the appropriate model selected for eliminating the gap, then the change agent must decide how to change the organization towards the appropriate model. He can be guided by the three basic change strategies in the organizational literatures of psychology, sociology, and management, which we described in Chapter 1. When we looked at cases in Chapters 3 and 4, however, we did not find interventions employing only one strategy. Our analysis leads us to the conclusion that organizational change efforts in LDCs, if not everywhere, are complex tasks that require team interventions and more than one tactic.[11] Development change agents need to know all three strategies, because they need to combine them for effective interventions.

Although the interventions in Chapters 3 and 4 do not reflect pure cases, three are practically exemplars of particular change strategies. The Colombian intervention for creating integrated rural development exemplifies the O.D. strategy. It effectively used group problem-solving techniques, which are common to both O.D. and organizational design, but also used T-groups and group discussion techniques, which are more common to O.D. The Jordan case is almost a pure organizational design intervention that focuses on structural change. There is no pure case of the use of an organizational theory strategy, but NIA and T and V nicely illustrate the principles of organizational theory.

The Nature of the Approach: Level of Intervention

It is no surprise that the higher the level of intervention within the organization, the more likely the intervention will be successful. Working down the hierarchy is easier than working up. Development change agents, however, do not always have a choice. Change agents must continually cultivate the support of the top leadership, as in the NIA intervention in the Philippines, the MOH intervention in Jordan, and the SMD intervention in Rio de Janeiro, Brazil. From these cases we observe that task groups are an effective tactic for maintaining leadership support. These are problem-solving groups at the top levels, and they engage the leadership in continual assessments of the organizational change.[12] According to Peters and Waterman, they also feature prominently in successful changes in major American corporations.[13]

The National Communal Irrigation Committee, a high-level problem-solving group in NIA led by an assistant administrator, was responsible for developing the communal irrigation program, evaluating and modifying it, and diffusing it throughout NIA. The group included central-level NIA officials, representatives of the community, organizers, and ". . . academically based members representing the disciplines of social science, management, and agricultural engineering."[14] It is important to note both the wide range of expertise in this working group and its closeness to the seat of power in the organization.

We highly recommend task groups as a tactic for continued involvement of the top leadership. As we noted at the end of Chapter 2, the top leadership can adapt solutions to the political and cultural constraints on the organization. Leaders are likely to be the best problem solvers. They are generally the most skilled at the very difficult task of adapting generic managerial technologies, organizational design rules, and even O.D. change tactics to the concrete realities of the organization.

There are two reasons for making the adaptation of the change to the political realities the problem-solving focus of the high-level task force. First, the adaptation problem will engage the interests of the leadership. Second, the task group can be a forum in which a variety of ranks and specialties can work together on implementation problems. The large organizational literature in the developed countries indicates that it is during implementation that access to the elites is especially critical.[15] High-level task forces also allow the development change agent—assuming that he or she is present in the discussions as was the case in Jordan—to learn a great deal about the *real politique* of the organization. This information is then critical in selecting a strategy for the introduction of some change, whether managerial technology or restructuring of the entire organization.

Finally, task forces at the top help identify opposition and convert it. At the top of an organization there are always some differences of opinion and political rivalries. The change effort can easily become a symbol of one or another political group and then be opposed by the others for the wrong reasons—"guilt by association." Task forces provide a forum in which these political problems can be worked out. However, task forces do not guarantee the reconciliation of conflicts and differences. Naturally, this depends on who leads the group and how it operates.

The role of the high-level task groups may begin to explain the subdued role of cultural values and of political influence. Cultural values will have less impact if a high-level task group treats these issues as problems to be solved. This task group adapts the changes to the cultural context. It is important to recognize this mechanism for overcoming the obstacles of cultural differences, because one could easily overemphasize the culture-free thesis. Instead, we suggest that cultural differences require some adaptation of general principles to specific cultural contexts. Again, it is worth reiterating that this is not obvious from the materials available to us, but is implied in them.

Another example of a high-level problem-solving group was the UNICEF multidisciplinary working group of four local consultants for the Urban Community Development Program, jointly sponsored by UNICEF and the Municipal Secretariat for Social Development (SMD) of Rio de Janeiro. This work group was charged with the task of devising a plan for community development in low-income areas. The point to note is that its structural location affected how it functioned. It was set up as an autonomous high-level unit in SMD, answering directly to the Secretary and left to function on its own. Its relative independence from SMD enabled it to function as a communications channel between SMD and the various community groups. Also, ". . . the identification of the working group with UNICEF, a non-political organization, was a positive factor in building up a working relationship with the community members."[16] Later, as the function of the group shifted from program development to guiding the implementation of programs, four highly qualified SMD staff were added to the working group. This step helped institutionalize both the working group and the new methodology involving high community participation in SMD. Later, UNICEF funding drew to a close and the unit was completely absorbed into SMD. It continued to meet weekly with the Secretary, however, and was included in the SMD Executive Committee.

This emphasis on the involvement of top leadership in problem solving does not mean an absence of involvement of rank and file in problem solving. Again, the successful interventions in the Philippines and in Jordan employed this tactic at multiple levels. The key issue here is that the problems of change are different at different levels and therefore there is a need to cultivate the interest and support at all levels. This is done best via the establishment of groups that attempt to solve the implementation problems. As we have seen in the case of NIA when problems could not be solved at one level, they were then moved upwards to another level for resolution. *The conclusion is that successful change efforts require multiple-level interventions and should have a problem-solving thrust.*

The Nature of the Approach: Tactics of Change

The case studies in Chapters 3 and 4 include a wide variety of tactics and usually several tactics employed together. *In fact, one of our major conclusions is that the more change tactics employed, the greater the effectiveness of the intervention, because organizational change is a complex task.* The tactics are applicable to a wide variety of situations although their content would be specific to the specific situation. For example, decree is a general tactic but to decree the decentralization of the Ministry of Health to a regional structure is applicable to very few specific situations. Being general, therefore, the nine tactics can be readily combined in almost any situation, with most cases of organizational change requiring several tactics. Implementing change is extraordinarily arduous and uncertain.[17] This is true whether one is trying to make an organization more mechanical or more organic, or to build effective local community associations.

Restructuring for long-term change.   Of the three strategies of organizational change presented in Chapter 1, O.T. is the most concerned about structural changes and emphasizes macrochanges, such as the addition of a new department as in the Jamaica case, a new level as in the Senegal case, or regional decentralization as in the Jordan case. Organizational design is also concerned about structural changes and focuses on the number of departments and how they are arranged. *In general, structural changes, whether planned or not, have long-lasting results.* They were important in NIA, T and V, and the interventions in Jordan, Jamaica, Brazil, Sri Lanka, and Senegal even though the change agents often focused on other tactics. Structural changes have the advantage of generally being institutionalized, and for lasting results it is generally better to create a new department than a task group.

Departments provide a power base for the supporters of change.[18] Without a departmental basis, the ardor and resolve of the team is likely to be dissipated, because the team is subjected to cross-pressures regarding what it should do and how it should allocate its time. We saw this most clearly in the Guyana intervention. Korten argues that creating a department is a way of protecting change in the initial stages. Another advantage of the department is that it encourages the presence of technological gatekeepers, individuals who try to keep up with the latest information.[19] These individuals play a critical role in ensuring that a department is effective.

Pilot studies. One highly successful tactic is experimentation or pilot studies. The change literature in the developed world demonstrates that first attempts have high failure rates. Pilot projects, however, provide feedback on problems and weaknesses so that corrective measures can be tried out during the experimentation stage. Many chemical firms establish pilot plants or pilot production lines within plants. Unfortunately, experimentation is rarer in the public sector. Experimentation, however, was used in the Philippine, T and V (India), Jordan, Guyana, Colombia, Brazil, Burma, and NDDB (India) cases.

Experimentation does not receive as much emphasis in the literature as it deserves. We believe the great value of experimentation is that it provides a mechanism for learning. We judge it to be the most important component of the Korten approach to learning by doing. As Korten points out, many changes fail because they are blueprints. Even the structured flexibility of the performance improvement approach to development suffers somewhat from this defect. Some change agents believe in one best general approach to the organizational problems of developing countries. While we agree that there are generic solutions, contingency theory argues that there are more than one. There are as many generic solutions as there are generic sets of conditions, and we presented four organizational models or generic solutions for four sets of technology/market conditions. A generic solution, however, must also be adapted to the specific cultural and political realities, and experimentation provides a way of doing this.

Experimentation also serves important functions in the implementation stage.[20] The two major causes of resistance to change in the developed world are overambitious goals and inflexible implementation. Experimentation can prevent both of these errors. It can also reduce resistance by allaying the fears of the organizational members. Pilot projects provide evidence about the correctness of the change and induce confidence during the large-scale implementation. Ideally, the change is introduced to the more adventurous organizational members or departments first, then gradually diffused throughout the organization.

We noted in Chapter 2 that the three approaches to development administration emphasize managerial tools and techniques including program planning, management by objectives, PERT, budget controls, and so forth.[21] Since these are thoroughly tested techniques one might assume that they can be introduced without experimentation. We advise against this practice, however, because even well-developed managerial tools have to be adapted to the specific culture and political realities of the organization. As a general rule simple tools should be used on a pilot basis first. As with heart transplants, even valuable tools can produce negative reactions. Most management-by-objective approaches have failed and quality work circles are largely now in abeyance in the United States, yet the basic ideas are laudatory. They might have worked better if they were tried on an experimental basis first and then adapted and perfected before implementation on a larger scale.

Successful pilot experiments do not necessarily become institutionalized as effective practices unless the transition is guided by a problem-solving group at the top of the organization. Pyle describes a case of the unsuccessful adaptation of a successful pilot study.[22] The translation went amiss. The central ministry did not adapt the successful elements of the pilot study but instead created a blueprint plan for implementation, which was in many ways the exact antithesis of the original flexible pilot study.

Group problem-solving.   Three tactics that were prominent in the case studies are often confused with each other: the group-decision approach, the data-discussion approach, and the group problem-solving approach. Each involves groups but in somewhat different tasks. Group data discussion is an effective tactic for recognizing output gaps. Group decision making goes beyond discussion because it involves genuine participation in decisions. It involves the acceptance by the organization of some of the recommendations of the group and is a more effective change tactic than group discussion, because acceptance of recommendations is rewarding and helps to reduce resistance to change. Unfortunately, the development administration literature has *not* kept clear the distinction between group discussion and group decision making.

Another confusion is between group decision making and group problem solving. *It is better to have groups solve problems than to have them just make decisions.* The reader may wonder how one can make decisions without problem solving. Unfortunately, this is all too easy. Problem solving is a high-order task. People usually have to be trained in how to solve problems. This is beautifully illustrated in both the Colombia and Jordan interventions. Furthermore, when quality work circles are effectively introduced, they require training in problem-solving techniques.

Group problem solving is common to both O.D. and organizational design strategies. It was part of the interventions in the Philippines, Jordan, Guyana, Jamaica, Colombia, Brazil, and Senegal, and crucial to their effectiveness. It is an effective mechanism for implementing change because implementation is a complex task. Plans never unfold as expected due to many unforeseen circumstances. The empirical research on quality work circles, one form of team effort, is in its infancy, but the existing literature indicates that these circles are more effective when: (1) individuals are trained in problem-solving techniques, (2) membership is voluntary, and (3) some of the first recommendations are accepted and implemented. These are basic tenants of an O.D. approach, although quality work circles are primarily a managerial technology.

An important component of the performance-improvement approach is the use of teams to introduce change. It uses teams mainly for training in managerial technologies. Since these technologies include skills in data collection, planning, and problem solving, however, these functions are performed as part of the learning-by-doing process, as illustrated in Guyana.

Training.   Training is a popular change tactic. All three development administration approaches discussed in Chapter 2 use training in one form or another. *All but one of the twelve interventions reviewed involved training people in leadership and/or technical skills.* The exception was Yemen and it was less successful specifically because it was an exception. Every organizational change necessitates significant changes in role behavior. Therefore, training for the new roles is required. This is another reason why experimentation and pilot studies are so important; they make clear how the roles change.

Most successful changes of organizational design in the United States involve extensive training of people for their new roles, obligations, and duties. The cases in Chapter 3 suggest that teams are effective training devices. Learning is faster in teams, as demonstrated in the Guyana intervention. Another training device, role playing from O.D., was used in Colombia and Jordan.

The action-learning technique of the performance improvement approach is a particularly effective training method and was the key to the success in the Jamaica case. The great advantage of this kind of training is that it increases involvement and makes the training more realistic.

Multiple tactics.   We repeat for emphasis the conclusion that *the more change tactics employed, the more effective the intervention.* We recommend using a combination of tactics in order to deal with the complexities of organizational change. The multiplicity of change tactics speaks to different motivational problems and potential causes of resistance. Decrees are swift and efficient when there is sufficient agreement on or acquiescence to the change. Data collection and discussion creates awareness of performance gaps. Group decision making or group problem solving can design changes and plan the implementation process. Training in new roles or skills is generally required. Experimentation and pilot projects help prevent costly mistakes. Structural change helps institutionalize the change. Multiple tactics are required for most successful organizational changes.

From our simple observation of the need for multiple tactics, we conclude that the change tactics in the learning process and performance-improvement approaches should be combined. The learning process approach emphasizes experimentation and decentralization, while the performance-improvement approach emphasizes training and managerial skills, including effective supervision. Both emphasize data collection and discussion, and group problem solving. Their objectives are somewhat at odds because management improvement seeks greater management control and efficiency while the learning process approach seeks greater participation and flexibility. Their tactics, however, are not necessarily antagonistic but can be complementary and, in our judgment, should be used together. The two approaches disagree more about ends than means. Although the rural development capacity-building approach as discussed by Brinkerhoff does use tactics from each, it still does not place as much emphasis as we are on the combination of experimentation, elite task forces, group problem solving, and training.

On the basis of our case studies and review of the literature, we recommend the following combination of tactics as a general guide. Data collection and discussion should be employed when there is not a strong perception of performance or output gaps. The change agent should choose structural changes for implementation on the basis of the contingency theory presented in Chapter 2. Then he or she should employ problem-solving groups at all levels to adapt and implement the changes and reduce their liabilities. People should be trained in their new roles and upgraded in their managerial and technical skills. Finally, the change should be tested in pilot projects before being implemented widely.

The Nature of the Approach:
Data-Collection Methods and Resources

Our general observation is that considerable effort goes into estimating the financial costs of organizational change but too little effort goes into estimating the temporal costs. The most effective interventions, however, are slow and steady. They need time to collect and analyze data, problem solve, experiment, design implementation plans, train personnel, modify plans, and adapt procedures. On the other hand, many successful interventions are relatively inexpensive.

The published materials on most of our cases disclosed little about their costs but we estimate that the economic costs of most were surprisingly low. In some instances $100 thousand went a long way towards effecting a major and long-term change, as in Jordan. Although our review of the development literature surfaced a large number of failures, we tentatively conclude that organizational improvement interventions generally pay for themselves from improved performances or outputs.

The time required for the more successful interventions was fairly long. Four or five years was a minimum, if we can generalize from the Philippines, Jamaica, Colombia, and T and V. It took time to do pilot studies and to experiment and diffuse the changes throughout the agency. The Jordan intervention was an exception because it accomplished a great deal in eighteen months.

Unfortunately, donor agencies such as USAID often work with too short a time frame. By insisting too rigidly on deadlines, they may force the pace of change beyond the capacity of the organization to manage it smoothly. The development administration literature is replete with stories of the failure of agencies to absorb and institutionalize change. Absorption can not occur if time has not been allowed for adapting general technologies and structural designs to the specifics of the organization.

Data collection is another cost which has received too little attention in the literature. Our case studies demonstrate the utility of data collection. First, it helps demonstrate output gaps, which provide the focus for the change effort. Second, data are frequently needed to determine the causes of the gap and point toward solutions. Organizational systems are complex, and the causes of poor performance are hard to determine without good data. Third, data collection can reaffirm the need for change when the going gets rough. Fourth, it can provide feedback during implementation, which then facilitates midcourse adjustments.

In general, a wide variety of data-collection methods are needed to handle the complexities of social systems. The interventions that used more methods had more ammunition with which to demonstrate and explain performance and output gaps. The Philippine intervention illustrates the advantages of using social science methodologies, which are thorough but costly. The Jordan case illustrates the advantages of the management consultant approach.

Environmental Context: Opportunities and Constraints

There is a surprising absence of discussion in the case studies about conditions that make change efforts easier, probably because change agents must concentrate on the obstacles (even these, however, are inadequately reported). Nevertheless, we notice in the case studies five conditions that created opportunities for changes: support from top administrators, equality of members, dynamic organizations, cross-cultural experiences, and professional personnel.

The reports for most of our cases do not say much about the basic macroorganizational structures of the organizations being changed, but the organizations seemed to be fairly centralized. Centralization generally is a constraint, but it may also be an opportunity when top management supports the change. According to the organizational literature decentralized organizations tend to be less resistant to change than do centralized organizations, other things being equal, because there is more equality among members. The high level of centralization of some of these organizations, therefore, was a constraint. On the other hand, strong support of the top administrator counts far more in a centralized organization. In these cases centralization might have been an opportunity.

In Chapter 3 we suggested that change agents should notice how many changes had occurred in the organization in the previous decade. The higher the number of previous changes, the more receptive the organization would be to future organizational changes. Dynamic organizations provide opportunities and static organizations, constraints. In the latter the change agent should start slowly and introduce a readily acceptable change with quick payoffs first. Future changes will then become easier and more probable.

The dynamic criterion for choosing an organizational site for an intervention is more concrete than the criteria used by the performance-improvement approach, which are a felt need for change, widespread commitment to change, and other facilitative conditions. We point out, however, that felt needs and commitments can change quickly, but past histories can not.

Administrators with wide and varied experiences provide another opportunity because they are more likely to perceive performance and output gaps. Cross-cultural experiences and especially American training, make administrators more critical and more capable of problem solving because they encourage dialectical thought. Change agents should build coalitions with these people. When high-level administrators have cross-cultural experiences, they tend to facilitate the job of change agents.

Certain occupational groups are easier for change agents to work with as we have already observed. People in occupations in which they are trained to use data and to problem solve are more likely to perceive output gaps and be motivated to do something about them. Certainly, this helped in the Philippines, Jordan, and the electric utility in Guyana.

A major constraint is staffing. Change interventions are doomed to failure in organizations that are short of staff. This was the problem in the Hydraulics Department in Guyana. Implementation of change requires extra work, time, and energy. It is very stressful. Therefore, interventions should only be tried if there are extra resources or if the organization is adequately staffed.

Special Third World Contingencies
and Organizational Forms

Too often social scientists apply their models of institutional development without testing whether their models work in the appropriate settings. Our contingency theory models work in developed countries but we had to test their utility in LDCs. Our literature review and case studies indicate that all four models worked as expected. Our review also identified conditions where none of these models worked effectively and we discovered two new successful models. We have discovered some new contingencies and some new forms, which are quite interesting. In fact, we have come to the conclusion that these Third World models can find useful applications in the First World, but this theme we will develop in another work. Nevertheless, our review of Third World cases to test contingency theory has resulted in its expansion. The two new organizational types that we have discovered can become new models for both organizational theory and change agents.

The contingency found in the Third World, but rare in the developed world, is a vast demand for basic services but almost no resources for providing them. *The major contingency not considered by contingency theory is an imbalance between what is known and demanded and what can actually be offered from available human and material resources.* This is the very special problem that the LDCs face. In many areas they see and want what the developed world has, but they do not have the resources even to come close to fulfilling these desires. Lerner refers to this as the problem of rising expectations.[23] The middle and upper classes of the LDCs demand and often obtain education, health care, and sanitation, which are provided universally in developed countries. The poor also want these services and the government wants to provide them, but it can not for lack of resources.

Why does contingency theory fail to consider this problem? The answer lies in the history of organizational development in the West. In the developed world there has been a rough balance between what was known and what could be offered (we ignore the problem of the internal distributions of wealth). Health care was primitive in the nineteenth century because not much was known, not because of lack of resources. The same can be said for all basic human needs. As the process of development continued, new products and services were created and new organizations gradually developed for producing them at low cost. These organizations fit the mechanical model and were capital intensive. Meanwhile, for other services the technologies improved and the craft organizations that provided them became more organic and human-capital intensive. It is difficult to attain these organizational forms if there is a shortage of human or physical capital and without these forms it is difficult to provide these products and services in the quantity and quality that is demanded in the poor countries today. What can be done in this supply/demand imbalance?

In attacking this dilemma some LDCs have produced interesting experiments that are worthy of study and even replication. Two new organizational models are implied in some of the cases of Chapters 3 and 4. One we call the truncated-craft model and the other the truncated-organic model. The critical difference between the truncated and nontruncated models is that the range of skills is severely narrowed. In the truncated model many of the skills associated with the craft in a traditional model or with the professional occupations in an organic model are not provided. The technology is truncated and reduced to a few elements, pieces of knowledge, and/or skills that can be taught in a very short time period.

The Truncated-Craft Model

One approach to the resource problem is the truncated-craft model. We see elements of this approach in both the Senegal and Burma interventions described in Chapter 4. The essence of the truncated model is to pick out only a few activities of the craft necessary to deal with a few major concerns—the most important diseases, most needed learning skills, or most severe administrative problems relevant to the locality—and ignore the others. For example, rather than train an elementary teacher for four years in a wide variety of different subjects, the teacher is taught only a few skills relative to teaching the fundamental skills of reading and writing. Another example is the nurse assistant; rather than spending four years in college learning a lot of different subjects, he or she takes a short course of one month or less to learn the very basics of the health care needed in a particular locale. The costs are obviously much less and, furthermore, the training can be routinized, as it was in the T and V system reported in Chapter 3.

The people selected to be trained do not need even a high school education; indeed, it would be better to work with people who had only a grade school education. People with a secondary diploma are likely to find the routinized work associated with the truncated-craft or truncated-organic models boring, as Leonard shows in his study of the Kenya Agricultural Extension Service.[24] Furthermore, more highly trained people are likely to be concerned about status and not want to live in the villages where the work needs to be done.

As soon as one recognizes new models, one can find precursors or analogs for them. For example, in the developed world, hospital corpsmen are trained in the U.S. Navy for some six months to handle a limited variety of illnesses, and they do a reasonable job. Tanzania, as well, has built its health care system on this model. Likewise, in the nineteenth century, primary school teachers in the United States were given only a couple of years education beyond grade school. In the Burma literacy campaign we saw volunteer university students with minimal training in education being used to teach literacy and to train village teachers to do the same, thereby extending the program.[25]

The truncated-craft model can be employed in all of the situations that are appropriate for the traditional-craft model simply by reducing the amount of training. It provides more services by using large numbers of inexpensive workers. The truncated-craft model can also be combined with a mechanical national service organization, serving as the local outpost of the service organization. Instead of making the clients come to the agency, the agency goes to the clients. A health system that depends entirely on regional hospitals requires that many people travel long distances to obtain medical care. The establishment of numerous health clinics throughout the region greatly facilitates health care. Even a widespread system of clinics, however, may inadequately localize health services; better still is a system of truncated-craft organizations ("health huts") in hundreds or thousands of villages. This form was used in the previously reported case of Senegal and in the case of primary health care in India as reported by Bogaert.[26] The quality of the professional service in the village health hut can not compare to the service in the hospital, but the health hut at least provides some basic services where no services were available previously. Furthermore, the more serious cases can be referred to the nearest clinic or hospital.

It is not necessary to detail the cases in which localization of services in truncated-craft organizations has led to greater agency effectiveness. The benefits and reasons for localization are clear. First, localizations make the services more available to beneficiaries, as illustrated by health care in Senegal and by two programs reported by Paul: the population program in Indonesia and the public health program in rural China.[27] Second, localization increases the understanding of the circumstances of beneficiaries and facilitates the adaptation of the services to those circumstances. This principle is widely recognized in agricultural research and extension as in the T and V system in India. For example, a research center will have satellite experiment stations or on-farm experimental plots to take into account local conditions. Likewise, extension services must be close to the farmers via regular on-farm visits and demonstrations to be effective.[28]

The truncated-craft organization is very small, with usually less than ten members. It is highly formalized and centrally designed. It relies heavily on local support as we have seen in the Senegal health huts, and, to a lesser but still considerable extent, in the Burma literacy campaign.

The truncated-craft organization adapts to a shortage of funds by using inexpensive workers and by obtaining material support from the local community for the teacher, health worker, or extension agent. In exchange, the local community controls the outpost organization. Community control, however, does not guarantee competent management or competent service. In fact, incompetence is to be expected unless the tasks are simple or training is provided. The failing Senegal health huts were turned into successes when the health committee was better trained in management practices. In summary, the service organization devolves control over the outpost to the village in exchange for the resources that the village generates, but the service organization must also provide training for workers and village leaders.

Another potential problem is the morale of the truncated-craft worker who may live in isolation without much professional contact. The worker will probably need supervising visits and the upgrading of skills to maintain motivation, or else should participate for only short periods of time as in Burma. On the other hand, the problem of living in remote areas disappears if local residents are used. The truncated-craft model is outlined in Figure 5.1 using the framework developed in Chapter 2. It features very low costs and requires minimum nonlocal inputs.

Figure 5.1   The Causes of Performance Level in the Truncated-Craft Model

Performances	Environmental Contingencies
Adapted to local needs	Large but local demand
Very low cost	Standardized activities
	No economies of scale
	Lack of resources
Structure	**Culture**
Components of a craft	Community Control
Centralized, formalized	Tradition of voluntary service
Resources	**Process**
Very little training	Participation by the community
Standardized technolgy	Agency provides training
Community capital/labor	
Very small size	

The Truncated-Organic Model

Another kind of organizational model discovered in the case studies is the truncated-organic model. It is designed for complex tasks under conditions of insufficient physical and human capital. Integrated rural development or community development are the most common examples. Interdisciplinary teams are needed but can not be provided; therefore, each worker is trained in a few carefully selected skills of an occupation and in team work. (An even more truncated-organic model substitutes a single person for the interdisciplinary team; he or she is superficially trained in a wide variety of essential tasks—for example, some community organizers are trained in this manner.) The truncated-organic model is particularly well-suited for low-funded integrated development, as in the two UNICEF urban development projects in Sri Lanka and Brazil.

One might assume that the Colombian project in integrated rural development is another example, but it is not. Instead, the Colombian project is a pure organic model involving a wide variety of professional specialists, well-trained and working in teams to solve very complex problems. In contrast, the problems in Sri Lanka and Brazil were much simpler, though multifaceted, since they concerned nutritional skills, sanitation, and birth control. Addressing each need is a relatively simple task once it is a worker's single focus. The necessary skills, however, were not all in public health and usually were associated with different occupations. In

Sri Lanka educators, engineers, and community mobilizers were needed in addition to several types of health professionals. This variety tended to cause coordination problems among agencies. The Sri Lanka case involved two lead agencies, the Ministry of Health and the Common Amenities Board, and several auxiliary agencies, including the Women's Bureau and the National Youth Services Council.

The truncated-organic model has all of the characteristics of the organic model except for the truncation of skills. The decision-making structure is decentralized and work is often done in teams. In most settings this model involves participation because community associations must provide resources and labor and help coordinate activities.

In both truncated models, human capital needs are reduced because occupations are simplified. They are not broken up into distinct tasks for specialized low-skilled workers as on an assembly line. Instead, a few occupational tasks are selected on the basis of the knowledge of the community or region. The occupation is not then made routine but is simplified.

We use the terms truncated craft and truncated organic for independent local organizations and for relatively autonomous outpost suborganizations of national or municipal service organizations. Since our research focuses on the national or regional service organization none of our twelve case studies involves an independent local truncated-craft or organic organization. The most autonomous of the truncated organizations discussed previously are the health huts in Senegal and the literary teachers in Burma. In both cases the local community paid or supported the workers. Nevertheless, in both cases the service organization established and supplied the outpost and trained the workers, so that autonomy is not complete.

The truncated-organic model is outlined in Figure 5.2. It features the adaptation of fairly complex services to local needs using minimally trained personnel.

In summary, we have derived from our case studies two new models of organizations: the truncated-craft model and the truncated-organic model. Tasks are simplified; resources are generated by voluntary associations or community organizations; and national or municipal governments usually provide training. These forms appear to be useful institution-building strategies for LDCs that have a scarcity of both human and physical capital but that need to meet large demands.

Figure 5.2   The Causes of Performance Level in the Truncated-Organic Model

Performances	Environmental Contingencies
Tailored to an integrated set of needs	Large but local demand
	Components can be standardized
Flexible	No economies of scale
	Lack of resources
Structure	**Culture**
Components of a number of crafts/professions	Community control
Decentralized	
Resources	**Processes**
Very little training	Participation by the community
Standardized components	Natural leadership
Community capital/labor	Agency provides training
Small size	

Conclusions

Organizations in LDCs have been moved in more than one direction, demonstrating the utility of contingency theory. Some were moved towards the mechanical model and some towards the organic model, depending on the emphasized performance. Finally, the contingency theory literature did not consider some of the contingencies found in LDCs. This has led to the recognition of several new organizational forms that we have labeled the truncated-craft and the truncated-organic models. They offer a number of possibilities for large gains at relatively low costs.

In this chapter we also analyzed why certain change strategies worked. Organizational change is a complex task. It requires strong pressures for change that are based on the recognition of performance and output gaps, a mixture of change strategies that includes both structural and process changes, and a number of change tactics and data-collection methods. It requires both money and time, but much less of the former and much more of the latter than many realize.

The higher the intervention level, the more effective the change. Top administrators, however, should be involved as problem solvers and not just as ratifiers. The most successful grouping of change tactics combines experimentation, data collection, group problem solving, structural changes (such as the addition of a department), and training. Together these provide a very powerful combination of tactics that can overcome problems and meet the exigencies of the situation. Data collection is necessary to demonstrate performance and output gaps, to determine their causes, and to uncover problems in the process of attempting to correct the output gap.

Notes

1. Robert Presthus, 1961, "Weberian vs. Welfare Bureaucracy in Traditional Society," *Administrative Science Quarterly,* vol. 6 (June); pp. 1-24.

2. Max Weber, 1951, *The Religion of China* (New York: Free Press).

3. Guy Gran, 1983, *Learning from Development Success: Some Lessons from Contemporary Case Histories* (Washington, D.C.: National Association of Schools of Public Affairs and Administration, Working Paper No. 9, (September), p. 4.

4. David C. Korten, 1980, "Community Organization and Rural Development: A Learning Process Approach," *Public Administration Review,* vol. 40, no. 5 (September/October), pp. 480-511.

5. Jay Galbraith, 1973, *Designing Complex Organizations* (Reading, Mass.: Addison-Wesley), Chapter 1; *also see* Jerald Hage, 1980, *Theories of Organization: Form, Process, and Transformation* (New York: John Wiley and Sons), Chapter 11.

6. John Montgomery, 1979, "The Populist Front in Rural Development: Or Shall We Eliminate the Bureaucrats and Get on with the Job," *Public Administration Review,* January-February, pp. 58-65.

7. Alfred D. Chandler, Jr., 1977, *The Visible Hand* (Cambridge, Mass.: Harvard University Press).

8. David Landes, 1969, *The Unbound Prometheus: Technological Change and Industrial Development in Western Europe from 1750 to the Present* (Cambridge: Cambridge University Press).

9. Samuel Paul, 1982, *Managing Development Programs: The Lessons of Success* (Boulder, Colo.: Westview Press), p. 188.

10. *See* Enyinna Chuta, 1983, "Upgrading the Managerial Process of Small Entrepreneurs in West Africa," *Public Administration and Development,* vol. 3, pp. 275-283; David Wilcock and Enyinna Chuta, 1982, "Employment in Rural Industries in Eastern Upper Volta," *International Labor Review,* vol. 121, no. 4 (July, August).

11. Derick Brinkherhoff, forthcoming, "The Evolution of Current Perspectives on Institutional Development: An Organizational Focus" in Brinkerhoff and Garcia-Zamor (eds.), *Political, Projects, and People: Institutional Development in Haiti* (New York: Praeger).

12. *See* Thomas Peters and Robert Waterman, Jr., 1982, *In Search of Excellence: Lessons from America's Best-Run Companies* (New York: Warner).

13. *Ibid.*

14. Korten, 1980, *op. cit.,* p. 483.

15. Jerald Hage and Michael Aiken, 1970, *Social Change in Complex Organizations* (New York: Random House).

16. Ana Maria F. Brasileiro *et. al.,* 1982, "Extending Municipal Services by Building on Local Initiatives," *Assignment Children,* vol. 57/58, p. 79.

17. Brinkerhoff, forthcoming, *op. cit.*

18. Thomas J. Allen, 1977, *Managing the Flow of Technology* (Cambridge, Mass.: MIT Press).

19. Korten, *op. cit.*

20. Jerald Hage and Michael Aiken, 1970, *Social Change in Complex Organizations,* (New York: Random House), Chapter 4; and Zaltman *et al.,* 1973, Chapter 3.

21. Brinkerhoff, forthcoming, *op. cit.*

22. David F. Pyle, 1982, *From Project to Program: Structural Constraints Associated with Expansion* (Washington, D.C.: NASPAA, Working Paper No. 3).

23. Daniel Lerner, 1958, *The Passing of Traditional Society* (New York: The Free Press).

24. David Leonard, 1977, *Reaching the Peasant Farmer: Organization Theory and Practice in Kenya* (Chicago: University of Chicago Press).

25. Nyi Nyi, 1983, "Planning, Implementation and Monitoring of Literacy Programmes: The Burmese Experience," *Assignment Children,* vol. 63/64, pp. 87-79.

26. Michael V. I. Bogaert, 1983, "Primary Health Care as Rural Communication," *Assignment Children,* vol. 63/64, pp. 59-67.

27. Paul, 1982, *op. cit.*

28. Willem Beets, 1979, "Relevant Cropping Systems Research for the Asian Farmer," *The Malaysian Agricultural Journal,* vol. 52, no. 1, pp. 58-64.

Epilogue

In this monograph we analyzed organizational change as a development strategy for LDCs. Our major focus was on improving organizations but the concern which drove the analysis was economic and institutional development. The previous chapters have fairly thoroughly addressed the issue of organizational improvement but they have not dealt in an integrated way with the larger issue of how organizational change can best serve societal development. We have made numerous observations on this connection throughout the monograph but now we would like to make a comprehensive statement about the strategy of organizational change for institutional development. The strategy that we propose has two parts: First, organizational structures should be chosen on the basis of contingency theory. As amended in Chapter 5, contingency theory provides six models from which to choose, and we shall describe in this Epilogue which models best fit the various economic sectors. Second, organizations should be changed by means of a complex multitactic intervention methodology. In this chapter we shall describe how the various tactics can be coordinated into an integrated strategy for changing organizations.

Our strategies of organizational change and institutional development are derived from the organizational change literature and grounded in Third World case materials. They are rationalistic yet adapted to the realities of LDCs. Nevertheless, some readers may wonder whether the interests of powerful groups and the scarcity of resources would allow interveners to change organizational structures in the direction prescribed by contingency theory. The two issues of power and the availability of resources need to be addressed, therefore, if our recommendations are to have any weight. We address them in the last section of this chapter.

The General Strategy: Choice of Organizational Model

According to our amended contingency theory there are four basic organizational models and two truncated models to utilize in a national development plan. The four basic models are designed for four sets of contingencies that are defined by the interaction of the level of technology and market demand. The two truncated models are differentiated by the additional contingency of scarcity of resources.

In Chapter 2 we divided the economy of a developing country into four major sectors that relate to the four sets of contingencies and the four models. In sector one the producers and providers have to be adaptive to local needs and tastes in areas that do not require high technology. In sector two the producers and providers have to produce inexpensively as much as possible of a standardized product or service in areas that do not require high technology. In sector three producers and providers have to produce inexpensively standardized goods or services at the same time that they continuously innovate using high technology. Finally, in sector four the producers and providers must produce relatively unique goods and services using high technology. Providers that invent appropriate technologies for the society would belong to this fourth sector. In the following sections we analyze these four basic sectors of the economy and propose a development strategy for the state in each sector. We also look at one or two common kinds of organizations within each sector as examples of the appropriate models.

Sector One: Small Farms, Small Businesses, and Local Government Services

Our narrow definition of an organization in Chapter 1 excluded social collectives with fewer than ten members. We thereby exclude many family businesses (including family farms), which predominate in developing countries. Our contingency theory of organizations, however, can be relevant to these social collectives by suggesting ways for a government agency to upgrade them through training.

First, we will consider the case of small farms. Typically, these are a major part of the total economy of a Third World country. The small farm is a craft organization, which needs technical assistance to be more productive. The state can help small farms through research and extension systems. The latter should be organized as a mechanical organization, such as T and V, when the crops are relatively standardized and the same technology essentially can be used over a wide area. When climate, topography, type of crop, farmers' resources, and other factors vary greatly, however, the mechanical form is inappropriate.

Instead, the state needs to develop appropriate technologies for each of the different situations that farmers face. If the variations are quite extensive the researchers would have to work very closely with farmers in order to understand their information needs. If this pattern were carried to the extreme, there would be no need for extension because researchers would work directly with farmers. The costs would be prohibitive, however, so a research and extension system must provide instead technologies that are somewhat standardized.

There are two solutions to the problem of providing appropriate technologies in moderately variable conditions. The first solution is to combine a fairly mechanical extension service with a very decentralized research system so that moderately variable technologies are channeled through a mechanical delivery system. The second solution is to combine a fairly centralized research system with a fairly organic extension service, so that fairly standard technologies are taught to extension agents who have relatively high skills and can adjust them to the various circumstances. Neither solution is practiced often in LDCs so that they are usually ineffective in providing appropriate technologies for highly or moderately variable situations. A third solution, which is beyond the capacity of LDCs, is to have highly educated farmers who know how to obtain the knowledge they need from research organizations and science information services.

We have discussed the structure of the agricultural research system as it relates to the extension system and to variability of conditions. Another factor that influences the structure of the agricultural research system is the availability from international agencies of technologies that can be adapted to local conditions. When appropriate technologies can be borrowed that require minimal adaptation to local conditions, the research system can feature many small, widely dispersed craft organizations (experiment stations) for local testing and adaptation. The more that the new and appropriate technology has to be domestically developed, however, the more the system has to feature organic organizations (research centers). This research system would also need experiment stations for regional adaptations of the domestic technologies.

Another role for the state in increasing the productivity of small farms is to provide inputs. The size of small farms does not allow for economies of scale in purchasing seeds, fertilizers, chemicals, and machinery. Theoretically, the government can improve the overall efficiency of this sector by purchasing inputs in large quantities and distributing them to small farmers at lower prices than found in the retail markets. In practice, it is not clear that this overall system is more efficient than the market. The state can also provide credit to small farmers at lower interest rates than the money lenders. These are popular programs and probably increase social justice but their economic rationality is being debated. The clearest role of the state in improving the small farm sector, therefore, is in providing research and extension since LDCs have no private sector alternatives.

There are also many non-farm small businesses in developing countries. Typically, these are not large enough to be considered organizations by our narrow definition: nevertheless, the principles presented in this monograph are applicable. The development objective of the state is to make these small businesses more productive. In the United States small businesses are upgraded by many thousands of workshops, seminars, courses, books, and consultants. Service markets handle the problem, but such are rare in LDCs. Instead, we recommend that the state provide outreach services to non-farm small businesses just as it does for farm small businesses. As with small farms, non-farm small businesses need two kinds of training: management skills and technical skills for their particular products or services. The management skills can be readily diffused by an extension service since they are relatively standardized technologies that the managers can adapt to their businesses. The same is true of the most widely demanded technical skills.

The state should direct its small-business extension service to goods-producing organizations because making them more productive would increase incomes, standards of living, and exports, while reducing imports. Economic development requires increasing both goods production and the provision of skilled services such as education and health; but it does *not* require increasing the provision of unskilled services such as retailing. In fact, underdevelopment is associated with underemployment, which results in millions of redundant service jobs such as stand-around-servants, mobs of shoe shine boys, excess salespeople, and the providers of unnecessary services. Developed countries also have a number of people who clean windshields at stop lights, but LDCs have millions of small businesses using small shops, stalls, or carts to sell a small number of widely available goods. To make these businesses productive would put many people out of work.

Some of the small-business producers make art and craft objects. Substantial incomes can be earned from these if international markets are successfully exploited as was done in the case of African masks and oriental rugs. The technical skill most needed for these businesses may be marketing in order for these products to sell at high prices and for LDCs to retain the majority of the earnings from them. Often these and other small businesses also can benefit greatly from upgrading in the technologies of production. We strongly recommend, therefore, the creation of research organizations that serve small businesses. The appropriate technology literature provides numerous examples of research teams that develop specific appropriate technologies for craft-business enterprises.[1] Usually, however, they are temporary teams working on a project basis. Permanent research organizations providing appropriate technologies for craft businesses are rare. One example is the Technology Consultancy Center of the University of Kumasi in Ghana, which charges fees for services. Another example is the research department serving hundreds of cooperatives of the National Dairy Development Board in India, as described in Chapter 4.

Another way to increase the productivity of non-farm small businesses is to upgrade small family enterprises into traditional-craft organizations by increasing their size. With increase in size some specialization of tasks can occur. The first great gains in productivity in the developed world were achieved via this method and it can benefit the newly developing nations as well.

A third major category in the craft sector is local government services. These frequently need strengthening in many of the same ways as do small businesses. They need upgrading in managerial technologies and technical skills. There is a need, therefore, for more research into appropriate technologies for fire and police departments, schools, public health departments, and the like, as well as a need for training in the appropriate skills. It is easy to overestimate the amount of education that these skills require. These local government services do not require people with high school educations, and certainly not college educations. As we have stressed before, Europe successfully eliminated illiteracy with primary school teachers who had only a few years of education beyond their students. This approach succeeded because the teachers worked with standardized curriculums. In other words, there were some elements of mechanical organization in the provision of these services.

In some countries, however, the resources are insufficient even to support these approaches, with the result that basic services are not provided widely. Some countries have developed new ways to provide services in these conditions of scarcity; they use truncated-craft organizations, voluntary associations, or some combination of the two. In the truncated-craft model, as illustrated in the Senegal health huts or the Burma literacy campaign, only one highly specific skill was taught. The organization could thereby provide one specific basic service over a wide area at low cost.

Some of our case studies provide examples of very poor developing countries providing some basic services via voluntary associations. When resources are scarce the state may have no alternative. In this context the state must play a supportive role, which includes provision of the required managerial and technical training, as it did in the case of the Senegal health huts and in some of the interventions of UNICEF.

When the state wants to increase the productivity of small farms, small businesses, and local government services, it can choose among three options: (1) provide training in managerial and technical skills only, (2) upgrade traditional organizations into true craft organizations (through increasing their size and providing managerial training appropriate for somewhat more complex and impersonal organizations), or (3) develop and utilize voluntary associations. The first is the standard approach when the state works with small businesses. The second is more venturesome but can move the community farther on the path of development. The third probably is the way to get the most out of the state's scarce resources by inducing considerable inputs from the community. This latter option is only appropriate for the kinds of basic services that most people in the community want and need, such as learning how to read, public health, sanitation, and feeder rural roads.

Voluntary associations are an effective mechanism for generating additional resources in the local community and, therefore, worth considering as a form of institution building when the tasks are simple and do not require much training. The key advantage of voluntary associations is that they can generate free labor to do such tasks as maintaining existing structures on even the building of new structures. Even though these tasks are simple, nevertheless, the state must provide training in technical and managerial skills.

The voluntary association approach is most viable when the local communities have few differences in wealth, status, and power. As we have seen this is partly a function of the type of crop or food-gathering technology, terrain, and other ecological factors. When inequality is pronounced, the state should provide services through other means.

The practice of relying upon voluntary associations is most effective when there is a collaborative arrangement between voluntary associations in the local communities and a national service organization. Relying solely upon either voluntary associations or national service organizations is generally less effective because a crucial component will be undersupplied. True development involves two sets of goals, which need to be balanced. The first is the pursuit of national goals and the second is the adaptation of programs to local needs. Unless the two kinds of institutions work together in a participative manner, one or both of these goals probably will be poorly addressed. Let us look, for example, at agricultural research and extension. Total attentiveness to farmers' needs might leave balance of payments problems uncorrected or urban food prices too high for political stability. Total attentiveness to national food issues might fail to address the farmers' most pressing needs.

In summary, there are many options available for increasing productivity in this first sector, and gains in this sector can have a major and positive impact on the rate of development of the economy as a whole because it is so large. It is also the sector of the economy that remains the most inefficient. Its inefficiency is not due to the absence of market competition—this sector is the *most* competitive; instead, low productivity results from low managerial and technical skills, little capital, and the diseconomies of small scale including low-task specialization.

Sector Two: Large and Standardized Government and Business Bureaucracies

All developing countries have need for standardized products and services. In the public sector the post office is perhaps the clearest example, but other examples would be railroads; the construction of bridges, highways, dams, and irrigation systems; the military; custodial mental hospitals; and the dispensing of welfare checks. Examples in the private sector would include standardized services such as insurance and banking, and standardized mass production such as steel, cement, rubber tires, bicycles, toys, cigarettes, flour and other processed foods, and many machine tools.

The mechanical organization is the best model for producing or providing standardized products and services. Since many national government agencies provide standardized services, they should be mechanical. However, most of these agencies are not mechanical in LDCs but are traditional or patrimonial bureaucracies. They deviate dramatically from the ideal bureaucratic form which is efficient and rational. Change agents can increase their productivity greatly by upgrading them into true mechanical organizations. There are many new managerial technologies that can make organizations more efficient and productive, as we have seen in a number of the interventions. The performance-improvement approach and management-improvement teams specialize in these technologies. In many cases, however, the poor performance of the agency is not due mainly to the lack of appropriate managerial tools, rather, the agency is controlled by a "baron" who diverts it from its goal of providing low-cost services on a mass basis.

Sometimes countries choose to provide locally diverse services rather than standardized services. An example in some countries is that of primary and secondary education. The government may choose to create one standard curriculum, as is the case in the French education system; it may choose to allow for local diversity as is the case with the British education system, based on local gov-

ernments and the private sector. The more standardized the service, the more mechanical the providing agency. The greater the
local diversity, the more craft-like the providing organizations.

Sometimes Third World countries lack the resources to provide
certain local services using craft or organic organizations, and
must provide them more inexpensively using mechanical organizations and standardizing the service. For example, a central government could provide a standardized public health service in market
towns throughout the country at relatively low cost, significantly
lowering the death rates of its people, when it could not afford to
build hospitals throughout the country. When conditions allow,
another example would be extension services to provide standard
technologies over a relatively large section of the country using a
mechanical organization.

Sometimes the resources are insufficient to allow a mechanical
organization to substitute standardized services for local craft or
organic organizations. Mechanical organizations require moderate
management skills and the money to support a bureaucracy. When
these skills and finances are absent, the agency might provide the
service using the truncated-craft form of organization. The service
is provided by people who have not received full craft training but
only training in one or a few elements of the craft. These workers
are not supported, managed, and supplied by a bureaucracy but are
supported and supplied by the community and are hardly managed
at all. The Senegal health huts and the Burma literacy campaign
fit this model. Health care and teaching of reading are usually performed by craft organizations and sometimes by mechanical organizations, but not in these cases.

Sector Three: Large and Semi-standardized
Government and Business Bureaucracies

In the developed world, sector three is very important and is growing as mechanical producers of goods and services add organic research departments or planning departments. In LDCs sector
three is underdeveloped because the technological and human-
capital requirements are too high. Nevertheless, LDCs need to
build research and planning capacity into some of their mechanical
organizations. An example is a large wood mill or lumber company
that experiments with processing new woods or developing new
tree strains for replanting its forests. The Jari lumber enterprise,

which billionaire Daniel Ludwig established in the Amazon, is this type of organization on a gigantic scale. Large mechanized operations with research departments can also be created in agriculture, but the costs in job displacement usually mitigate against this. A possible example in the public sector might be a public health service with a mechanical system of delivering services combined with an organic research group that develops the service packages. In the private sector, the production of chemicals, electrical goods, drugs, and computers requires the mixed mechanical-organic form. In general, only the larger and more wealthy developing countries can provide the necessary investments in this sector.

Sector Four: Small and Non-standardized Government and Business Organizations

The future for many developing countries lies in the development of appropriate technologies for farms, public health agencies, small craft businesses, and many other productive enterprises and service agencies. *The research of sector four is needed to make sector one effective,* underlining the importance of a coordinated development strategy. The research, planning, consulting, and training organizations in sector four should fit the organic model so that they require highly skilled personnel working in teams and often with sophisticated equipment. Nevertheless, the human and physical capital requirements are not too great for most LDCs to spawn some of these organic organizations.

Sector four includes more than research organizations. In the public sector it includes hospitals and universities that require complex technologies and attempt to provide a variety of services that are frequently adapted to individualized needs. The organic form is most appropriate for providing these complex and varied services.

In the private sector there are opportunities in electronics and bio-tech that developing countries can exploit with organic organizations. Korea and Taiwan have made small investments and created new improvements in electronic products which have given them large trade benefits. A large amount of new products can be developed also in bio-tech with relatively small investments in research and development. One person with a degree, an idea, and some laboratory equipment can do wonders in this field. There are other areas besides electronics and bio-tech where small-batch production and innovation are possible, and LDCs should consider their resources and seek niches of this type.

Scarcity of resources (mainly of money and highly trained personnel) often prevents LDCs from creating organic organizations. In this situation truncated-organic organizations might provide the service until resources increase to the level that can support organic organizations. The truncated-organic organization uses a locally trained individual in place of the multidisciplinary team of the organic organization. For example, community development is a complex task requiring the integrated contributions of a multidisciplinary team of experts. Most LDCs can not afford to field such teams but they can afford to field community developers. They will not be as effective as the community development team, but can accomplish some simple projects with the help of the community and justify their employment.

General Strategy: Choice of Change Tactics

The choice of organizational model involves mutually exclusive choices but the choice of change tactics does not. A change agent can use all of the change tactics and combine them in a great variety of ways. In fact, we have recommended using multiple tactics because organizational change is a complex task. Nevertheless, we think there is *one* major combination of tactics that has proved to be effective in a variety of situations. It is the combination of data collection and discussion groups, problem-solving groups, experimentation, and training.

The first step in an intervention is to demonstrate that there is a performance or output gap if it is not yet widely perceived. A minimal tactic for this purpose is discussion groups, but where possible it is better to first collect data either to demonstrate the gap or to make it more concrete and visible. The greater the demonstration of ineffectiveness, the more commitment that can be mobilized to improve the organization in concrete and objective terms. Typically, organizations keep records that can help in this process, as we have seen in the Jordan and Philippine interventions. Discussion groups can help interpret the data and allow the change agent to discover the level of commitment to the organization's goals.

As we have noted in the previous chapter, it is also important to keep reminding key individuals of these gaps. An institutionalized data-collection system can be used for this purpose and help maintain the commitment of organizational members to the change effort. This continued support will often be essential to the success of the change because organizational change requires an enormous effort and great dedication.

Once a performance or output gap is widely perceived a solution must be devised. If a standard solution is required, such as making the organization more mechanical through managerial technologies, then the change agent can devise the solution. Most likely, however, unique aspects of the situation will make it necessary to use a problem-solving group to devise a solution.

The next step is to experiment. The solution should be tested on a small scale and revised before being implemented widely. A high-level problem-solving group is useful during this stage to adapt the solution to the political and cultural realities of the organization and to confront unforeseen impacts. As the experiment unfolds, new problems requiring new solutions become evident. A data-collection system increases the speed and accuracy of the perceptions of these problems and provides an information base for the problem solvers.

Problem-solving groups at several levels of the organization are useful for implementing the change and responding to additional problems that may be generated. The high-level problem-solving group would be out of touch with the realities at lower levels. Also, implementation requires the active participation of a large number of people and this participation is most effective through problem-solving groups.

In the implementation stage training is used to teach new roles, skills, and procedures. A particularly effective training method is action learning in groups as illustrated in the management-improvement approach. Training in groups is appropriate since the changes will involve new interaction patterns.

In summary, we recommend an intervention process as follows: Data collection and discussion are used to develop and pinpoint the performance or output gaps. Problem-solving groups at several levels, including the top, design a solution and plan its implementation. The solution is implemented on a small scale on an experimental basis. As the experiment unfolds, problem-solving groups are adapting the solution to the cultural, political, and technological realities of the organization. Once a successful model is demonstrated, then training is conducted to teach people the new set of skills, behaviors, and interactions that are required.

The Problem of Power

We have presented a fairly rational guide to improving organizations. Our work has benefited considerably from careful reviews by a number of experts in theories of organizational change or in development administration. Most reviewers support what we have done, but some have expressed concern about what we have not done. In particular, they doubt whether our framework can deal with the major obstacle to changing organizations to make them more effective—the power of key actors who do not support the change. There is some truth to this criticism. We would expect the power factor to be involved in most cases in which our recommendations failed. However, some of our recommendations deal with power issues which we summarize and expand upon in this section.

The major way our framework recognizes and attempts to deal with power is in the demonstration of performance and output gaps to the influential people, inside and outside the organization, in order to obtain the necessary support for the change. If these influentials have no interest in productivity, efficiency, innovation, or adaptiveness, then our framework has little utility. In our research, however, we have found such cases to be rare. We find many cases where the personal goals of influentials limit the pursuit of productivity and other indicators of effectiveness, but within these limits influentials favor performance improvement. In fact, for many public services there is much more demand for the service than the agency can provide, and both influentials and the general public think that increasing the provision of these services is essential and desirable. There are always some exceptions, as in the case of birth control in Arabic cultures, but these are rare. Even when elites are unconcerned about the lack of services for the poor, they will become interested when pressure for change builds from below, and data gathering can help build this pressure for change by documenting the gaps.

The second major way our framework deals with power issues is in the use of problem-solving groups, especially at the top of the organization, to adapt the change to the political and cultural realities of the organization. We frankly recognize that the proposed change must leave undisturbed some benefits that powerful elites derive from the existing circumstances. The adaptation of the model means leaving some of these benefits unaffected in exchange for elite support. Frequently, elites overestimate their potential costs from organizational change and underestimate their potential benefits. One of the tasks of the problem-solving groups is to make the changes benefit the elites and inform them accordingly. In fact, elites should be members of the high-level problem-solving groups or work closely with them. Furthermore, elite opposition is usually partial. If some of the elite support the change, the high-level problem-solving group might persuade the opposition to concur via group discussion and pressure. The process of discussion can build legitimacy for change; whereas without the discussions of the problem-solving group, the opposition might resort to active or passive sabotage when the change is introduced.

Improvements in the performances of organizations and the expansion of the volume of output normally mean the generation of new resources that can benefit the elites as well as the members of the organization. Organizational improvement produces more winners than losers contrary to the fears of many traditional elites in many developing countries. One of the contributions of problem-solving groups at the top level is the dispelling of a zero-sum mentality. Elite members, not the change agents, convince the resisters that nearly everyone wins.

We naturally began our discussion of power in organizations with elites. Non-elites also have power that can make or break an intervention; resistance to change can occur at many levels and for many reasons. The change tactics that we have discussed in the previous section are designed to deal with a variety of these resistances. Experimentation and data collection undermine the naysayers; group problem solving tries to answer real objections and criticisms; and training prepares people for the changes and their new roles, while indirectly dispelling doubts.

One of the common themes in the literature on development is the importance of participation. As we observed in Chapter 4, participation has many meanings; however, we define it to mean participation in decision making. This type of participation has been found to be very effective in helping organizations change. Participation, however, is not desirable in all situations. Participation, decentralization, and democracy are dysfunctional in mechanical organizations, which depend on routines or assembly lines to coordinate specialized tasks and on centralized decision making to direct the large organization. On the other hand, the lack of participation in organic organizations would be fatal.

We propose that the value of participation depends upon certain contingencies. The following two situations reveal places where participation within organizations is especially effective:

1. Whenever the tasks are complex, as in organic forms or in the organic part of a mixed mechanical-organic form, power should be decentralized. Research is the most common example but it is not the only one; others include the provision of complex services such as hospital medical care or university education.
2. Participation by teams in decision making is necessary to make them effective either as task groups or as quality work circles. There is no point creating problem-solving teams unless the inner circle or elite of the organization accepts some of their recommendations. Over the long term this means some implicit sharing of power but not necessarily decentralization of the power structure.

Outside of organizations, there are several situations where participation also can have an important impact:

1. For voluntary associations to be effective, it is necessary for them to rely upon widespread participation among their membership in order to maintain morale and motivate volunteering. While organizations can be both centralized and effective, voluntary associations can not. When individuals contribute their labor for free, they usually want to be compensated by sharing in the power.
2. For collaborative relationships between a national service organization and voluntary associations to be effective, it is necessary that there be genuine participation between them. In other words, the service organization must accept the recommendations of the voluntary associations and vice-versa. Trust is built via the sharing of power and information. The voluntary associations have much to contribute in information on the local situation and local attitudes; their recommendations deserve respect. In addition, building trust between separate social collectives is very important for long-term effectiveness.

3. For effective linkages between independent agencies to achieve integrated development, it is necessary to have participation between them, that is, each organization accepts the recommendations of the others. The reasoning is the same as presented previously. Collaboration is essential to effective relationships and accepting recommendations is essential to collaboration.

To summarize, our framework deals with the problem of power in several ways. First, support for the change must be generated among influentials by demonstrating performance and output gaps through data collection and data discussion. Second, involving influentials in high-level problem-solving groups helps to adapt the change to the political and cultural realities of the organization. These groups also help dispel the zero-sum mentality, which overestimates potential losses and underestimates potential gains. Third, problem-solving groups at middle and lower levels can help prevent sabotage at these levels by building commitment to the change. Fourth, experimentation and training also reduce resistance to the change. Finally, allowing genuine participation or power sharing within the organization, and between the organization and other organizations or voluntary associations, reduces opposition and gains support.

These suggestions do not cover all the problems of power but they cover many of them. Our framework provides no answer when the elites are united against a project except to advise against implementing the project under these conditions. Another problem that we fail to solve is that of elites that support a project but then along with others do little to help the project overcome obstacles. Red tape, lack of vehicles and other equipment, poor pay scales for project personnel, and political infighting can prevent success, and the elites must help the organization get past these obstacles. Our solution is to use elites in problem-solving groups to address these problems.

The Problem of Scarce Resources

By definition, developing countries lack many of the resources required for development. They lack money, equipment, infrastructure, qualified managers, skilled personnel, and appropriate technologies. The literature suggests that the most critical shortage is of qualified personnel. We agree with this judgment but point out that solving this problem through increasing years of schooling is *not* the answer. The formal education approach is currently being oversold in the literature. Many LDCs presently spend much more on education as a percent of their budgets than did Western Europe and the United States during the nineteenth century. We doubt that they need to provide as much formal schooling as they are doing; it is not cost effective and it spawns wasteful status games. Instead more emphasis should be put on short-term training in specific skills.

The human-capital needs in sector one are fairly low. Craft and artisan organizations mainly require apprenticeships or on-the-the job learning and could also benefit from short-term training in managerial and technical skills. As previously noted small farms, small businesses, local government agencies, and voluntary associations frequently need both leadership (or management) and technical training; but their need is for workshops and two-week courses rather than more years of schooling.

The human-capital requirements in sector two are fairly low but mechanical organizations do need well-qualified repair people and top managers to succeed. Most sector two jobs are unskilled or semiskilled and well-suited to Third World labor forces. In the poorer Third World countries, however, there is a shortage of repair people and qualified top managers and many mechanical organizations fail as a result. In fact, one of the main arguments for modest scale businesses, made in the appropriate technology literature, is that they can be adequately maintained by available repair people, and led by available entrepreneurs and managers. Heller reports on two large government sugar plants that went bankrupt due to mismanagement and the lack of spare parts, while, nearby, two small sugar plants succeeded because the smaller plants were more manageable and maintainable.[2]

In contrast, sectors three and four, the mixed mechanical-organic and organic organizational forms, require much higher investments in human capital, although selected organic or mechanical-organic organizations have only moderate requirements. (For example, as we have already observed, a bio-tech firm might need only one or two researchers with some ideas and relatively inexpensive laboratory equipment.) Both kinds of organizations, however, require formal college training, which can not be avoided. When organizations should be organic but can not find or pay for qualified personnel, the truncated-organic organization may be the necessary form, as argued in Chapter 5.

In summary, the critical scarcity in LDCs is in human capital. In craft organizations this scarcity is mild and can be rectified largely by short-term training programs. In mechanical organizations there are two human-capital shortages: qualified repair people and top managers. In some cases the solution is appropriate technology, i.e., moderate-size organizations using simple technologies that are manageable and maintainable. In organic organizations human-capital requirements are high and often unattainable. One solution is the truncated-organic organization, which adapts to this scarcity. In mixed mechanical-organic organizations the human-capital requirements are high and out of reach for most LDCs—the solution, therefore, is to avoid this form. However in select areas and on a smaller and more appropriate scale, they may be workable for the more resourceful LDCs.

We have related resource scarcities to organizational forms. We also want to discuss skill scarcities that affect organizational change possibilities. First, participation requires some skills to be effective; it may require working in teams and learning new models of analysis. There is much evidence that participation often fails because the individuals involved have not been trained in the "rules of the game." Team training in groups is a good mechanism for instilling the necessary skills for participation.

Another skill that may be scarce in LDCs is group problem solving. We have stressed the centrality of this skill in any attempt to change an organization. Although highly trained people are likely to have these skills, individuals with less than college educations are not likely to be good at problem solving without special training. The key to success in quality work circles, a major type of problem-solving team and one that is employed with rank-and-file workers, is training in the skill of recognizing and solving problems. These training programs are short and cost relatively little.

The third skill shortage that needs special mention is managerial skills. This monograph presents ample evidence of the need for improvements in management skills and managerial technologies in LDCs. It also documents how substantial improvements can be obtained at low costs. The Guyana, Jamaica, and Jordan cases feature this method of improving organizations. We therefore recommend that management improvement be a major component of the development strategies of LDCs and donors.

The fourth skill shortage is technical skills. This problem is widely recognized and needs no further documentation; what needs comment is the method for providing these skills. We emphasize cost-effective methods such as short-term training and extension classes, and recommend against providing most of these skills through increasing years of expensive schooling. The drive of individuals for education is strong in LDCs because educational credentials earn tremendous status gains; it is usually unnecessary, therefore, for governments to add to the pressure for education as a development policy. Investment in human capital has high pay-offs, but it is the kind of investment that must be selected carefully.

We briefly discuss two other scarcities: time and money. The need for monetary resources is acute and is the focus of much attention in the development literature. The monetary cost for organizational change, however, is relatively small as we have seen in those few interventions that reported their costs. Finances therefore are not a major obstacle for organizational change. Many times the greater obstacle is a scarcity of time allowed for the intervention. Unfortunately, donor agencies frequently provide enough money for effective organizational changes but not enough time. In our judgment smaller interventions over longer time periods would be more effective.

When all the scarcities of resources are considered together we make the following five observations: First, craft organizations are appropriate for the conditions of scarce resources. This is why they are so dominant in LDCs. Development requires that they be improved through technology transfer in farming and through training in managerial and technical skills in non-farm enterprises. Second, mechanical organizations greatly increase production for mass markets over that of craft organizations. Resource scarcities require that appropriate technologies are used in mechanical organizations, rather than state-of-the-art technologies. Third, the truncated-craft organization is an effective organizational model for providing widely demanded craft-type public services under conditions of resource scarcities. Fourth, the truncated-organic organization is an effective organizational model for providing relatively widely needed organic-type public services under conditions of resource scarcities. Finally, when resources are scarce, organizations should consider mobilizing inputs from voluntary associations and beneficiaries.

Conclusions

We feel that the contingency theory of organizations, expanded to include the two truncated models found in developing countries, offers a coordinated attack on the problem of development. It suggests different interventions in different sectors of the economy and it can be employed with both public sector agencies and private sector firms. It teaches how to make organizations either more efficient or more innovative/adaptive.

This monograph has also focused on how to change organizations so that they better approximate the organizational model that is appropriate for the specific conditions. The strategy of identifying performance gaps, collecting data, creating problem-solving groups, experimenting, and training can overcome resistance, build commitment, and implement the change.

The two major obstacles to development, powerful actors who block change and the lack of resources, have been considered in some detail. Our change strategy recognizes these obstacles and addresses them in a variety of ways.

In this book we analyzed a very promising strategy of development—organizational change—and considered how to strengthen and mobilize voluntary associations. Since organizations and voluntary associations carry out *most* of the development activities in the Third World, if they can be made more effective, the speed of development will be considerably accelerated. To this end we offer our framework.

Notes

1. Marilyn Carr, 1976, *Economically Appropriate Technologies for Developing Countries: An Annotated Bibliography* (London: Intermediate Technology Publications); and Peter B. Heller, 1985, *Technology Transfer and Human Values: Concepts, Applications, Cases* (New York: University Press of America).

2. Heller, *op. cit.*

Index

About the Authors and the Book

Jerald Hage is director of the Center for Innovation and professor of sociology at the University of Maryland. He has published six previous books on organization theory, including *Social Change in Complex Organizations* (with Michael Aiken) and *Theories of Organizations*. Kurt Finsterbusch is associate professor of sociology at the University of Maryland and is also affiliated with the Center for Innovation. His previous publications include *Understanding Social Impact* and *Social Research for Policy Decisions* (with Annabelle Bender Motz).

Seeking methods to improve organizations in developing countries, the authors ask whether, given the great variability of institutions within the Third World and between the Third World and the developed states, the organizational models of the West are applicable to LDCs. The answer they find, through studying case materials from the Third World, is a definite yes.

Their case studies also confirm the thesis that the structure of an organization has a profound effect on its productivity. The authors analyze when the major types of structure are effective—and when they are not—and suggest how each can best be used to achieve particular development goals. Calling on agents for change to construct a variety of organizational structures within a single country —there is no single panacea—they outline, as well, specific tactics for effecting desired change.